The COMPLETE

IDIOT'S
GUIDE TO

Getting the Job You Want

by Marc Dorio

alpha
books

A Division of Macmillan General Reference
A Simon & Schuster Macmillan Company
1633 Broadway, New York, NY 10019-6785

International Standard Book Number: 1-56761-608-9

Library of Congress Catalog Card Number: 94-073567

97 96 95   9 8 7 6 5 4 3 2 1

Interpretation of the printing code: the rightmost number of the first series of numbers is the year of the book's printing; the rightmost number of the second series of numbers is the number of the book's printing. For example, a printing code of 95-1 shows that the first printing occurred in 1995.

Printed in the United States of America

Publisher
Theresa H. Murtha

Associate Publisher
Lisa A. Bucki

Manuscript Editor
Judy J. Brunetti

Production Manager
Kelly Dobbs

Designer
Kim Scott

Illustrations
Judd Winick

Manufacturing Coordinator
Paul Gilchrist

Production Team Supervisor
Laurie Casey

Indexer
Jeanne Clark

Graphic Image Specialists
Jason Hand
Clint Lahnen
Laura Robbins
Craig Small
Todd Wente

Production Team
*Heather Butler, Angela Calvert, Kim Cofer, Jennifer Eberhardt,
Tricia Flodder, Joe Millay, Erika Millen, Gina Rexrode,
Erich J. Richter, Christine Tyner, Karen Walsh*

Contents at a Glance

Contents

17 In Limbo or Out the Door: How to Profit from Inaction and Rejection 211

18 Preparing for the Interview: How to Plan for Spontaneity 221

Foreword

If you're looking for a job in the 1990s, this is the book you need. At some time in our lives, all of us have had occasion to crack the cover of a job search self-help book. What have we felt? Intimidated. Turned off by touchy-feely talk. Overwhelmed. Bored silly. Mad at ourselves for shelling out perfectly good money for some hackneyed truisms that are clearly seriously dated. Not this time.

This book is talking to you, the individual who's put the lid on the ego, and is gladly consulting a book that demands on its very cover that you make some plucky admissions to yourself. Congratulations. You've already completed Step One: Acceptance of the fact that, yes, I could use some help here. You've got spirit.

Every job search book gives good advice. Wholesome bromides. But few do as good a job as this one at getting you to look at your problem in a fresh way. A way that gets you thinking. And acting.

For most of us, job searching is stressful. When we're stressed, we tend to go a little haywire. The brain is either on idle or in overdrive. Emotions—frustration, anxiety, you know them all—interfere with thinking and acting. This book is the antidote. Sensible, simple mental exercises…Get You To Focus. Focus is 90 percent of the solution. It's better than luck, right now. And it's something you can control. By now, most of us have come to the realization that the pattern of our lives is going to include more than one career. Job searching may be a stressful undertaking, but we've already mastered a lot of other stressful projects, and we can call on those skills. Take vacations, for example. Planning vacations and even taking them can be stressful. If we took only one or two vacations in our whole lives, each one would be loaded with stress. But we've all gone through the process enough times that we've overcome our distress. Now we make lists. We check them twice. We look upon the prospect of a trip with composure. Are job searches so different? Not if we are mentally prepared for more than one job search in our life. Not if we know how to make the right lists. This book teaches us to make the right lists. For example, one of the most helpful sections of this book gets you to look at the job search process as a marketing project. A series of manageable steps helps you discern the advantages you bring to a prospective employer, and how to communicate them successfully. This is a critical proficiency. I see far too many résumés myself that try to sell a job candidate, but fail to consider what I, the prospective employer, may need. We advertise, say for a director of manufacturing, and we get résumés with an introductory paragraph stating the desire for "meaningful employment in a responsible…." When you read this book, you won't be making that mistake, or scores of others.

What do employers want? At the MidAtlantic Employer's Association, a group of some 1,200 small and midsized companies throughout a four-state region, we spend a sizable portion of our time serving as a sounding board to chief executives and human resources professionals. They have made their needs perfectly clear: The Number One concern is finding good people.

This book lets you in on a few secrets about how we, the employers, think. This book is so accessible, you probably won't notice how well-informed it is by the principles of the professional discipline of human resource management, including the latest thinking. A firm grasp on the fundamental principles anchors this book to today's work search realities.

Reality. This is the 90s. It's time to take out your computer. Consult the Internet; that's a new skill for nearly all of us. This book will show you how to put your name in lights, thousands of pixels' worth. Nationwide. Global. This is a whole new ball game, and you've just bought the rule book. Grab that disk from the back of the book, and plug it in.

You are ready for this.

Good luck and good hunting!

Dianne E. Reed, Ph.D.
President, MidAtlantic Employer's Association
Valley Forge, Pennsylvania

August 1995

Introduction

What's *happened* to you?

You've just graduated (or are about to). You've been laid off, you've been "terminated," you've been fired, or you're just sick and tired of your present job. Maybe you woke up this morning and asked yourself, "Where's my future?" Maybe you've reached the conclusion that you're in a dead-end job in a dead-end industry: typewriter repair person in the age of the personal computer, carbon-paper sales representative in the age of the office copier.

Or maybe your current job isn't all that bad, but, the fact is, you deserve and you want better.

Anyway, you shake your head and rub your eyes. No two ways about it. You are officially "out there" in the job market.

For better or worse, you are not alone. At any given moment in the United States, 2 out of every 14 workers are unemployed; 6 out of 14 are working, but seriously worried about losing their jobs; and out of every 12 workers, 1 is in the process of changing careers. In your parents' or grandparents' day, the custom was to hook up with a company early in life, stick with it through much of your life, rise through the ranks, and retire unscarred and unscathed. Today, you can expect to change *jobs* ten times before you call it quits because of age. Today, you can expect to change *careers* three times. Today, the average job lasts only four-and-a-half years. As this century winds down and the next one kicks in, the breakneck pace will only quicken.

Better hang on to this book. Hang on to it not just for dear life, but also to help you find and grab the opportunities that are multiplying for you. You see, the upside of this employment frenzy is that, while no job is *safe* anymore, just about no job is out of reach anymore, either. And there are, plain and simple, a lot *more* jobs out there than ever before.

Only a *complete idiot* would allow him- or herself to be left out of it all. But you've bought this book, and so I know that the one thing you're not is a complete idiot. However, I also realize that you're not a veteran job hunter or career changer. I suspect, too, that you don't feel like an "insider," and maybe you envy the "insiders"—the folks who *always* get the "Good Jobs." My guess is that you're looking forward to hunting for a new job about as enthusiastically as you'd look forward to root-canal work.

This book is for you, then.

Part 1: But What Is "the Job You Want"? shows you how to create an effective job-hunting attitude, how to take stock of your skills, talents, and qualifications, and how to decide where best to put them to work.

Part 2: Finding a Home on the Range—of Career Options surveys the spectrum of opportunities waiting for you: moving up within your present company, moving to a better job in a different company, or boldly changing careers. You'll also find a complete guide to moving to another region or another part of the world.

Part 3: A Résumé Handbook provides a new and far more effective approach to designing and customizing your résumé, as well as the cover letter that helps sell it.

Part 4: The Search and Interview is your complete guide to *proactive* techniques for uncovering "hidden" job markets. It lets you in on the secrets of the want-ad jungle, and it shows how networking can transform you into the "insider" you've always wanted to be. You'll also find a comprehensive primer on using the electronic information super-highway to find and research job opportunities and to communicate directly with potential employers. You'll learn how to heat things up with a dynamite cold letter or cold call, as well as when and how to use employment agencies and headhunters. We also face the hard facts about job hunting when you are out of work—as well as how you can turn unemployment to your advantage.

Feeling rejected? Chapter 17 will show you how to profit from rejection as well as indifference.

A suite of chapters maps out the most effective strategies to prepare you for the employment interview, including doing your pre-interview homework, dressing for the occasion, and giving the right answers as well as asking the right questions. Then the big moment: negotiating the best pay at the peak of your qualifications.

Part 5: More Strings to Your Bow tells you what to do if your job hunt stalls out, including self-review techniques, freelance and part-time alternatives, and even advice on setting up on your own. It also shows you how to get started with the special edition of *JobHunt 6-in-1*, the terrific job-search software that comes with this book.

You'll also find a useful Glossary to help you learn the language of successful employment.

Wonderful thing about a book: You don't *have* to read it front-to-back and cover-to-cover. Feel free to pick and choose what's most useful to you. If you're at a loss—or just wide open to new possibilities—start with Parts 1 and 2. If you need a résumé fast, begin with Part 3. And if you're ready for serious searching or you need to prep for an interview, plunge into Part 4. You have options. And that, in the proverbial nutshell, is what this book is all about.

Extras

In addition to advice, guidance, explanations, and examples, this book offers other types of information to point you in the direction of getting the job you want, that define buzz words and jargon, that give you tips for going the extra mile, and that point out pitfalls to be avoided. Look for these easy-to-recognize signposts in boxes:

Buzz Word
The road to fulfilling employment is littered with jargon, catch phrases, euphemisms, and hot-button words. These boxes will tip you off to the most important ones.

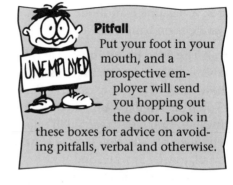

Pitfall
Put your foot in your mouth, and a prospective employer will send you hopping out the door. Look in these boxes for advice on avoiding pitfalls, verbal and otherwise.

Jump Start
These are tips about better ways to get things done and nuggets of knowledge that will help put your job hunt in perspective.

Winner
Here are "extra-mile" tips for getting the edge on the competition and winning jobs by influencing employers.

Case Study
I've told you: You are not alone. Here are short stories from other job hunters.

Acknowledgments

I would like personally to thank the following individuals and colleagues, who contributed research material or illustrations that added value to various chapters in this book:

Bruce Doherty, Director of Human Resources, Aquarium Pharmaceuticals Inc., Chalfont, Pennsylvania

Jeanette Hutwagner, Vice President-Investments, Dean Witter Reynolds Inc., Ridgewood, New Jersey

Elwood Lichack, Assistant Director, Employee Relations, Howmedica Inc., Pfizer Hospital Products Group, Rutherford, New Jersey

Drew Von Tish, Total Quality Facilitator, International Flavors Fragrances, Dayton, New Jersey

In addition, I would like to thank the many individuals throughout the country whom I have met over the years in my Outplacement and Career Transition programs. Their willingness to share openly their job-hunting questions, fears, and concerns played a major role in the development of the innovative techniques and tips found in this book.

If you have any job-hunting success stories you want to share with us, I would like to hear from you. Write to me at Dorio Associates Inc., 6 Maddock Road, Titusville, N.J. 08560.

May you get the job you want!

Marc Dorio

Special Thanks from the Publisher to the Technical Reviewer...

The Complete Idiot's Guide to Getting the Job You Want was reviewed by an expert who not only checked the technical accuracy of what you'll learn here, but also provided insight to help us ensure that this book gives you everything you need to know to make the next move in your career. Our special thanks are extended to:

Ron Smith is a management consultant and writer. Previously, Ron was a Senior Systems Analyst with Mobile Oil Corporation for nine years. In addition to being responsible for network computer support and training, he's taught university courses on various computer subjects. He has published three books on application development, and ten related computer articles. Ron also is President of the Greensport Area Toastmasters in Houston, Texas, and enjoys racquetball.

Part 1
But What Is "the Job You Want"?

Most job-hunting books begin by assuming that you know what you want and all you need is help getting it. I'd like to have begun that way, too. It would have made for a shorter, less expensive book—not that this one isn't worth every penny. The catch is, I've talked to many job hunters, and I've been impressed by how little thought most of them—let's face it, most of us—give to making one the most important of life's many decisions.

May as well give a chimp a bundle of darts to throw against some want ads pasted to a wall. That's about the equivalent of the amount of deliberation most of us spend when it comes to "choosing" a career.

So let's begin by examining some common—and thoroughly destructive—job-hunting attitudes and then go on to taking a thorough and revealing self-inventory.

Put away your darts—and your chimp.

Chapter 1

Attitude 101

In This Chapter

➤ Overcoming negative job-hunting attitudes

➤ Formulating proactive strategies for today's job market

➤ Identifying your transferable skills

➤ Using transferable skills to get the job you want

➤ Redesigning yourself

I can tell you what you're feeling. You're not happy. That much is for sure.

Then at least two of the following three things are also true. You're bored and discontented. You need or want more money. You're even a little scared.

How do I know these things?

If you were happy, you wouldn't have bought this book. You cannot be happy if you are not *in some way* fulfilled by what you do for a living. Now, if you're just getting out of school and looking for your first "real" job, well, you're going to be anxious, uncomfortable, and in a physical as well as spiritual sense *hungry* until you find one. And, if you are "between jobs"—laid off, fired, or quit in disgust—it's just about impossible to enjoy life.

The other things—boredom and discontent, needing or wanting more income, fear—they're all factors that send you looking for a new job (or *any* job, period). Or maybe you've found yourself in layoff limbo—that one- to six-month period in which you've been put "on notice" that you are about to be laid off.

So here's the problem. Job hunting is a major undertaking, which requires a major effort. It is an enterprise on which your life—physically and spiritually—depends. It requires energy, dedication, perseverance, concentration, and an ability to remain optimistic. Hardest of all, it requires these things while you are, by definition, unhappy, bored or discontented, and very probably scared.

Oh, boy.

Five Attitudes Guaranteed to Fail

Job hunt. It's one of those phrases so thoroughly worn out that we hardly think about what it means anymore. Look at it. How do you feel about that phrase? *Hunt.* That suggests adventure, challenge, and exhilaration.

Just a minute. So, you're thinking, *Here it is. This is where the happy talk begins. Finding a job, getting a career is "challenging." It's an "adventure." It's a "real thrill." Blah, blah, blah.*

Well, there will be no happy talk here. Because everyone knows that the word *job* in front of that word *hunt* seems to cancel out all positive connotations. What's left is a vague notion about having to grope around ("hunt") for something you desperately need ("job"), but probably will have a very hard time finding. It's not a pleasant thought, and the negative energy it generates inside of you puts you in a frame of mind that does anything but help you get a job, let alone the job you want. Here are the five attitudes most job hunters have in common. All are 100 percent guaranteed to help you fail in your job hunt.

1. I have to find a job.

2. Somebody, somewhere will recognize what I have to offer.

3. I have nothing special to offer.

4. If it ain't broke, don't fix it.

5. I must love my job.

I Have to Find a Job

Maybe you're one of these people, or maybe you live with one: somebody who is always misplacing things. Off hand, I can think of two sentences guaranteed to create anxiety in the heartiest soul: "It's a letter from the IRS" and "Where *did* I put my keys, anyway?"

Most of us equate *getting* the job we want with *finding* the job we want. It's as if we've been born into some cruel, cosmic Easter-egg hunt. The jobs are out there, somewhere, waiting—but very, very well hidden. You have to catch a nonrefundable, supersaver flight to your once-in-a-lifetime Paris vacation. The plane leaves at 11:30. It's 10:45 now. The suitcases are standing by the door. "Now, where *did* I put my keys?"

That, I submit, is more or less the way most of us feel about job hunting. A certain amount of anxiety is normal, but we tend to make it much worse by thinking about job hunting in the same way that we think about looking for something we have lost and that we desperately need. True enough, the world can be a pretty stupid place. I don't understand why we can't figure out how to stop war. How to end world hunger. How to cure the common cold. How to build a supermarket so that the slowest checkout line is not always the one I'm in.

But the world is not that stupid. Nobody has deliberately hidden the jobs. The time has come to abandon that anxiety-producing notion. Instead, consider these two propositions:

Businesses need many things. They need paper, pencils, offices, computers, a decent coffee machine. But, most of all, they need people to do the work they do. By all means, hide the key to the office petty cash drawer, but don't hide the jobs.

> **Jump Start**
> Think there are no jobs? Think again. Even in the worst markets, job vacancies run an average of 2.5 percent or higher. In the United States, about one million job vacancies are filled each month by the unemployed.

Don't even bother looking for a job. Instead, try looking for needs—not your needs, but the needs of all those employers out there. Then create a way to satisfy those needs. I will discuss how to address employer needs in more detail at the end of the chapter. And if you miss it there, don't worry. It's about the most important theme of this book, and you'll find it discussed and repeated many times.

Somebody, Somewhere Will Recognize What I Have to Offer

Most job-hunting books most of the time contain mostly advice about writing cold letters, résumés, and cover letters. That stuff usually takes up the first half of the book. The second half—oh, the second half—it's the payoff for the first. It's all about the interview, which happens only if the résumé is successful.

Well, a good résumé is important. But it's not as important as you may think, and, certainly, it is not as important as most job-hunting books would have you think. Don't worry, you'll find plenty of help with cold letters, résumés, and cover letters in *The Complete Idiot's Guide to Getting the Job You Want*. But you need to be aware that putting all your eggs in one résumé is an act of faith—and nothing more. Your belief—your hope, your faith—is that somebody, somewhere will recognize what you have to offer. I said the world of business isn't so stupid that it deliberately hides the jobs. True enough. But it's also not bright enough that you can count on somebody appreciating your talents and skills just because you put yourself out there with a spiffy résumé. Companies desperately need talent, and you'd think, therefore, that they'd employ full-time "talent scouts" to find it. A few do. Most don't. Therefore, you need a set of *proactive strategies* to market yourself actively, rather than just exhibit yourself passively. Most of this book is devoted to helping you develop such strategies.

I Have Nothing Special to Offer

This is a particularly pervasive negative attitude, and, regrettably, it invites such happy talk responses as *You* are *special because* everybody *is special.*

Ugh.

Pitfall
Only 1 in 1,470 unsolicited résumés produces a job offer. No kidding.

The antidote to the poison of this negative attitude is most definitely not to induce vomiting with such smarmy clichés, but to invest some time in discovering *for* yourself just what special qualities you do have to offer. One option is to visit a professional career counselor (see Chapter 15, "Agencies and Headhunters") or you can work with the material you'll find in Chapter 2, "Where Do You Want to Be (and Should You Really Go There)?"

If It Ain't Broke, Don't Fix It

Tyrants, dictators, and despots thrive on this attitude. A cliché, it is bolstered by other clichés, all of which pass for prudence: *Leave well enough alone. A bird in the hand is worth two in the bush. Don't rock the boat. Let sleeping dogs lie.* If your present job is good enough, don't even think of looking for something else. If your present set of skills are good enough, don't even think of adding to them.

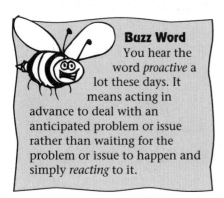

Buzz Word
You hear the word *proactive* a lot these days. It means acting in advance to deal with an anticipated problem or issue rather than waiting for the problem or issue to happen and simply *reacting* to it.

A desire to make changes—to fix things that ain't broke—is usually written off to restlessness, and restlessness sounds like an unpleasant feeling to be avoided. In fact, it's the condition of even the simplest forms of life on earth. Even an amoeba keeps changing shape. Why should you be any less evolved than a unicellular animal?

Never define yourself absolutely. A willingness to change may not create peace and quiet, but it does open you up to new possibilities in your present position, in a new position, even in a new career.

I Must Love My Job

Whoa! Just hold your proverbial horses. Isn't finding a job you love the be-all and end-all of a job hunt and career search? More to the point, isn't finding such a job precisely what books like this promise and guarantee?

The nice thing about rhetorical questions is that they're easy to answer. Yes, it is true that job-hunting books customarily promise to help you find happiness, but, no, you don't have to love your job.

Most jobs neither promise—nor require—a lifetime commitment. A few generations ago, this was not the case. Typically, a man (and it *was* a male-dominated job market) dedicated himself to a profession or vocation, and he attached himself to a company or institution that would pretty much give him a job for life. That hasn't been the case for some time now. On both sides, employee and employer, commitments are much more tentative and temporary.

Is this to be regretted? I don't think so. Sure, the contemporary employment environment has done wonders for the makers and sellers of antacid products, but the new facts of vocational life also encourage experimentation, personal growth, creative risk-taking, and, ultimately, vocational fulfillment. Here's a rule of thumb that may help: Always *love* your spouse (or your "significant other," or your family, or your parakeet). For now, at least *like* your job. (You can always try another.)

You Don't Have to Be What You Do

When is the last time you were at a backyard barbecue, and a stranger, burger in hand, sidled up to you, introduced himself, and asked, "What is your identity?"

Jump Start
The average worker changes employers seven times during his or her career. He or she changes careers three times.

Unless your neighborhood harbors an extraterrestrial or two, it just doesn't happen this way. Instead, the question, sooner or later, is "What do you do?" And the answer does *not* begin, "I do …" or "I work as a …," but, simply, "I'm a …."

I'm a lawyer. I'm a doctor. I'm an accountant. I'm an editor. I'm a systems analyst. I'm a car mechanic. I'm a sales representative. I'm a cop. I'm a teacher.

Our language is telling us how we think about what we do. Consciously or unconsciously, we equate our job with who we are, as if it were a permanent part of our identity. *I am a plumber.*

Well, what's wrong with being a plumber?

The answer may shock you: No one should be a plumber. However, it is perfectly fine (and can be highly profitable) to work *as* a plumber. What you should be, however, is a human being.

Buzz Word
Human being, for the purpose of getting the job you want, is defined as an upright biped with *transferable skills*. Please read on for a discussion of the latter.

Think about it this way. Right now, more than one-third of American households have personal computers. Virtually all American offices have them. The average computer (at this instant; for the prices change more often than a politician's promises) costs about $2,000. A decent electric typewriter, if you can still find one, costs maybe $300. A pocket calculator—well, many businesses give them away *free* nowadays, instead of a wall calendar featuring a picture of snow-capped Mt. Whitney.

Why, then, spend so much more on a personal computer? Because it is a machine that refuses to define itself simply as a typewriter, or a calculator, or, for that matter, as a telecommunications device, a fax machine, a copier, a drafting tool, a means of video amusement. A computer is all of these things, and more. It is a device with a set of transferable skills and, therefore, indispensable. As a human being, you are at least as versatile as a computer. You are loaded with transferable skills.

How to Win the Lottery

Question: Why is it so hard to win the state lottery?

Answer: Because you don't know in advance what numbers to pick.

So why go about looking for a job the same way you play the lottery? Most job hunters prepare a résumé, dutifully listing what they believe are their "skills" in the fervent (but truly forlorn) hope that their particular set of skills will make them "right for" a particular job. Bingo. Maybe the tumblers will click just right—this time.

Buzz Word
Transferable skills are the building blocks of any career you choose. They are specific to you rather than to a particular job. They always describe a function: that is, how you work with people, data, or things. Communicating effectively, negotiating, advising, analyzing, synthesizing—these are all examples of transferable skills.

Maybe. But probably not.

Most résumés fail to produce job offers because the writer of the résumé fails to list his or her transferable skills. Instead, he or she reels off a set of traits and/or narrowly defined job experiences.

The eyes of potential employers glaze over with reading such words and phrases as:

➤ Dependable

➤ Detail-oriented

➤ Determined

➤ Energetic

➤ Intuitive

➤ Learns fast

➤ Persistent

➤ Punctual

➤ Well-focused

➤ Works well under pressure

➤ Works well with people

These are traits, desirable traits, to be sure, but everybody who applies for a job lays claim to these or a similar set. Your goal is to demonstrate to a potential employer what sets you apart from the other 143 applicants for the target position.

Then there is the other approach. Under the heading "Experience," the applicant may list:

Word processing with MicroWonder Lexikon 3.4 on ABM-compatible systems

This is wonderful, *if* you happen to know that the target employer uses that software on that system and if you are content to define yourself exclusively for a particular job requiring this particular experience. If neither of these things is true, however, this item on a résumé is not likely to get you the job.

You'll learn more about the specifics of writing résumés in Part 3. I only mention résumés here because job hunters believe they are supremely important and because they reflect—usually—everything that is wrong about how job hunters approach the job hunt. Most importantly, the résumé shows how job hunters think about themselves. In all too many instances, this self-image is inaccurate, ineffective, and unfair.

By emphasizing general *traits*, you make yourself look like a one-size-fits-all person, no different from anyone else milling around outside the employer's door.

But, on the other hand, by defining yourself too narrowly, strictly in terms of what you have done or have been trained to do, you risk being too different, too narrow to make a comfortable fit in the employer's organization.

Redesigning Yourself

Not just to write a résumé, but, far more importantly, to adjust your job-hunting attitude, you need to convert the common stuff of the ordinary résumé into the uniquely valuable qualities all employers lust after. You need to translate general traits and overly specific fragments of experience into the expression of transferable skills.

Remember: A transferable skill is always expressed in terms of function—doing something with people or data or things. "I am persuasive" is a statement of a trait. "I am a salesperson" is a narrow job description ("narrow" because it pigeonholes you—like calling that $2,000 personal computer a calculator).

Combining the trait with the narrow job description is a step in the right direction. "I am a persuasive salesperson" is a small step toward getting the job you want. Take another step by transforming the adjective describing the trait into a verb describing a transferable skill: "I am persuasive" becomes "I persuade."

Now work on expanding that all-too-confining job description. The easiest way to do this is to decide whether "salesperson" primarily involves a function with people, data, or things. The answer, of course, is people. Your description of a transferable skill now becomes "I persuade people."

You have now expressed a skill that is of great value in many jobs. You could even use this phrase in a résumé. But its more important purpose, at this stage of the job hunt, is to build an attitude that will help you define and get the job you want.

So, where are you right now? You've taken a persuasive person, whose particular job experience is as a salesperson, and redesigned him or her into someone who persuades people. That's another step toward getting the job you want. But you can go farther.

Transferable skills are hierarchical, rising from simple to complex. Persuading is more complex than merely communicating, just as communicating is a more complex "people" skill than taking instructions or following directions. However, persuading is less complex than supervising, and, in turn, supervising is less complex than instructing. Higher up on the ladder of complexity comes negotiating. At the very top, perhaps, is high-level teaching or mentoring.

The ultimate step toward creating an attitude that will help you define and get the job you want is to lay claim to the most complex—the highest—transferable skills possible. If, based on your training and past performance, you can honestly say, "I persuade people," can you declare with equal legitimacy, "I negotiate with people"? Negotiation is persuasion at a higher level. It presupposes the ability to persuade, but involves a greater degree of problem solving. Persuasiveness is great in a salesperson. Negotiation skills are essential to an account executive. Now, ratchet the skill level up to, say, mentoring, and you have the makings of a Director of Sales or a Vice President for Sales.

The Best Job-Hunting Secret: Never Apply for a Job

Depending on a lot of variables—where you live, the job market, the economy, your experience, and so on—applying for a job can be a snap or an arduous undertaking. But, easy or hard, is it worth it?

Stupid question, huh? I mean, barring a rich maiden aunt who's just been considerate enough to pass away, what is the alternative?

Don't apply for a job.

Let that sentence hang in the air a moment. Look: A good salesperson makes a sale. But a great salesperson creates a customer. He or she doesn't take the easy way out, saying and doing whatever is required to make a fast sale of an item or two, but, instead, invests time and energy in making certain the customer will be sufficiently satisfied to give the firm more business and to recommend the firm's merchandise to others.

Take a hint. Don't apply for this job or that. Don't make the job hunt a frustrating series of one-shot shots in the dark. Instead, invest time in redesigning yourself so that, rather than applying for a job, you market yourself among the pool of employers who need—who desperately need—remarkable individuals with great transferable skills.

Redesign yourself in each of the functional areas. You've already touched on the "people" area, which includes transferable skills ranging from the relatively simple ability to follow instructions, up through the greater complexity of persuading, then supervising, instructing, negotiating, and mentoring. The other two areas involve working with data and working with things. Transferable skills related to *data* range from the simplest, the ability to compare, and travel up through complexity with such skills as copying; collating, compiling, and computing; analyzing; coordinating; and, finally, synthesizing and innovating. The transferable skills related to *things* start at the low end with handling, go up through tending, then operating or driving; next comes controlling, precision working, and setting up; then creating, innovating, and inventing.

Higher skill levels presuppose mastery of the lower ones as well. Be aware that the lower skills tend to involve responding, following instructions, following prescribed routines, and fitting in, while the higher levels involve greater degrees of creativity and proactive initiative. The higher the level of transferable skill you can claim, the more effectively you can market yourself as a uniquely valuable asset to any organization. At the higher skill levels, you will also be given greater latitude and responsibility for defining your own job rather than having to fit into one that is rigidly prescribed. Finally, to the degree that you market your high-level transferable skills, your competition will simply melt away.

Thinking about, expressing, and effectively marketing your transferable skills is a kind of skeleton key. It can unlock the doors that hold back the positive energy you need to charge up an effective job-hunting attitude. It can raise the lid on job possibilities you may never have thought of or that you simply thought were beyond your reach. Finally, it can unlock the doors of more employers, giving you more choices and more opportunities. How? The details are in Chapter 2.

The Least You Need to Know

➤ Recognize and abandon the five common negative attitudes that hinder job hunting.

➤ Don't search for jobs. Identify needs—what employers need—and create ways to satisfy those needs.

➤ Identify your transferable skills.

➤ Translate your good traits into marketable skills.

➤ Invest time now in redesigning yourself, not just for this or that job, but to market yourself for a lifetime of optimum employment.

Chapter 2

Where Do You Want to Be (and Should You Really Go There)?

In This Chapter

➤ Taking a self-inventory of skills and interests

➤ Measuring your current job satisfaction

➤ Positioning yourself in the job market

➤ Assessing your salary needs

Up there (or *down* there), along with pride, avarice, lust, gluttony, anger, and sloth, comes the fourth of the Seven Deadly Sins: envy. I suspect it's really the most popular of them all—more of us are envious than prideful, slothful, or the rest—and I'm willing to venture another speculation as well. There are many things in the world to envy: good looks, sex appeal, powerful automobiles, majestic yachts, cash, a reserved parking space near the front entrance of the plant—you name it. But I'm willing to bet that what most of us envy most is the person who has found his or her calling in life, who has found a true vocation, who has found a *meaningful* way to sustain and prosper his or her family.

I can't promise that reading this chapter will lead you straight to a meaningful career. But, as Confucius said, "A journey of a thousand miles begins with a single step." Here's an opportunity to step.

Taking Inventory of Yourself

You know, it might really be very simple. You may already have a good idea of the kind of work that would both sustain and satisfy you. Or you may at least be closer to that idea than you think you are. Let's start by testing the assumption that you know what you want to do.

In a single declarative sentence, describe the job you want. For example, "I want to be an electrical engineer."

Maybe you are even prepared to be more specific: "I want to be an electrical engineer, specializing in the design of integrated circuits to accelerate computer graphics calculations." It is most helpful to be specific.

If you cannot write a sentence like this, go to the next exercise. Equally important, if you *can* write the sentence, but, after reading it over, you either

    A. Don't like what you wrote,

      or

    B. Believe that aliens abducted you and forced you to write it,

you should also proceed to the next exercise.

If you can't, right off the bat, state a vocational goal that feels right to you, try inventorying those transferable skills discussed at the end of Chapter 1, "Attitude 101." Perhaps you recall that these fall into three categories: skills in relation to *people*, to *data*, and to *things*. Now, take three blank sheets of paper. Write **PEOPLE** at the top of one, **DATA** at the top of another, and **THINGS** at the top of the third. Below these headings, on each sheet, write **I am good at....** Next, complete that sentence in as many ways as you can for each transferable skill category: people, data, and things. For example,

> PEOPLE
>
> I am good at...
>
> Persuading
>
> Selling
>
> Helping people make purchase decisions
>
> Explaining
>
> Explaining how machinery works
>
> Being patient
>
> Listening

And so on, covering the areas of DATA and THINGS.

You may find that the free-form approach, working with a sheet of paper that is blank except for the heading and the first part of the sentence, either lubricates your thought process very nicely or gets it right off to a grinding halt. If the latter is the case, you may find the Skills Worksheets in this chapter helpful. Rate your skill level from 1 to 4, with 4 being the strongest.

People Skills Inventory

Rate each of your skills from 1 to 4, with 4 being the strongest. Circle the number for the rating that applies.

When dealing with individuals, I'm good at...

Following instructions	1	(2)	3	4
Serving	1	2	(3)	4
Listening	1	2	(3)	4
Communicating verbally	1	2	3	(4)
Communicating in writing (letters, memos)	1	2	(3)	4
Diagnosing, evaluating, and analyzing	1	2	3	(4)
Persuading	1	2	3	(4)
Recruiting and motivating	1	2	3	4
Selling	1	2	(3)	4
Instructing and training	1	2	3	(4)
Coaching and mentoring	1	2	3	(4)

When dealing with groups, I'm good at...

Communicating	1	2	3	4
Representing	1	2	3	4
Guiding group discussion	1	2	3	4
Persuading and motivating	1	2	3	4
Formal public speaking (including TV, and so on)	1	2	3	4
Performing and entertaining	1	2	3	4
Managing and supervising	1	2	3	4
Consulting and advising	1	2	3	4
Negotiating and resolving conflict	1	2	3	4
Pioneering (leading innovation)	1	2	3	4

Data Skills Inventory

Rate each of your skills from 1 to 4, with 4 being the strongest. Circle the number for the rating that applies.

When dealing with data, I'm good at...

Sorting:

Data entry	1	2	3	4
Record keeping and filing	1	2	3	4
Retrieving information efficiently	1	2	3	4
Helping others retrieve information	1	2	3	4
Memorizing and paying attention to detail	1	2	3	4

Gathering:

Compiling	1	2	3	4
Searching and researching	1	2	3	4
Observing (in order to gather data)	1	2	3	4

Managing:

Copying	1	2	3	4
Comparing (similarities? differences?)	1	2	3	4
Computing	1	2	3	4
➤ Analyzing	1	2	3	4
Organizing, systematizing, prioritizing	1	2	3	4
Step-by-step, goal-oriented planning	1	2	3	4
Visualizing (drawing, creating graphics, and so on)	1	2	3	4
Synthesizing, developing, improving	1	2	3	4
Problem solving	1	2	3	4
Developing the "big picture"	1	2	3	4

Creating:

Daydreaming	1	2	3	4
Imagining	1	2	3	4
Improving	1	2	3	4
Designing	1	2	3	4
Inventing and innovating	1	2	3	4

Things Skills Inventory

Rate each of your skills from 1 to 4, with 4 being the strongest. Circle the number for the rating that applies.

When dealing with things, I'm good at...

Working machinery and vehicles:

Operating	1	2	3	4
Controlling (including driving)	1	2	3	4
Maintaining	1	2	3	4
Repairing	1	2	3	4
Assembling	1	2	3	4

Working with materials:

Sewing, weaving, basic woodworking, and so on	1	2	3	4
Finishing	1	2	3	4
Carving	1	2	3	4
Sculpting	1	2	3	4
Precision handwork	1	2	3	4

Construction work:

Rough carpentry, framing, and so on	1	2	3	4
Finish carpentry	1	2	3	4
Remodeling	1	2	3	4

Working with living things:

Gardening	1	2	3	4
Farming	1	2	3	4
Caring for animals	1	2	3	4
Training and handling animals	1	2	3	4

Body skills:

Strength	1	2	3	4
Endurance	1	2	3	4
Dexterity	1	2	3	4
Athletics	1	2	3	4

Within each of the skill areas—people, data, and things—the skills are arranged in approximate order of complexity, from lowest to highest. That is, under the "People" category, for example, "Following instructions" (the first item listed) is a simpler skill than "Coaching and mentoring" (the last item). In completing the worksheets, try to identify the highest transferable skills you can honestly claim. Why?

Jump Start These worksheets and the next exercise are hard work, but you should enjoy it. Take a break if it gets boring. The more relaxed you are about it, the more accurate the results will be.

First, the higher your transferable skill level, the more unique you are as a candidate for employment. More directly put: The higher your transferable skills, the less competition you will face. Second, jobs that require higher levels of transferable skills generally pay more and are more interesting than jobs calling for lower levels of these skills. Third, jobs requiring higher levels of transferable skills tend to be genuine careers; that is, they tend to be jobs with a future. Finally, the higher your transferable skills, the more latitude you are likely to have on the job. For you, employment will be less a matter of fitting in than of your creating a job to fit you. Positions requiring only the lower levels of transferable skills are usually quite prescriptive. The employer tells you what to do and what not to do. At the higher levels, positions tend to invite and require you to be creative and inventive.

Let's Tell a Story

Let's pause at this point for a question: Is any of this working for you? Have you been able to identify your transferable skills? Are you beginning to feel some direction to your drift?

I hope your answers are yes, but I wouldn't be surprised if they aren't. You see, very few people do what you're doing now—that is, *think* about what they're doing. It's hard work, a strain on the imagination, and a strain on the brain. If, then, you're having trouble taking your self-inventory, maybe it's time you told yourself some stories. Not bedtime stories, but wake-up stories.

In a few paragraphs, recall one successful action or achievement for which you were responsible. It can be job-related, but it need not be. However, the structure of the story should not be entirely free-form. In fact, it should follow this narrowly prescribed plot line:

1. Begin by stating a goal: What you wanted to do or accomplish.

2. Most good stories involve conflict or a problem. Your story should be no exception. Describe a problem, conflict, or obstacle in the way of achieving your goal.

3. What did you *do* to overcome the obstacle and achieve your goal? Describe this process step by step.

4. Describe the outcome. What did you accomplish?

5. Evaluate your achievement objectively. If possible, quantify the results.

What about material for the story? You don't have to have single-handedly wiped out your firm's competition, nor climbed Everest solo. Humbler achievements will do. Here's one from my more or less real life:

> I wanted to fix the knob on our front door. It kept slipping, at times making it almost impossible to open the door. It is a very beautiful antique knob and plate, which I certainly did not want to replace. Nor did I want to pay a locksmith $50 or $100 to come out to the house. Unfortunately, however, I had never tried to repair a doorknob mechanism, and I knew nothing about them. Nevertheless, I decided to investigate the problem.
>
> First, I examined the knobs themselves and discovered that they were held onto a shaft with two little set screws. I loosened the screw on one knob and was able to pull the knob. This allowed me to pull out the shaft from the hole in the plate covering the lock mechanism.
>
> Just by looking at the shaft, I could tell what the problem was. The shaft was so old and worn that it slipped within the locking mechanism. Reasoning that a worn shaft must be a fairly common problem, I concluded that the local hardware store would probably have the part I needed. I unscrewed the other knob off the shaft, and I took the shaft with me to the store. It is a very well-arranged store, so I had no trouble finding the door-hardware department. Sure enough, there was a shaft that matched the worn part. It cost $1.49.
>
> I took the new part home, put one knob on one end of the shaft, inserted the shaft into the lock mechanism, and tried the door.
>
> It worked much better, but the shaft still slipped somewhat. Would I have to spend money on a locksmith after all? I peered into the lock mechanism with a flashlight. I concluded that the square hole into which the shaft fit was, like the old shaft, also worn. However, I knew that I did not have the skill to remove and disassemble the entire lock mechanism. What I needed to do was to thicken the shaft slightly. I remembered that I had some metallic tape. I wrapped three turns of the tape around the middle of the shaft and reinserted it into the hole. It was now a nice, snug fit. I tested the doorknob assembly. The mechanism worked perfectly. After putting the other doorknob on, I was done.

I had a fully functioning door, complete with our beautiful antique knob and plate set, and I saved $50 to $100 by fixing it all myself.

Okay, so it's not Pulitzer Prize material. But it does tell me something about my skills. I can take the checklist of people, things, and data skills and compare it to the content of the story. I can decide which skills the story exhibits, and to what degree (1, 2, 3, or 4) it exhibits them. If I write at least a half dozen short stories about myself—each starting with a goal, introducing a problem, explaining my solution, stating the outcome, then objectifying the outcome—I will begin to have an inventory of my transferable skills.

Winner

When you describe yourself, your experience, and your skills, whether you are writing for these exercises, composing a résumé, or participating in a job interview, concentrate on specific activities and events, not vague descriptions of your admirable traits. Provide evidence: nouns and verbs relating to real things.

The skills demonstrated by the stories necessarily limited by what you'll find in the checklist. For example, I may conclude from my story that I have about a number 2 transferable skill level in *repairing* machinery. The problem is, while I did derive satisfaction from repairing the door mechanism, and while, in objective, quantifiable terms, doing so was valuable, I have no real desire to become, say, a locksmith. Fortunately, that's not the point. It's not just that I might make a good locksmith, but that I have a willingness to investigate a problem for myself and the initiative to try to fix it myself. Moreover, I was able to diagnose the problem and to arrive at a simple and inexpensive solution to it.

After writing and analyzing six or more of these kinds of stories, I could expect not only to find a pattern of transferable skills emerging in my checklist, but also other valuable information about my skills, aptitude, likes and dislikes, imagination, and even character.

Try to compile a list of six to eight of your strongest and highest-level transferable skills. Then put each of these in a complete sentence, beginning with, "I am good at ...."

Let's say you've concluded that *negotiating* is one of your top skills. You might write, "I am good at negotiating." That certainly says something, but it does not say enough. Always include an object in your sentence: "I am good at negotiating prices." Now we're getting somewhere. Try developing the sentence further with an adjective or adverb: "I am good at negotiating prices that are satisfying to both buyer and seller."

In this step-by-step manner, you should be able to identify your top transferable skills and to define them in a way that not only describes you accurately and vividly, but also sets you apart from the other several million folks jostling around the job market.

Where Are You Now? Measuring Current Career Satisfaction

Identifying and describing your transferable skills is always useful, to yourself and to potential employers. It is also a great help when you are not sure exactly how you feel about your current job or career path. In this case, I suggest you use your list of transferable skills as a yardstick for evaluating how the current situation suits you or fails to suit you. Most likely, however, you do have some definite feelings about your current situation. There's no magic formula for evaluating these. I suggest getting out a piece of paper—yes, *another* piece of paper—dividing it into two columns, and heading one **I like** and the other **I don't like**. Then inventory everything you like and don't like about your job.

You will find yourself listing much more than transferable skills. Your list will include items related to the workplace (including physical environment as well as the kind of people with whom you work), the kinds of tools involved in the work, the salary it pays, and the demand the work makes on your time, in addition to such skill-related items as the object or goal of the job, the nature of the tasks involved, the specific talents and skills required, and the knowledge required.

Part 2 of this book explores job- and career-changing in depth, but we should acknowledge right here and now that your current job experience tells you a great deal about what you like and don't like and what you need and do not need or do not want. Use your current job experience as a strong reality check on what your inventory of transferable skills tells you.

Marketing 101: If You Don't Know What You Want, Somebody Else Will Tell You

You've just spent a lot of time learning various ways to discover and sort out your skills so that you can select a career path from among the vast available array. The fact is that whatever your particular job or calling, you are, before everything else, a marketer. Now, that's not the same thing as a salesperson, who tries to persuade a customer to purchase a product or service and who does whatever is required to facilitate the transaction. Nor is it the same as the advertising specialist, who uses an array of techniques to inform and persuade a pool of potential customers. Successful job hunting usually involves some form of salespersonship and advertising, it is true; but to make sales and advertising effective, marketing must first take place.

Buzz Word
Positioning is how a product or service (or an entire company, for that matter) is perceived by the best potential customer for that product, service, or company.

At its most basic, the marketing process begins by identifying a market for your goods or services. Put another way, marketing begins by identifying your best potential customer. When you are hunting for a job, effective marketing requires that you define just what it is that you offer and then define which employers are best suited to what you have to offer. This need not be a passive process: *I offer XYZ; therefore, my task is to find an employer who wants XYZ.* Instead, you can practice the central activity of marketing, which is *positioning*.

A *position* is a marketplace image or a set of beliefs created by a company. Ideally, all advertising and all sales are based on positioning. As a job hunter, your product, service, and company are *you*, what you offer to a potential employer. Once you have defined your strongest set of transferable skills, your next task is to use them so that you can position yourself in the job market.

Whether your product is a widget or yourself, there are three components to positioning:

➤ **Benefit**: The essentially emotional reason to "buy" your "product."

➤ **Target**: Your best potential "customer."

➤ **Competition**: The others in the marketplace vying for the same "customers."

Benefit: Let's Get Emotional

This is a little tricky. Having determined your transferable skills, you know how to describe what may be called your product *features*. For example, the sentence "I am good at negotiating prices that satisfy both the seller and the customer" describes one of your "features." To position yourself in the job market, however, you need to translate such features into *benefits*. How will a particular "product feature" or set of features benefit the "customer." Benefit is essentially an emotional perception. For example, a certain body deodorant tells us that it "takes the worry out of being close." This is a product benefit—in contrast to the main product feature, which is that it masks disagreeable body odors. Similarly, a certain express shipping company has positioned itself not as an expert in overnight shipping (overnight shipping is the principle *feature* of its product), but as a way to stop worrying about whether the package you sent will arrive on time. Relief from anxiety is the benefit of this product.

Positioning yourself in the job market also involves defining emotional benefits. "I am good at negotiating prices that satisfy both the seller and the customer" can be translated as, "I create satisfaction" or "I will make your life easier, Ms. Smith [the sales manager], by creating satisfaction for us and for our customers." Here's some good news: You will soon discover that defining the benefits of your "product features" as a job candidate is much easier than defining the benefits, say, of a bar of soap or particular brand of running shoe. Retail customers present a wide range of emotional motives for buying—or *not* buying—a given product. Your "customer," however, the potential employer, generally has a single overriding motive: making more money.

Always try to translate your set of transferable skills into factors that will benefit the employer's bottom line. "I am good at negotiating prices that satisfy both the seller and the customer. That means I not only make the sale, but I make every sale a good sale. Because my customers are satisfied, I create repeat business. All of that adds to the bottom line—and not just in a single quarter, but consistently, quarter after quarter." Chapters 8, "Looking Good on Paper," and 9, "Judged by Its Cover: How to Write Great Cover Letters," which discuss résumés and cover letters, explore strategies for translating your skills into benefits and for expressing benefits in terms of dollars.

Target: As in "Right On"

Inventorying your transferable skills is the first major step toward defining what potential employers to target in your job hunt. The chapters of Part 2 in this book explore the range of targets.

Competition: Beat It

Strongly positioning yourself by vividly defining the benefits you bring an employer will alone set you apart from the competition. It is helpful to know, however, what kinds of specific qualifications other job candidates bring to the table. How do you gather this information? Two methods are effective.

1. Talk to people who currently hold the kind of position you seek. Ask them about their background, their training, and their experience. Be sure to ask, "Are there any specific skills or qualifications that you've found indispensable for your position?"

2. Be sure to follow up on any rejections you may receive. Don't just send a thank-you note, or make a thank-you phone call, ending with, "I wonder if you could tell me about anything you were looking for that I just didn't offer. The information would be very helpful to me."

> **Pitfall**
> It is a mistake to be discouraged by rejection. Yes, a mistake. Used correctly, rejection presents an opportunity for learning about yourself and about the market for the job you seek. Never waste an opportunity. Exploit every rejection you get.

23

This thank-you note exploits a potential of rejection. Don't ask for a favor. Ask for help. Most people respond enthusiastically.

GRANT HELM
644 Treeline Drive
Weston, NY 10309
555-555-5555
Fax: 555-555-4444

August 2, 1995

Susan Whitaker
Sales Manager
Schwartz and Dunlap
1515 West End Drive
Virtual, NY 10135

Dear Ms. Whitaker:

I greatly enjoyed our meeting on Wednesday. Of course, I'm disappointed that Schwartz and Dunlap have decided to go with another candidate, but I am grateful for having had the opportunity of speaking with you.

It would be very helpful to me if we could discuss--briefly, by telephone--some of the reasons behind your decision. I'd like to know how I might offer more in the future. I would very much appreciate your taking my call next week.

Sincerely,

Grant Helm

Grant Helm

Dough: How Much?

One of the main reasons for getting a job is to earn a living. The character Uncle Charlie in Arthur Miller's great play *Death of a Salesman* provided the best answer to the question, How much is enough? "No man," he said, "has enough salary." It's the "best" answer because, let's face it, this is the way most of us feel about what we're paid. Our feelings range from "I'm a wage slave" (at the low end) to "It could be better" (at the high). Still, having identified your transferable skills and having targeted a career area or even some specific potential employers, you need to formulate at least an acceptable minimum salary range.

> **Pitfall**
> Beware of the expenses associated with a new job that eat away at your net income. Do you have to relocate? Do you have a costlier commute? Do you have to buy a new car? Do you need a whole new wardrobe?

How do you determine these figures? You could begin by looking at your present situation. Are you meeting your monthly expenses *and* putting a bit aside? If not, how much more do you need each month? Establish a minimum figure, making sure that you take into account such areas as housing, food, clothing, automobile and transportation expenses, insurance, medical expenses, support for other family members, charity, education, pet care, bills and debts, taxes, amusements, and gifts; then add 30 percent to the total. This will give you a good idea of your target salary from the perspective of living expenses.

You may also think of the target salary in relation to your present salary. If you are changing jobs principally to secure a salary increase, you should expect a minimum jump of 8 to 10 percent over your present salary. Do not take this as a hard-and-fast rule, however, especially if you are changing jobs for reasons of personal interest, self-fulfillment, or other motives unrelated to salary.

So, you can probably figure out how much of a salary to look for, but this will still leave you, at the end of an interview, asking yourself: *Could I have gotten more?* That question nags even the most experienced negotiators (they just learn to live with it), and I don't believe that anything I can tell you will keep that ugly phrase from popping into your mind. However, you will find guidelines for negotiating salary in Chapter 22, "Negotiating Salary and Other Matters," that are designed to make you feel more confident about the figure you negotiate.

The Least You Need to Know

➤ Take a comprehensive self-inventory to assess your strongest skills and greatest interests.

➤ Learn to see—and describe—yourself as a problem solver.

➤ Position yourself effectively in the job market, being vividly clear about the *benefits* (in addition to the *skills* and *experience*) you offer an employer.

➤ Translate the benefits you offer into quantifiable terms—most effectively, into dollars that will be earned or saved for the company.

➤ Calculate your target salary needs.

Part 2
Finding a Home on the Range—of Career Options

If you are on the street and starving, you don't have to read this part. Best thing to do in your situation is spin the wheel of fortune and take the first job that comes your way. Don't worry too much about making the "right" move. For you, any move is the right move.

I suspect you're not quite so bad off, and, that being the case, you'd better plan your job move. They come in three different directions: up, down, or lateral. You don't need an MBA to conclude that, usually, up is the best choice. However, sometimes a lateral move (and, in rare cases, a step down) are wise strategic choices.

Then there are the domains that define your move: within your present company, to a new company, to an entirely new industry and career, or to a different region or part of the world.

Chapters 3 through 7 will help you plot your course.

Chapter 3

Same Ladder, Higher Rung: Upward Mobility within the Organization

Clichés are like little tin toys. Just wind 'em up, and watch 'em go. Here's one: "The grass is always greener...." (It's so timeworn that nobody ever bothers to get out all of it.) A life led by cliché is tedious and narrow, yet there is a reason why such little homilies, once wound up, never quite run down.

That reason is truth. Most clichés contain at least a grain of the stuff.

This chapter invites you to explore the green grass in your own backyard: the growth potential within your present organization.

A Lesson from the World of Sales: Your Best Customer Is Your Present Customer

Not long ago, I ran across a disarmingly frank statement from the CEO of a major mail-order personal computer manufacturer. He said, "These days, any idiot with a screwdriver can make a PC." Sure, that's an exaggeration, but the point is, despite the buckets of ink spilled in advertising them and the pages of PC consumer magazines devoted to reporting on their technological innards, just about all personal computers, whatever the brand, do the jobs they were designed to do.

So what separates the winning PC makers from the runners up? It's not price, because most of them charge just about the same money for similar machines. It's not advertising, because most of them have well-developed ad campaigns. It's not technology, because no one has any secret weapons. Instead, the most significant differences come in the availability and quality of customer service. Consumers are no longer content with high-quality hardware at a reasonable price. They expect their dollars to buy support as well.

Now, as the availability of high technology becomes increasingly universal throughout the worlds of industry and commerce, what's true for personal computer makers is rapidly becoming the case with all business. Customer service has become a hot feature of just about any product.

Jump Start Customer service, traditionally a back-office, low-profile obligation most businesses took on grudgingly at best, is now a growth area. There are good careers here. For example, software giant Microsoft hired some 1,600 new staffers just to handle telephone customer support when it released its Windows 95 operating system in August 1995.

But there is more to it than that. The winners in all industries are those firms that understand who their best potential customer is. No, it's not the folks who fit a certain demographic profile, nor the ladies and gentlemen impressed by an entertaining TV ad or an elaborate magazine spread (although companies routinely lavish millions upon millions of dollars to reach these people). The real winners know that their best potential customers are their current customers—provided, of course, these current customers are satisfied customers. So it has become the business of customer service departments to create customer satisfaction to help the sales department cultivate the company's own backyard, harvesting a bumper crop of customers *there* rather than spending so many more advertising and promotional dollars in search of new fields, which may or may not prove fertile.

Perhaps you are interested in customer service as a career. Perhaps not. That's not my point. I have dwelled a bit on this subject because the practice of creating customer satisfaction to maximize repeat business, while a very traditional idea, is creating a revolution in the way we work. And I strongly advise any job hunter to take heed of the lessons of this revolution. Work at creating satisfaction in your employer, then look to your *current* employer for a *new* job. He or she is your best potential "customer."

Keep Your Eye on the Stars—but Your Ear to the Ground

Now, I don't want you to get the idea that, by simply doing a good job, your employer will put an arm around your shoulder and tell you that he's "kickin' ya' upstairs." Many rags-to-riches books and movies have been telling us for years that this is how it happens. Sometimes, I suppose, it really does happen like this. Sometimes, people hit it big on the state lottery, too.

Begin at the Very Beginning (It's a Very Good Place to Start)

Have you noticed that many new-car TV commercials don't just extoll the beauty of the automobile, its technical excellence, and its safety, but also promise that the visit to the dealer—the very act of making the purchase—will be pleasurable and rewarding? These advertisers believe that customer satisfaction should begin at the beginning. Of course, *you* also want employer satisfaction to begin at the beginning. I mean, that's how you get the job, right, by making a great impression at the interview? We'll spend plenty of time in Part 3 and Part 4 talking about just how to accomplish this. But, right now, let's stand the opening situation on its head. You're at the job interview. You want to create satisfaction in your employer, sure. But always remember: This is a transaction, a two-way street. The interview is also your opportunity to give your potential employer the message that *you* likewise expect satisfaction.

An important aspect of your satisfaction is opportunity for advancement. You need to let the employer know this while he or she is still a *potential* employer.

> **YOU'RE HIRED!**
>
> **Winner**
> Put the question in an attractive frame. "I'm very excited about the challenges of a position like this. I realize how critical it is to the company's performance. What do you see as the opportunities it offers for even more advancement and growth?" This suggests that, while growth is important to you, you don't see the present position as a mere stepping stone.

One of the interview questions you should always ask is, "What avenues for growth and advancement does the position offer?" While you don't need to use exactly these words, it is important that you structure the question in just this way. Don't ask, "Does this job offer any opportunity for advancement?" This question calls for a simple yes or no. While few employers are going to answer with a pointblank *no*, a simple *yes* is not very helpful, either. Asking *what* ("What avenues…," "What opportunities…") rather than *does* will elicit a more thoughtful, specific, and helpful answer. Even more important, it tells the potential employer that advancement and growth are important to you and that you *expect* such opportunity to be a part of the job. It positions you proactively rather than passively. It is the first step toward *creating* opportunity for advancement. Setting growth as priority right from the start will make it easier for you to raise the issue of advancement and promotion during annual performance reviews. You may remind the employer of what you shook hands on when you were hired.

Using Job Listings and Postings

Most larger organizations have a system for internally posting available positions. Make it your business to find out the following:

➤ Where the positions are posted

➤ When they are posted

➤ How often they are updated

It's about time for another cliché: The early bird…. You know the rest. Respond to the postings as soon as possible. If you find out that they are posted in Place X before they are posted in Place Y, make an expedition to Place X part of your routine, even if the difference between the two postings is a matter of hours. A growing number of companies post available positions over the internal computer network. Monitor this regularly.

A posting is not worth much if it fails to include someone to whom you can respond. If you are offered a choice between responding to someone in Human Resources and someone at the department posting the job, always respond directly to the department. In fact, you should try to respond directly to the source of the position even if you are *not* explicitly given the choice.

Rule 1: If possible, respond directly to the source of the position.

Optical Engineer II
Job description: Contributing to the development of optical assembly and testing of new lenses, as well as solving lens production problems.
Requirements: BS in Physical Science or Engineering (MS preferred) coupled with 3 yrs of industrial experience. A solid knowledge of testing lithographic lenses for distortion, focus vs. CDs and astigmatism is essential. Key to your qualification is a strong background in classical optics (esp. In lens design and optical testing), computer literacy and superior written/verbal skills in English. A plus is knowledge of statistical process control.
Contact: Human Resources at 5896.

Posted at a high-tech imaging company. Before contacting Human Resources, contact the head of Optical Engineering.

Rule 2: If possible, avoid going through Human Resources.

Is this subversive?

Well...yes, by all means. But it's not a subversive tactic for the sake of subversion. Human resources departments perform a wide array of very valuable services, including such things as administering insurance programs, arbitrating disputes, addressing grievances, and so on. In the area of hiring, many companies pervert the truest and best function of Human Resources, assigning it a mandate not to *search for* job candidates, but to *screen* applicants. Now, why subject yourself to a screening in a company for which you already work? At the very least, it consumes your time and energy. At worst, you may get screened out.

If the name of a department manager is included in the posting, respond directly to him or her. If no name is given—only someone in Human Resources—try calling the department directly anyway. Look up the name and extension of the department's manager or supervisor and call:

"Mrs. Perkins, I'm John Dillard in Special Sales. I saw your posting for a sales supervisor. It's a position I believe I'm very right for, and I'd like the opportunity to talk with you about it."

Make no reference to Human Resources or to having looked up her name and number in the corporate directory. Just make the call. If she insists that you go through Human Resources, don't argue. Go through Human Resources.

Jump Start
Only 15 percent of businesses have human resources departments. However, this minority includes the nation's largest employers.

33

An internal e-mail job posting from a university. The two "specialists" listed are the human resources contacts. If you were serious about moving into one of the positions listed, you would try to bypass the "specialists" and contact the department managers directly.

WHERE THE QUALIFICATIONS FOR A POSITION ARE DESCRIBED IN TERMS OF FORMAL EDUCATION OR TRAINING, PRIOR EXPERIENCE IN THE SAME FIELD MAY BE SUBSTITUTED.

POSITIONS WITH FULL DESCRIPTIONS ARE THOSE MOST RECENTLY POSTED.

MEDICAL SCHOOL
Specialist: Ronald Story/Janet Zinser

ASSISTANT MANAGER II (05057JZ) Assist manager with overall operation of optical shop; assist with supervision and provide directions to patients and physicians; work closely with manager to evaluate optical wear; repair lenses and other optical materials; assist in instruction of house staff about lenses techniques, bifocals and prisms for patients. Qualifications: BA/BS or equivalent; three yrs. experience as an optician; must be licensed as an optician. Grade: P2; Range: $21,700-28,200 5-18-95 Ophthalmology

CLINICAL RESEARCH COORDINATOR(06091RS) Responsible for general management of study; recruit/screen patients; organize recruitment programs; coordinate patient activity; interview and meet with patients, family members and physicians; oversee faculty and ancillary staff; maintain study documentation; communicate with IRB concerning status of study; prepare and monitor budget during grant period; prepare annual report; attend national meetings. Qualifications: BA/BS in scientific or related field required; four yrs. experience in field; related research experience is desirable; certified ophthalmic technician desirable. Grade: P5; Range: $28,800-37,600 Ophthalmology

COORDINATOR II (07076JZ) Prepare & process exempt & non-exempt personnel appointments from search process; interact with faculty and central administration offices; monitor & journal payroll charges to research grants for HUP employees on department inter-fund account; generate payroll roster for staff for payment from various grant accounts; process personnel forms for payroll and on-line payroll system; reconcile & justify efforts reports; place ads in scientific journals & newspapers; monitor department information database on all employees. Qualifications: BA/BS required; one-three yrs. experience in fiscal operations; bookkeeping course work experience desirable; strong organizational skills; demonstrated oral & written communication skills; experience in MAC Excel, Microsoft Word, FileMaker Pro desired; knowledge of Penn salary/personnel systems preferred. Grade: P2; Range: 21,700-28,200 7-19-95 Radiology

Visiting Human Resources

I'm not saying Human Resources doesn't do a good job. It's just that the job it does will not necessarily help you advance within the organization. Remember, in all too many organizations large enough to have a human resources department, the primary hiring function of Human Resources is *screening* rather than *recruiting*. This said, you should pay a visit to Human Resources so that you can discuss your interests and goals. Let them know that you are interested in growth and advancement. Just make sure that you keep it positive. Never tell a human resources "counselor" that you are bored or dissatisfied with your job. In fact, take the opportunity to report your success within the position. Emphasize that you are committed to the organization and that you want to continue to grow within it. Then get into your interests, aspirations, goals, and objectives.

Just don't count on any of this getting you a better job. It may turn up a posted position that you somehow overlooked. It may even turn up one that somehow failed to get posted. It may result in getting your name in a file that a hiring department head may peruse. Just don't count on it. Don't wait for Human Resources to connect you with a job. Use that department as just one more resource while you actively pursue positions directly.

Climbing the Grapevine

Everyone knows that any company employing more than a half-dozen people is really two organizations. It's the organization depicted on a hierarchical branch diagram in the annual report, and it's the unofficial organization in which John A always tells Joe B all the gossip, or Mary X gives Tom Y better customer leads because she likes him more than she does Jane Z. Around the rigid official structure of almost any organization, a richly organic grapevine soon twines and intertwines. It never fails to amaze corporate managers how efficient the grapevine can be. News seems to travel faster on it than across the electronic grid linking the firm's personal computers.

Don't ignore the grapevine. If it makes you feel better, go ahead and dignify it with the term *network* (we will discuss *networking* in detail in Chapter 12, "Making Networking Work for You"), but don't overlook what your friends and colleagues have to say about positions in other departments or in your own. Here are some grapevine *dos* and *don'ts*:

Do:

➤ Keep your ears open for word about opportunities within the company, in your department and in others.

➤ Follow up on any leads that interest you. Again, identify the source of the position and contact him or her directly. Avoid Human Resources, if possible.

➤ Put out the word that you are interested in moving up. Be as specific as you can be. ("I really want to get into a sales supervisor position.") Keep it positive. ("With the success I've had in working in selling this line, I'd really like to direct a department—get into a sales supervisor position.")

Don't:

➤ Depend on the grapevine. This is a passive approach.

➤ Complain about your present position. This will not spread the word that you are looking to move up. It will just create gossip that you hate your job. And, make no mistake, your expression of *mild* discontent will be rapidly magnified into, "Kent just cannot stand his job. He hates it. He's going crazy in it. He's going to have a breakdown any day now."

Managing Your Boss When You Want to Make a Move

Before moving on to a new job in a different department, you should consider the possibility of promotion in your present department. Depending on your relationship with your boss, seniority considerations, and the needs of the department, it is usually easier to move up within a department than to move out and up.

Promoting Yourself

Now that you are contemplating remaining in your current department, should you seek a promotion or remain in your present position and seek a raise in salary? In part, this depends on your feelings and needs. Obviously, if you are satisfied with your current duties and responsibilities but you need more money, you should go after a raise. In many organizations, however, specific positions have formal or informal salary ceilings, and the next step up the compensation ladder is a loftier position: a promotion.

Is it harder to get a promotion than it is to get a raise? This question recalls the classic query posed to differentiate optimists from the pessimists: Is the glass half empty or half full? The pessimist will tell you that it's harder to get a promotion because you are asking for two things, more money *and* more responsibility. Of course, the hardcore pessimist will also point out that getting a raise is also

Jump Start
This chapter assumes that you are working in a large organization—an organization big enough to be divided into departments. Just for the record, though, 80 percent of all private businesses employ 50 or fewer persons, yet this 80 percent generates two-thirds of the new jobs.

difficult, because you are asking for more cash without doing anything more to earn it. The optimist, in contrast, will tell you that it's easier to get a promotion than a raise, because you are giving the powers-that-be a better bargain—they're giving you more money, but you are accepting more responsibility for it. On the other hand, that optimist may tell you that it's easier to get a raise, because bosses are more willing to yield on issues of money than power.

If you feel I've tied you up in a Gordian knot, just emulate Alexander the Great, and use your sword on it. Don't argue the point. Instead, arbitrarily take the optimist's position on both issues: the raise and the promotion. Most folks will go for the promotion, and the best way to begin is by holding on to the principle that you are taking on more work, more responsibility, exercising a higher-level set of transferable skills in fair exchange for greater compensation. Keeping this principle uppermost in your negotiations will not only give your boss the right feelings about parting with more cash, but, even more important, it will allow *you* to feel less like a hat-in-hand supplicant and more like a good businessperson. You are, after all, not simply asking for more; you are offering value for value in a way that shows respect for yourself and commitment to your company.

Going after the promotion rather than the raise is the more prudent of the two approaches. If you are turned down for the promotion, you can still negotiate a raise in your present position. In contrast, you cannot fall back from asking for a raise to asking for a promotion.

Assuming you have performed well in your job, you come to the negotiating table armed with something the outsider lacks: a track record with *this* department and *this* boss. Just don't depend on your boss being intimately familiar with that record. Come into the discussion fully armed with a list of solid accomplishments—not a canned spiel consisting of self-laudatory adjectives. Do what the great novelists and poets have always done. Use words to show rather than tell. Exhibit results, not empty verbiage. And, whenever possible, exhibit those results in dollars: dollars made and dollars saved.

Out and Up

There are many compelling reasons to seek opportunities outside your current department. You may well have gone about as far as you can go in your present spot. You may find a more appealing position in another department. You may not agree with your present boss. Whatever the reason, better remember just one more cliché. It's about burning your bridges behind you.

Don't do it.

Sometimes you are fortunate enough to enjoy a special, genuinely mentoring relationship with your boss. In these all-too-rare cases, your boss may encourage you to move on and develop. Unfortunately, this is an exception to the rule. In most cases, your boss will be far less interested in your personal growth than he or she is in making sure that the department is not disrupted. Additionally, your boss may feel that he or she has invested time, talent, and energy in developing you, only to "lose" you to another department. There may also be a personal element. Like a spurned "significant other," your boss may (to some degree) feel offended and affronted. Be sensitive to these feelings.

Whatever your reasons for transferring to another department, your "terminal" conversation should be positive. Cast yourself, your soon-to-be-ex-boss, and the department in the best possible light. This does not mean that you should lie: "I love this job, and I love you, and it just kills me to move out and up." Obviously, if this were really the case, you wouldn't leave. However, avoid stressing the negative reasons that have motivated the move: "I'm transferring because this is a dead-end job in a nowhere department." Instead,

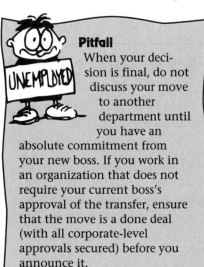

Pitfall
When your decision is final, do not discuss your move to another department until you have an absolute commitment from your new boss. If you work in an organization that does not require your current boss's approval of the transfer, ensure that the move is a done deal (with all corporate-level approvals secured) before you announce it.

leave with something like, "I've decided to accept a position that, at this time, is a better match between my skills and the needs of the company." Not only does this statement take the burden off you *and* your boss by suggesting that your move is in the best interest of the company—the larger team, of which you are both members—but the phrase "at this time" leaves the door slightly ajar after you walk out. Remember, no exit is more offensive than one accompanied by the shotgun sound of a slammed door.

Well, why bother with all this? Let's say your boss has been a real jerk. Why not get the satisfaction of setting those bridges ablaze?

The object is not to soften the blow of your departure, or even to make your boss feel good. It is, rather, to demonstrate that you are a valuable person, an important asset to the firm, and that you are fully aware of your value.

Leaving the discussion gracefully and gratefully, with honesty tempered by courtesy, demonstrates your self-image. It is the difference between quitting and moving on to something better—better for you and better for the company. In more directly practical terms, it is also well to remember that the two of you are still in the same organization. It is highly probable that you will need to continue, in some measure, to work together. (If you were able to move, so can your former boss. He or she may end up as your supervisor again, or he or she may be reporting to you.) By all means, grow. Change positions when it is right for you to do so. But don't destroy relationships in the process.

Up Is Not the Only Way

The titles of some of the chapters in this book reflect a fact we all take for granted. Vocational or professional or career growth is always upward: moving up the ladder of success, to higher floor, or climbing every mountain to loftier and loftier heights. It's a powerful and pervasive metaphor, and, like all metaphors, its appeal is to the emotions rather than to the intellect. The fact is, while up is generally the direction in which we all want to move, it is not the only strategically viable direction all the time. Or maybe it's just that we tend to define "up" too narrowly. For most of us, "up" simply means "more money." And, what's more, we think that's the way it *has* to be.

But the contrary idea, that we don't live by bread alone, is at least as old as the Gospels. Moving "up" can also mean moving up into a position that is more person-ally satisfying—intellectually, spiritually, whatever. Of course, it *is* certainly more convenient when the job that offers us more spiritual satisfaction and intellectual challenge also comes with a bigger paycheck. But that is not always the case.

> **Buzz Word**
>
> A *lateral move* is one to a position offering the same salary as your current job or, at most, a compensation increase of three percent or less. Any move involving a decrease in salary, no matter how small, is likely to be seen (at least by others) as a downward rather than lateral move.

There is yet another reason to avoid thinking exclusively in upward terms. Sometimes, a lateral or even a downward salary move is necessary to position yourself for greater growth in the long run. Sometimes such moves are necessary to avoid getting locked into a career track with less income—and/or personal fulfillment—potential than you deserve.

Lateral Moves: Why, When, and How

You may make a lateral move simply because a position in another department is, for whatever reason, more personally appealing to you. Hey, it's your life, and that is reason enough to make the move. Your lateral move, however, may also be motivated by long-term strategic goals. For example, you may have good reason to believe that a certain department offers more room for advancement than your current department. Making a lateral move *now* will position you for greater advancement later. Or you may recognize that another department offers a job that will position you for greater growth within your industry.

Case Study

You are currently a sales representative in the Buggy Whip Division of Acme Enterprises. A position as sales representative in the Microchip Division opens up at the same salary level. Should you make the move? (Probably a good idea.) You'd better. Make it your business to track industry trends to avoid getting caught in the squeeze when one technology edges out another.

Well, here's a helpful statement: Lateral moves are both easier and harder to make than moves up the salary ladder. Easier? Yes, because you are on strong ground. Obviously, your move is not motivated by salary, but by a genuine desire for the position. To your potential new boss, this suggests commitment and even passion. Harder? Yes, because it will be more difficult to avoid the possibility of ill will from your current boss. He or she will have an easier time gracefully accepting a move made for salary reasons than one motivated by a desire for—what?—greater challenges? Greater spiritual satisfaction? More of a future? Avoiding a conflagration of your bridges in this case requires particular sensitivity.

Pitfall

Avoid serial lateral moves. If you make it a habit to move from one same-salary position to another, you will be perceived as unreliable. No supervisor wants to invest time and energy in a subordinate who is likely to leave.

The lateral move is also more difficult in that it is possible that your grand strategy may fail. The potential of the new department may suddenly contract rather than expand. In this case, the move may retard your growth. It may be more difficult to explain as an item on your résumé. ("Why didn't you get a raise when you moved from X to Y?") These are real risks, and they mean that you should not make a lateral move lightly. Unless you have a strong personal motive for making the move, be certain that you have a sound strategic reason for it. Carefully weigh the possible strategic gains against the risks.

Should You Take a Strategic Step Down?

In a word, the answer is *no*. In two words, it's *probably no*.

The deliberate step down is always a very high-risk move. Maybe you have a pressing personal reason for doing this. A hot new department in your company is offering an opportunity you really want to take, but at a lower salary. Just make sure that your personal need is pretty overwhelming before you make the move.

You may consider taking a step down for the same overall *strategic* reasons that motivate a lateral move: a perception that another department offers ultimately greater opportunities. This may be quite valid, but it is a substantial gamble. The problem is that the ladder-of-success idea is so deeply ingrained in all of us that anyone reviewing a résumé or salary history indicating a decrease will have a difficult time believing that the move downward was voluntary. Most generals will tell you that the phrase "strategic retreat" is usually a euphemism for defeat. To be sure, the strategic step down is an option, but it requires great insight, careful judgment, and nerves of steel.

And, for Do-It-Yourselfers...Building a Position from Scratch

I believe the most successful job hunters are the most proactive. They anticipate opportunity rather than respond to it when—and if—it comes a-knocking. The most extreme proactive approach is not to *hunt* for opportunity in your current department or other departments, but to *create* opportunity.

The most feasible way of creating a new position is to work within your current department, which, after all, you have firsthand experience with and in which you have created credibility—a track record. Make it your business to learn how your department works and how it works with other departments. Then go hire yourself as a consultant (you can name your own salary), and report to yourself on how your department could be improved by the addition of such-and-such a position or by replacing one position with another. Work this out in detail, as if you were reporting not just to yourself, but to the powers that be.

The secret is to take this self-assignment seriously, but also to feel free to play with it. Create scenarios demonstrating the benefits of the new position, then demonstrate how you are the ideal candidate for the position. When you have worked out a set of scenarios and matched yourself seamlessly to the job, take it to your boss.

Here's how *not* to approach him or her: "I've got a great idea that will get this department into shape." Why is this a bad approach? Well, it will make your boss feel that you have somehow left two words off the end of the sentence. They are: "you idiot."

Rather than begin by implying that the boss doesn't know how to run the department, put the emphasis on yourself in relation to the department: "I'd like to talk to you about how I may make more of a contribution to this department. I want to get your take on a few ideas I've been working out." Put the emphasis on yourself as an asset to the department. Do not begin by stating the need for creating a brand-new position. In fact, as you explain to your boss how you see your new role, he or she—ideally—should be the one to point out that you are really talking about redefining your present position or creating a new one. Let the concept of a redefined or new position come from the boss, not you. Let it be his or her idea, so that he or she will feel an ownership stake in it, which will greatly multiply its chances for becoming reality.

The Least You Need to Know

➤ Take a lesson from the world of contemporary business, which has learned that your best *potential* customer is the customer you already have. Cultivate your current employer as your best potential employer.

➤ Start working on your growth within the company from the very beginning.

➤ Use your company's human resources department effectively, but know when and how to avoid that department and go directly to the source of your target position.

➤ Make judicious use of the office grapevine and actively develop your networking skills.

➤ Know when promotion within your current department is your best option and when it is time to look elsewhere within the company.

➤ Make your current boss a partner in your advancement. Never burn your bridges.

➤ Consider a lateral move (in rare cases, even a downward move) when it serves your long-term strategy.

➤ Don't limit yourself to the menu of available positions; consider creating a new opportunity for yourself and for your company.

Chapter 4

Up Another Ladder: Moving to Another Employer in a Company Similar to Yours

In This Chapter

➤ How to assess opportunities in your industry

➤ Making contacts and securing references

➤ Scoping out your industry via the "information superhighway"

➤ How to use headhunters and employment agencies to help you move within your industry

➤ Hunting jobs without arousing suspicion

The Iron Curtain has rusted away, and the Berlin Wall is dust. The fact is that totalitarian regimes, despite their brutal muscle, don't have much staying power. Few people are willing to live without choices, and that goes for economic systems as well. The ones that try to outlaw competition are doomed from the get go. Just as you are free to vote for the candidates of your choice and buy whatever brand of frozen pizza you like best, so you are almost never restricted to climbing the corporate ladder of the company in which you started. Your birthright is to choose another ladder.

So, we're agreed, it's your right to move on—provided, of course, you have a place to go. How do you know what's out there? Begin by measuring the size of your particular universe.

Exploring the Universe: Filling Your Pool of Potential Employers

If you're in retailing, you have perhaps thousands of firms into which you can move. Of course, the more specialized your area of retailing expertise, the smaller that universe becomes. If you specialize in selling devices for safely handling plutonium, your universe is quite small. Also, if you work in an industry that is concentrated in a given city—say, meat packing in Kansas City or publishing in New York—mobility is easier than if changing jobs means moving from Los Angeles to Seoul.

In a locale rich with firms in your industry, moving to a new company does not necessitate uprooting yourself and your family. If, however, an out-of-town move is required, you will have to decide whether or not to pull up stakes. Chapter 7, "Yet Another Move: To Another Region or a Different Country," discusses pros, cons, strategies, and tactics of long-distance job moves.

Depending on the size of your industry and how well you know your business, it may be a very simple matter for you to draw up a list of companies similar to yours. You may even know whom to contact about a job. If, however, this kind of information is not at your fingertips, you have all the sources discussed in Part 5 of this book, plus the resources listed and commented upon in Chapter 26, "Search Resources." For people planning to move from one company to another, at least four kinds of resources are especially relevant: the network of references in your own files; certain publications; electronic, on-line resources; and specialized headhunters and placement agencies.

Harvesting Your Files

Start the search with yourself. Most firms in similar businesses are competitors, but within that atmosphere of competition, there often are overlapping areas of collaboration and cooperation. You may see your peers and colleagues at social gatherings, at conventions, and at professional meetings and seminars. You may also work cooperatively with those in other companies when, for whatever reason, you refer a client or customer to another firm (maybe the service requested is too big or too small; maybe you are out of stock of a certain item of merchandise). You may embark on a joint venture. You may share a contract. Whatever the occasion, take advantage of these collegial circumstances to get to know names and faces at other companies. Collect business cards, and keep a file. Also keep these contacts alive with an occasional friendly phone call or, if appropriate, a breakfast or lunch. Pretty soon, you'll find that you have something much more meaningful than a file of names. You have a network.

Your underlying motive in building contacts may be—or may not be—to expand your employment horizon. Whatever the motive, however, please remember that the keynote of all these contacts should be collegiality. Do not let your interest in your counterparts be construed as either industrial espionage—an attempt to cajole corporate secrets— or overt job hunting. There *is* a time to discreetly put out the word that you are interested in moving out

Winner
Don't forget the personal and professional friends you've made in a company you left. Former coworkers don't just fade away. They remain as lively nodes in your employment-opportunity network.

YOU'RE HIRED!

of your company and into another, but, at this stage, you are merely gathering information and making contacts. At the most basic level, you are collecting contacts so that you can locate the person who has the power to hire you. In general, the companies drawn from your files are your best prospects for a new position.

Your network serves two purposes. The first is informational. Each of your contacts is a potential source of news about a job. The next step beyond information is referral. Potentially, you may call on each of your contacts to recommend you for a position.

Potentially.

In actual practice, you must review your list of contacts carefully before calling on any for references. Make certain that the person you tap for good words will, in fact, have nothing but good words to offer. Beware of hidden agendas, and always ask yourself whether so-and-so may be a potential competitor for your target position.

Once you have identified a contact as a good—and safe—prospect for a reference, how do you move from basic networking to asking for the referral?

Don't hem, haw, and beat around the bush, but do begin your phone call with a pleasant exchange of small talk, industry chatter, and an inquiry about the welfare and activity of the family. Then invoke the magic words: "Mary, I want to ask your advice." No request is more likely to yield a positive response. Everyone likes to be flattered by being instantly deemed a guru.

Next, succinctly summarize your current situation. In general, it is always best to keep this as positive as possible: "You know, we've had a great year at Acme Widgets, and while we're riding the crest of this particular wave, I thought it would be the perfect time for a career move." Being positive does not mean lying. If Acme has had a bad year, it is very likely that this fact is known within the industry. It is most definitely not a good idea to broach your request for a reference by being caught in a lie. Be upfront about a bad situation, but neither desperate nor feckless: "Mary, I want to ask your advice. It's no secret that Acme Widgets has had problems this year. Frankly, I think *now* would be a very good time for me to make a career move."

Winner

Some savvy job changers and job hunters ask a friend to do a "dummy check" on references. Posing as a potential employer, the friend calls the reference and listens to what he or she says about the "applicant." At least one professional service, Taylor Review (at 810-651-0286), will, for a fee, check your references.

Pitfall

Former coworkers— people you worked with at a job you've left—can be good references. Depending on the circumstances of your leaving, however, caution and prudence are required. Make sure that you've left behind no hard feelings, and be aware that your reference will likely be asked to say something about why you left.

Move on to the climax: "We both know how important references are, and a reference from you would carry a lot of weight with just about anyone in our industry. Would you have any reservations about my using you as a reference?"

The approach is dual pronged. You begin with undisguised flattery, but you follow up by offering the opportunity to decline. This is *not* a sales situation, where your object is to avoid giving your prospect an opportunity to turn you down. If your contact has any reasons not to provide an enthusiastic, 100 percent positive reference, you want those reasons to surface right *now*, before any harm is done.

In most cases, the response to your request will be positive. Now you're about halfway home. But this is no time to sit back and let your reference do the rest of the work. Do not depend on his or her knowing what to say about you. On the other hand, you do not want to appear to be cramming words into his or her mouth. Instead, give your enthusiastic thanks and then offer information: "Hey, thanks a lot, Mary. I hoped you'd be able to help me out. This is great. Let me just update you on what I've been doing most recently, and I'll also tell you a bit about the kind of opportunity I'm looking for."

Spend two or three minutes enumerating some key accomplishments. Be specific, and put the greatest emphasis on projects you worked on together. List for your reference your half-dozen most important duties and responsibilities. Mention at least three of your greatest strengths. You could also go over some of the questions your reference may be asked. Finally, offer to jot down all of this in a note. Either mail the note or send it via private e-mail. Unless you know that your reference has a dedicated fax machine to which only he or she has access (a rarity in most offices!), do not send the note by fax, where it is likely to be seen by any number of prying eyes.

PARRINGTON GIFTS

443 S. Homestead Blvd.
Clifford, Ohio 23456
555-555-5555
Fax: 555-444-4444

August 2, 1995

Mr. Harold Better
Director of Special Sales
Rex Publishing Company
561 Third Avenue
New York, NY 10002

Dear Mr. Better:

It is a pleasure to tell you about Jane Chan, whom, I understand, you are considering for the position of Special Sales Director.

Jane and I have worked together on many projects over the past three years. As assistant director of special sales at Carlton House Publishers, she was key to my decision to order Carlton's "Inspirational Moments" series for our exclusive gift catalogue. I know this represents a good piece of business for Carlton, and I can tell you that it has proved a real profit center for Parrington Gifts. I am very grateful to Jane for having turned me on to the series.

It is not just that she is an effective salesperson. She has worked to make us all partners in success. She is, in fact, less interested in making any particular sale than she is in creating a satisfied customer--a customer who develops a buying relationship with her firm. I feel that, because of her, I have bought not only a product line, but the backing, the support, and the responsiveness of her entire company.

Mr. Better, Jane Chan is the kind of person you want leading your special sales team. Please call me if you have further questions.

Sincerely yours,

Vernon Parrington

Head Buyer

A good letter of recommendation is not only enthusiastic and unreserved in its praise, but also is specific, citing a particular project or set of accomplishments.

Be sure to follow up with your reference after you have closed in on a specific job. Tell him or her to expect a call from so-and-so at So-and-So, Inc. Review the salient areas the potential employer may want to discuss.

Using Published Sources

As someone moving from one company to another within the same industry, you are by definition an insider. Congratulations.

That said, don't neglect the published sources of job information and job news listed in Chapter 26, which, of course, are available to everybody, insiders and outsiders alike. You should also *creatively* monitor newspaper want ads. Check out Chapter 11, "Trekking the Want Ad Jungle."

Jump Start One of your most valuable job-hunting tools is a public library card. You are seriously and unnecessarily handicapping yourself if you do not obtain one.

Those moving from one company to another within the same industry should also use the trade and business publications produced by and/or for the industry. You probably are familiar with the ones that apply to your business. If not, go to the handiest public library and consult the following:

➤ *National Trade and Professional Associations of the United States* (Washington, D.C.: Columbia Books)

➤ *Reader's Guide to Periodical Literature* (available in the reference department of most libraries)

National Trade and Professional Associations lists not only associations relevant to your industry, but also any publications the association may produce. Finally, the *Reader's Guide* is an ongoing and monumental source of information. You look up a subject—say, "widget wonking"—and this remarkable reference will list relevant articles in a wide variety of periodical publications. This will allow you to identify not only relevant magazines, but particularly relevant articles in those magazines.

Your use of trade and business periodicals should not be limited to searching the want ads you may find in them. To be sure, these are a valuable resource, but you'll find the articles devoted to specific companies and industry issues even more valuable because of the insight they provide. Explore industry-related periodicals for the following:

➤ Company-focused articles, which will tip you off to hot firms and solid opportunities

➤ Industry-focused articles, which will inform you about trends and developments, suggesting growth areas that may guide your job move

➤ Names: names of article authors (if they are industry professionals) and the names mentioned in the articles. Both of these are potential job contacts

➤ News about promotions, executive moves, retirements, and—yes—deaths. These help you identify possible openings at specific companies

➤ Product and service ads, which tip you off to companies that are producing hot new merchandise and offering trend-setting services

Remember, industry publications are *interactive* publications. No law says that all you can do with them is read them. Think about being a contributor, writing an article, a news item, or even a letter to the editor. Getting published or even quoted in a trade periodical gives you instant credibility and broadcasts your name throughout the industry.

Start and maintain a clipping file of articles that generate job leads. Also copy into your address book any potential contact names.

UNITED SCENIC ARTISTS

NEWS

NEW YORK • CHICAGO • LOS ANGELES

UNITED SCENIC ARTISTS
Local 829

AUGUST 1995

Regional Membership Meeting Schedules:

New York: Sept. 12 6:30pm Tuesday
Location: Local 802 Meeting Rm.
322 West 48th Street

Chicago: Aug. 7 6:00pm Monday
Location: USA office/Midland Hotel
176 W. Adams-Ste. 1712

Los Angeles: Aug. 12 1:00pm Saturday(Exec. Bd.)
1:30pm Saturday (GMM)

COMPUTER FAIR:

The office has received a great many applications from members who are interested in the Aug. 26, 1995 Computer Fair. If you have not signed up, fill out the application below and sent it in as soon as possible.

We have decided to expand the scope of the fair and include more lighting design. Tom Simitzes has agreed to coordinate this area of interest. We are looking at several venues to accommodate the fair. We need at least one theater space to demonstrate lighting options involving computers and a large area to set up workstations for drafting and graphics and smaller viewing area for the animation. If you have work or products you would like to present, please contact Don Padgett in the office. We are asking vendors to come and present their products (programs, workstations, etc.)

Applicants will be informed by mail about location and time.

FROM 401(k) OFFICE:

A number of our employers will be matching the first 2% of our contributions to the 401(k) Fund starting in the fall. The value of this matching money is considerable. Assume you are 40 and work until 65, you currently make $50,000, you contribute 10% of your income, and you experience a 2.8% increase in contributions each year. If you elect the Equity fund and it performs at the level it has over the last 5 years,* your contributions will be worth $661,296 and combined with the company match, your fund value will be $793,555. This will produce $47,613 in annual income at 6% return without depleting your fund value. *(Net 10.5% per year)

Under current tax law, none of the contributions are subject to current state or federal income tax. All withdrawals will be taxed at the then current rates.

This example is provided for your information only and your experience may differ from this projection. Calculations are made from Quicken 4 for Windows.

COMPUTER FAIR
A great deal of interest has been expressed in the "Computer Fair" held in the office on June 17, 1995. The event was organized when we discovered that so many of the members have an interest in classes in computer design programs. We had a very difficult time arranging a "one size fits all" class and decided to present some of our members who are using computers to design and draft talk about the demonstrate the different forms (IBM and MAC) and directions (CAD, ILLUSTRATION, ANIMATION, ETC.) available. We had more than expected turn out and would like to have a list of members who would like to attend an expanded version. If you are interested, please fill out the form below and send it to the Union Office.

NAME _____

ADDRESS _____

_____

PHONE (___) _____

I USE:

☐ IBM   ☐ MAC

☐ VELLUM   ☐ AUTO-CAD

☐ PHOTOSHOP   ☐ ILLUSTRATOR

☐ _____   ☐ _____

You don't have to get published in a prestigious trade journal. Send letters and other communications to the editors of newsletters and bulletins, such as this publication for the members of a union.

One last point: Should you invest in a subscription to any or all the relevant publications? Some of these subscriptions can be fairly expensive, and, chances are, your office already subscribes. However, it is likely that the office copy passes through many hands before it reaches yours. Employment information is timely. If you are serious about making a move, you should invest in a subscription. It is a good idea to specify delivery to your home address to make an end run around would-be borrowers at the office.

Getting Online

Chapter 8, "Looking Good on Paper," and Chapter 13, "Cruising the Infobahn," provide extensive discussions of the newest avenue to a new job, the electronic information superhighway. Chapter 8 tells you how to put your résumé online, while Chapter 13 gives you techniques and strategies for navigating the often bewildering range of job-related databases available on the Internet as well as on such commercial services as CompuServe.

The information superhighway offers seven opportunities for job seekers:

➤ You can post your résumé online.

➤ You can send cold letters and résumés to specific companies (and specific individuals within those companies) through electronic mail (e-mail) instead of "snail mail" (computerese for what the U.S. Postal Service offers).

➤ You can search for job postings.

➤ You can find job-hunting help.

➤ You can research facts about an array of companies and industries.

➤ Through "forums," "chat rooms," and "news groups" (the names vary with the on-line service you use), you can make live, interactive contacts.

➤ Once you have a hot lead or significant prospect, e-mail can be an efficient way of transmitting follow-up information fast.

Pitfall
Don't expect on-line miracles. The potential of the electronic superhighway is great. But leading career counselors and employment authorities estimate that, at present, most on-line methods will be less than 10 percent effective in getting you a job.

Here and now, let's consider the two on-line options most directly useful to those looking to move from one company to another within the same industry. The other options are potentially important, however, for *anyone* seeking a job, so please consult Chapters 8 and 13.

A growing number of companies maintain a so-called "home page" on the World-Wide Web (WWW, also called simply "the Web") accessible through the Internet (or "the Net"). Others are accessible through "ftp" Internet connections. (See Chapter 13 for specifics on accessing the Internet and WWW.) Other firms maintain freestanding on-line bulletin board services (BBSs), usually accessible via modem and telephone (you just dial an ordinary phone number) and sometimes at least partly open to the public. The publicly available areas of a private BBS usually offer such items as company profiles and copies of recent press releases. Even if your target companies don't offer Internet or BBS services, they may be accessible through an e-mail address. You can use this to transmit a request for information.

Chapter 13 includes a list of guides and directories that will help you navigate the Internet, commercial on-line services, and the vast sea of bulletin board services. Some of these guides mention a popular service available on most commercial on-line services as well as throughout the Internet: the chat room, the discussion forum, or the newsgroup. Whatever a particular on-line venue may call it, these way stations on the information superhighway offer opportunities to make interactive (that is, two-way) contact with experts in your industry and with the people who actually have the power to hire you. Most commercial on-line services maintain electronic directories of their members and their forums. You can search these directories simply by typing in a keyword or two.

Headhunters and Placement Agencies

You will find an entire chapter—Chapter 15, "Agencies and Headhunters"—devoted to working with employment agencies and headhunters. Of most use to you, as someone looking to change jobs within an industry, are the headhunters and agencies who specialize in your industry. Most *general* employment agencies are inefficient at connecting you with a job, especially at the higher levels of employment. But, depending on the industry, companies in search of specific personnel do make use of industry-specific placement firms. (Larger employment agencies or executive recruiters often have divisions or departments devoted to specific industries.) It therefore behooves you to identify the relevant agencies. How do you find them? Start with the Yellow Pages and look under "Employment Agencies." Usually, the firm's ad will describe its specialties, if any. Many trade associations and even commercial business publishers publish industry directories, listing names and numbers of various services useful to the industry. Consult these guides, if they are available. If trade publications specific to your industry are available, these usually contain ads for specialized placement agencies.

You should understand that there are three kinds of agencies available to you. There are permanent employment agencies, where the prospective employer pays the fee (and you pay nothing). Want ads placed by such firms often specify "fee paid," meaning that the fee will be paid by the employer, not you. There are search firms that an employer may retain to fill a particular position. (This is what most people mean by "headhunter," and, again, you pay no fee.) Finally, there are permanent employment agencies that you pay for. In the first two cases, the employer, not you, is the client. In the third case, the agency is working for you. Chapter 15 tells you how to check out an agency's credentials and credibility, which is especially important if you are paying the bill. For most people who are changing companies within an industry, the employer-paid agencies or head-hunters are the most effective and least expensive alternative. Don't even bother to pick and choose among them. Simply visit all of them.

Don't waste your time mailing in a résumé to an agency. Make a phone call and set up a face-to-face interview. Consult Chapter 15 before each interview. Depending on the salary level of the job you are looking for, you will probably visit either an agency or an executive recruiter. Agencies generally handle lower-level positions (in most industries, those at the manager level and below, paying under $60,000 or $70,000), while executive search firms are retained to fill upper-level posts ($70,000+). Don't be intimidated. If you feel you are ready to move into upper management, pay a call on an executive recruiter. Just be aware that these firms are hired by employers to fill specific positions. Unless your résumé suggests a perfect fit, the recruiter is likely to keep your résumé on file, but not likely to get you a job any time soon. The fact is that executive recruiters are hired to be proactive. They make calls and go out in search of likely candidates. They do not rely on walk-ins.

Pitfall

No reputable executive recruiter will ever charge *you* a fee. If any self-styled "professional" offers to find you a high-paying job in exchange for a fee, get up, go out the door, feel for the presence of your wallet or purse, and keep walking—at a very brisk pace.

Looking before Leaping: How to Assess the Work Environment of Another Company

One of the "Ten Interview Questions You Should Always Ask" is, "How would you describe the 'weather' in this company? Stormy? Hot? Cool? Breezy? Calm? Brisk? Or what?" Making the idea of workplace climate something literal will catch the interviewer off guard, make him or her think, and most likely produce an honest answer that represents a reasonably realistic perception of what it's like to work at the place. Even if you are fairly miserable where you are now, don't assume there is greener grass in a new venue. Ask the question, and weigh the answer.

Even before you get to the interview stage, however, you can begin to assess the work environment of your target company. Do people in your industry talk about the company? What do they say? Any consistent pattern to the remarks, pro or con? Ask—in a friendly, social way—folks who currently work at the target company how they like it and why. If you can identify someone who recently left the firm, ask him or her why. Try to assess the turnover rate at the target company. Do people stay on board for more than three to five years? Finally, fall back on common sense. If you can meet some current employees, ask yourself whether you would enjoy working and socializing with these folks.

Beyond talking to people and listening to the prevailing word, read the company's literature, including advertisements. Look for statements of company policy in these materials. What are the firm's stated—or implied—values?

And then there is the product or service itself: How good is it? What kind of reputation does the company have among consumers? Sure, it is possible for an utterly despicable firm to produce an excellent product. Possible. But not likely. Excellence, fortunately, tends to be highly contagious. If it is present in one aspect of what a company does, it is likely to pervade the entire operation. It is not easy for mean-spirited, miserable, unfair, or unimaginative people to produce a good and valuable product.

Putting Out Feelers without Raising Eyebrows

Researching job possibilities and putting out the word on your availability involve some hard work. What makes the work even harder is that you have to probe and advertise without drawing attention to yourself in your own company. Now, you may be tempted to let on that you are looking for a new job. Maybe you feel that you've been under-appreciated or even mistreated. Maybe you're unhappy about being passed over for a promotion. You want to say to your present employer, "Look. I'm not trapped here. You're not the only game in town. I'm a hot item." This is understandable, and the sentiments it embodies indicate a healthy, positive self-image and attitude. But actually saying or doing something that transmits this message is counterproductive at best and very dangerous at worst. The least risk you run is being perceived as a grumbler and malcontent. The greater risk is being judged as disloyal.

Either of these extremes—but especially the latter—can get you fired. Certainly, the perception of your negative attitude will tend to hold you back. (What do you care? You don't plan to stick around anyway. Look at that sentence carefully. The critical phrase is *don't plan to*. Regardless of your plan, you may be with your present firm for quite a while.)

Said Confucius: "Silence Is a Friend Who Never Betrays"

Don't talk about your job search to anyone in your company. It's that simple. You will be tempted to speak to your friends and presumed confidantes, swearing them, of course, to secrecy. But you may as well post a notice on the bulletin board in the coffee room.

53

As for your conversations with those outside your company, try to keep your research inquiries at a social level whenever possible, except for those individuals from whom you solicit referrals. In trying to get information on a prospective employer from other colleagues, try asking questions such as, "How are they treating you at Acme Widgets?" Then draw out the conversation from that point, without, however, implying that you are looking to leave your present firm.

Job Searching in a Close-Knit Industry

Job Changer A is worried that Prospective Employer B, to whom A has just spoken, will call Present Employer C, blab to him about A's desire to defect, thereby leaving A to twist slowly, slowly in the wind.

The bad news is, it's a possibility. The good news, however, is that it's a *remote* possibility. Even in small, close-knit industries, where everyone knows everyone else, the overwhelming majority of prospective employers keep applications in confidence. In part, this is due to a basic sense of decency. Blessedly few people enjoy deliberately inflicting injury. Keeping the confidence also results from a desire to withhold information from a competitor. And if these two motives are not sufficient, there is also the specter of legal liability. If Prospective Employer B spills the beans to Present Employer C, thereby prompting C to fire Job Changer A, A may have a solid damages suit to bring against B. Prospective Employer B would be foolish indeed to risk such exposure.

Despite the likelihood that your inquiry or application will be kept in confidence, do stress to the prospective employer that your inquiry or application is strictly privileged information. Use that phrase—*privileged information*—and do not go beyond it. Do not mention what is obvious: "My boss has no idea that I'm looking around." Do not express a fear by saying, "My boss would can me in a New York minute if she knew I was looking around." Remember, you are trying to persuade your listener to be your *new* boss. Implying that you are skulking around behind your present boss's back is insensitive, to say the least.

As part of your unobtrusive effort to maintain confidentiality, give careful consideration to how you want the potential employer to communicate with you. Unless your office mail comes directly to you, ask that all communication be sent to your home address. Likewise, if you do not have a completely private voice mail system, accessible only by your password, ask that the prospective employer leave no sensitive messages. (It is usually impractical to ask calls to be directed to your home. During business hours, you are not home. You are in the office.) Finally, beware of the fax machine. In many offices, it is virtually a bulletin board. Tell the prospective employer that the office fax machine is in a hallway and is neither secure nor private. Unless you have your own fax machine in your own office, caution your prospect to transmit no sensitive material by fax.

Crossing the Rubicon—without Burning Your Bridges

Breaking the news about your move can be difficult. In many industries, such moves come with the territory, and your boss has long since learned to accept them more or less gracefully. But it is a real possibility that your news will be greeted as a defection, a betrayal, and a veritable knife through the heart. Your boss's emotions may be akin to those that accompany a divorce, and he or she may try to inflict on you a sense of guilt commensurate with his or her own pain. In a case such as this, the most you can do is remind your boss—gently but firmly—that your move is a matter of business and that it is not intended to convey a personal message of any kind. Keep it positive. Avoid statements such as, "We never really saw eye to eye, so I decided it was time for a change." This may be perfectly true. It may, in fact, be the reason for your move.

It is better, however, to draw the focus away from the company and the boss you are leaving and to concentrate the spotlight solely on yourself: "The time is right for me to make the move." If you are pressed to give a fuller account of your motives, do so, but maintain the focus on the opportunities the new company offers rather than why the company you are about to leave has become intolerable. In enumerating the new opportunities, keep the discussion general. Be careful not to betray any of your new company's proprietary information ("Oh, yeah. They're bringing out a dynamite new line of widgets, and I'll be directly involved with it. Nothing else like it in the business! Top secret!")

It is the practice of many companies these days to conduct so-called exit interviews. If asked to participate in one, you should make an effort to cooperate. Resist the temptation, however, to be overly frank. Don't complain. Don't criticize. Again, keep the focus positive.

Why bother with all of this? And what if working at Acme Widgets truly was a hell on earth? Shouldn't you avail yourself of the cathartic satisfaction of delivering your pent up spleen in all its blazing glory?

If the company you are leaving is 100 percent guaranteed to self-destruct—like the tape-recorder tape on a *Mission Impossible* rerun—immediately after you walk out the door, then by all means fire away. But the fact is that the company and the people who work there will not evaporate. You may work with some of them again, somewhere, sometime. Though it may at the moment be the furthest thing from your mind, you may even return to the company. Do your best to preserve a modicum of good feelings.

The Least You Need to Know

➤ Do all that you can to learn about your industry. Establish contacts and build a network.

➤ Acquire a kit of job-hunting research tools, and learn how to use them.

➤ Identify individuals with the power to hire you, and identify individuals willing to give you persuasive endorsements and recommendations.

➤ Learn to conduct your job search without creating suspicion and anxiety in your present firm.

➤ When you leave, make a graceful exit. Remember that, even in your new position, you are not an island.

Chapter 5

Should I Leave the Ladder to Climb the Mountain? Deciding whether to Change Careers

In This Chapter

➤ Reasons for changing careers

➤ Making the career-change decision

➤ The two-step method of changing careers

➤ Getting the training you need—if you need it

➤ Changing work style instead of career

Depending on the size and scope of your industry, the opportunities it offers, and your enduring interest in it, you could spend your entire working life happily moving from one company to another—the kind of move described in the previous chapter. A growing number of us, however, are making the more dramatic move from one industry to another: getting out of publishing and going into teaching, leaving customer service in the auto industry to go into software marketing, and so on.

Somewhere between these extremes—moving from one company to another without changing careers versus transitioning from a career in one industry to a career in another—is the alternative of moving to a new career within your current industry, maybe even within your current company. Perhaps you are a publisher's sales representative looking to become a book editor. Or maybe you work in the customer service department of an office-machine manufacturer and you want to move into Human Resources.

In recent years, the corporate landscape of America has been transformed by vertical integration, so that, for example, activities as apparently diverse as book publishing, television production and broadcasting, and movie making may be seen as the business not of three or four separate industries, but, rather, one "communications industry." Indeed, all of these activities may be the business of a single "communications company." It is now possible—in fact, not uncommon—for workers to change careers *without* leaving their company.

While the previous chapter focused on the tactics and strategies for changing jobs, this chapter is designed to help you decide if it is time to change careers. It goes on to provide a set of guidelines for career-change alternatives as well as alternatives to career change itself. The chapter that follows this one walks you through the strategic details of career changing.

Why Change Channels?

Some people say television is a terrible thing. I say television is a *wonderful* thing. A *terrible* thing would be television with only a single channel.

Why change channels? Because you are bored with the current program. Because you see a program that is of greater interest to you. Because you see a program that will teach you more. Because you see a program that will—in whatever sense—enrich you more.

Televisions were always manufactured with variable tuners, capable of receiving a variety of channels. In fact, the trend is toward more and more channels. In the world of work, such was not always the case. Before World War II, in this country, people tended to find a job, build a career out of it, and remain in that career—in the same industry, perhaps even in the same company—for the rest of their working lives. This was not only the norm, it was, at least in part, a measure of success. Increasingly, during the postwar years, it became more common not only to move from company to company, but to try different career paths. In part, this is undoubtedly due to the speed of technology, which has spawned a host of brand-new industries, each with brand-new employment needs. In part, it is due to the changing role of the American employer, from corporate father figure to an organization that grants workers more freedom but in return makes fewer guarantees of "job security." Finally, the transition to greater vocational mobility comes from a growing desire to work in fulfillment of your own dreams rather than someone else's corporate vision.

What I'm saying is this: Want to make a big change? There is nothing wrong with you, and you are not alone.

Your Pre-Flight Checklist

You're not alone if you're thinking about changing careers, but do you have a good reason for taking off? Okay, only you and you alone can answer that question. Is that a cop-out? You bet it is. But it also happens to be the truth. Nevertheless, I can offer a list of general reasons for changing careers. Think of it as your pre-flight checklist. Unless he or she has a secret desire to crash and burn, no pilot takes off without one.

➤ You're bored, fed up, sick and tired. And *bored* is no way to live.

➤ You want more money.

➤ You want more challenge.

➤ You want the stimulation of greater risk or greater risk for greater reward.

➤ Your current career may have changed (so to speak) right out from under you. Perhaps the nature of the market for your work has changed, forcing you to deal with products, services, or customers you don't like. Perhaps technology has changed the nature of the work in a way you can't stand. Perhaps your company has moved to a place you hate. Perhaps changes in ownership, management, supervision, or personnel have turned a great job into a daily disaster.

➤ You're eating lunch with a coworker or client. With fork poised midway between plate and mouth, you hear a voice from within ask, "Is this really what I want to do for the rest of my life?" And the answer isn't yes.

➤ You're buying your second roll of antacid tablets, and it's only 10:30 in the morning.

➤ Your current career demands too much of your time—or maybe too much of your spirit. You feel you are neglecting your family. You never see your children. Or you simply feel that your career leaves you with neither the time nor energy to enjoy life.

➤ Your current career is approaching a dead end: It's 1981. A company called IBM has just introduced something that looks like a typewriter with a portable TV set on top of it. They call it a "personal computer." You sell typewriters.

➤ Your current career has ceased to hold *meaning* for you.

Possible Moves, Impossible Moves, and the Right Moves

Those of us who were blessed with loving, nurturing parents have been told more than once, "You can be anything you want to be." Then we leave our parents, go out on our own, and the realm of possibilities seems to contract with each step we take. Depending on the industry you are in, it may be relatively easy, relatively difficult, or pretty much impossible to move from one career to another within the same industry. Similarly, it is not likely that, after working 30 years as a shoemaker, you will be able to make the career change to neurosurgeon. Even writers of self-help books have to face certain realities.

This said, take heed of two additional realities:

1. As far as the prevailing attitude of business and society are both concerned, career changing has never been easier than it is today.

2. The continued development of vertical integration—a trend that will usher in the corporation of the twenty-first century—will continue to encourage career changers.

And here's more good news if you want to change careers. Let me put it this way. I have a real weakness for foot-long submarine sandwiches: ham, cheese, salami, and absolutely everything on them. However, if a law were passed requiring that such a sandwich had to be consumed in a single bite, I'd switch to *nouvelle cuisine*. Fortunately, no legislation of the kind is likely to be enacted. It is just as fortunate that no law says you have to take a career change at one swallow, either.

A career—in fact, any job—consists of nine parts:

➤ **Where you work:** Office, store, farm, and so on.

➤ **Stated goal(s):** To teach math, to repair air conditioners, to sell widgets, and so on.

➤ **Assigned tasks:** For the widget sales representative—be fully familiar with Acme's line of widgets and all their features, prices, and availability; identify and target potential customers; contact potential customers; persuade potential customers; provide information; close the sale; transmit the customer's order to the warehouse; follow up with the customer to ensure satisfaction.

➤ **Tools of the trade:** For the widget sales representative—a telephone, beeper, personal computer, contact-management software, samples and sample case, attractive wardrobe, automobile, and frequent flier card,

➤ **A salary:** Includes all income, tips, commissions, and so on.

➤ **Time:** Few careers are truly limited to eight hours a day, five days a week.

➤ **Talents and/or traits required:** For the widget sales representative—ability to think on your feet, a "people" knack, a good memory, a pleasant telephone voice, a competitive spirit, and a "can-do" attitude.

➤ **Skills required:** For the widget sales representative—persuading people to buy; organization skills.

➤ **Knowledge required:** For the widget sales representative—must be familiar with widget technology and advances in the widget industry; must be able to drive; must be able to operate contact-management software for a personal computer.

Once you break down a career into these constituent parts, you come to realize that, although a career change *can* involve changing all the parts, it rarely does. The core of a career change is found in at least two and at most three of these areas. Changing careers always involves acquiring new skills and acquiring new knowledge. Often, it also requires you to call upon talents or traits your old career did not tap.

When you contemplate a career change, always begin by considering what new skills and knowledge you will need. Can you acquire these? Are you willing to invest the time and effort required to acquire these? Do these new skills and areas of knowledge require you to draw on a new set of talents or traits? Do you possess these? If you have never shown any flair for music, your contemplated career change from accountant to concert violinist will almost certainly fail.

> **Buzz Word**
> Chapter 1 introduced the concept of *transferable skills*—general skills you can take from one job (or life experience) to another. Most jobs also require *specific skills*—that is, skills more or less specific to the particular job. Carpentry is a specific skill, whereas an ability to work with materials is a transferable skill. Carpentry, the specific skill, is a subset of working well with materials, the transferable skill.

Once you have answered these questions, you can go on to consider the other career parts that may change. But, first, take the basics a bit further. Consider that the chief *specific* skill a job or career calls for is usually embodied in the general title of the job. A carpenter's chief skill is carpentry. A physicist's chief skill is physics. Consider next that the principal area of knowledge required in a given field is usually embodied in the descriptive name of that field. If the field is construction, the knowledge required is a knowledge of construction.

Now, think of your current job title. Then think of your current field. The two form a unit that concisely describes your career. Attempting to move, in a single jump, to a career with a new job title and a new field is the vocational equivalent of trying to swallow the submarine sandwich whole. Hard work with poor odds of success and quite possibly fatal results. The more feasible career change is at least a two-step process, in which you begin by changing *either* the title *or* the field, then, in your next career move, make a transition that changes both. For example:

> You are a sales representative for a book publisher. You want to be an advertising copywriter for a maker of computer games. You find a position in your current company as an advertising copywriter. You work at this for many years. Then you become an advertising copywriter for a maker of computer games.

Or you do it this way:

> You leave the publishing company to become a sales representative for a maker of computer games. Later, you make the transition from the sales department to the advertising department.

The first career move—which changes only the job title—may be easier to make without leaving your current company. However, based on your experience in publishing, it is possible to move to a *new* company in a *new* position. The same is true of the second transition. You might move from the sales department to the advertising department in your present company, or find an employer who will hire you not as a sales representative, but as a copywriter.

Do I Need to Retool?

Does a career change always require going back to school? The answer is simple, no—but it depends on the career. Every state in the union frowns on the practice of medicine without a license, and all licensing agencies require candidates to possess a medical degree. But perhaps the more important question to ask is, "Will going back to school help me change careers?"

The answer is a definite maybe. There are some careers for which a certain academic degree or certificate of achievement or number of classroom hours are required. But earning the degree or putting in the hours does not guarantee you a job. For most career paths, it is usually a fairly risky strategy to go back to school on the firm assumption that your degree will automatically produce a job. You should also be aware that classroom education rarely teaches you everything you need to know in order to do the job in the so-called real world.

Pride and Prejudice: Easing the Move from One Career to Another

While the two-step career change process makes even fairly dramatic moves more feasible, you may encounter resistance from employers—and, subsequently, coworkers and supervisors—who are understandably leery of someone who has crossed the boundary separating career paths.

Approach such resistance with understanding. Emphasize your *transferable skills*, but also make it clear that you are eager to learn *specific skills* from those around you. To be sure, do your job, but don't be shy about seeking help and advice.

> **Winner**
> Asking for help will not reveal you as weak or incompetent or unsure of yourself. Rather, it will encourage others to make an investment in you, an investment of their time, their skill, and their attention. Once such an investment is made, resistance tends to dissolve.
>
> YOU'RE HIRED!

A Change of Career or a Change of Style?

Today more than ever before, it is possible to make a dramatic career move without changing careers. I have pointed out that a career (or a job) consists of nine parts and that the essence of a career change is found in two, sometimes three, of those parts. At least some aspects of the other six parts can be changed without necessarily changing careers. Where you work, the stated goal(s) of what you do, your assigned tasks, the tools of the trade, your salary, and the time commitment required by the work, all can be changed significantly without changing careers. Instead, it is often possible to change the *style* of your employment.

Chucking Your Suit for a Pair of Jeans: The Anti-Corporate Transition

"Beware of all enterprises that require new clothes," Henry David Thoreau declared in his 1854 *Walden*, thereby underscoring the superficiality in which we often quite literally garb the work we do. In the 1950s, the ubiquitous gray flannel suit was a corporate uniform, a sign of the conformity that was often mistaken for a prerequisite to being a "team player." Today, of course, we are still concerned with "uniforms": "power" suits for men and women, "power" ties, "power" suspenders, and the like. However, the classic suited dress code has vanished from many white-collar industries and workplaces. In many offices, jeans are commonplace, at least part of the time.

Maybe freedom from the suit is important to you. Or maybe you're thinking, *So what? Give me a six-figure salary, and I'll wear any blasted thing you want me to!* The significance of the transition from suit to jeans, however, has less to do with fashion than with symbol.

Relaxation of spoken and unspoken dress codes is only one aspect and sign of general changes sweeping the world of work and the corporate world in particular. Even big companies are learning to value diversity in their employees, if not from motives of social responsibility, then from a realization that a diverse workplace reflects the increasing diversity of their customer base.

Jump Start
Just because corporate policy may be flexible on such things as dress and office hours, don't assume your supervisor will be. If these issues are important to you, make certain that you understand company policy, but, even more important, make sure that you understand the views of your prospective supervisor.

Without looking as hard and as long as you may think, it is now possible to find companies that accept and even welcome ethnic, gender, and lifestyle diversity. Many employers provide day care (Why lose a great employee because he or she has a family?), flexible hours (Why put a worker in a foul mood by subjecting him or her to the peak of the rush hour?), part-time and retainer-based work arrangements, and, most dramatically, telecommuting: going to work without leaving your home.

If you are discontent in your present job, consider changing styles as an alternative to changing careers. Most companies that embrace diversity and flexibility put a high premium on creativity and imagination, so those two traits are golden keys into such firms. When you are looking to change, don't approach the target company by declaring that you're sick and tired of wearing a suit or that you can't take battling the same rush hour day after day. Instead, emphasize your desire for a greater range of creative options, and that you want to work for an organization that rewards imaginative problem solving. In other words, don't address the outward manifestations of the target company's philosophy—liberal dress requirements, flex time, and the rest—but the underlying, motivating philosophy itself.

Trading in a Pair of Jeans for a Brand-New Suit: The Corporate Transition

Let's not be simplistic. *Corporate* does not necessarily equal *close-minded*. While the trend may be toward more outward flexibility in corporate America, there are plenty of companies that still stress certain traditional values, including the necessity of keeping regular hours in an assigned office and an expectation of a certain standard of dress. Such trappings of tradition are especially prevalent in "money businesses"—banking, lending, brokering, and the like, where conservatism, regularity, and restrained elegance are important to communicating confidence to customers.

If you are contemplating a transition from jeans to suits, be fully prepared to respect the traditions and the trappings and, most importantly, the values they represent. Avoid calling attention to the personal drama of the transition: "Man, it's going to take some getting used to a suit and tie again!" Instead, underscore your transferable and specific skills. If you've been working on your own, talk about the transition to the corporate environment in glowingly positive terms. "I am eager to bring the skills I've honed working one-on-one with my clients to an environment that offers such tremendous resources." Your task will be to avoid being pinned with the label of *maverick*. Yet beware of appearing to condescend. Don't fall into the simple-minded trap of confusing being a team player with being a mindless conformist.

Going Home: Is Telecommuting for You?

About two decades ago, just as personal computers were beginning to make serious inroads into the workplace, we were deluged with predictions of the "paperless office." In fact, although the electronic revolution has made much paperwork unnecessary, it seems to have generated a mountain of paper anyway: faxes, photocopies, and data printouts in multiple drafts.

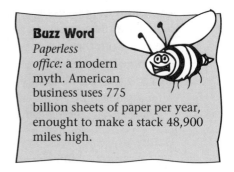

Buzz Word
Paperless office: a modern myth. American business uses 775 billion sheets of paper per year, enought to make a stack 48,900 miles high.

What the electronic revolution may well succeed in producing, however, is the employeeless office. In many industries, the telephone, combined with the personal computer (with modem) and the fax machine, has made it superfluous for warm bodies to transport themselves to and from a designated central office. Much of the work can be performed from home. And the technology of telecommuting, already far advanced, is improving almost daily. It is possible to hold conferences, complete with voice, video, and data transmission, in "real time" and with little more effort or thought than it takes to make a phone call. A host of commercial on-line services, plus the Internet, have made it possible to transmit and receive e-mail over any distance more quickly and efficiently than memos were ever transmitted within a physical office. These same services also allow access to vast libraries of data, research, and records.

For many businesses, then, telecommuting is not only feasible, but desirable. Most employees love it. Rush hour becomes a thing of the past. Companies can downsize office space, saving significant overhead costs.

Is there a downside? From the point of view of the employer, you should be aware that there are fears of relinquishing too much control over the employee. There is something to be said about having your troops physically present and accounted for. Others argue that there is simply no substitute for face-to-face meetings and discussions. There is a fear that unmonitored employees will loaf around in pajamas, watch the soaps on TV, and make frequent trips to the refrigerator.

Some of this, of course, is quite valid. In part, many of the employer objections to telecommuting can be addressed by combining telecommuting with in-office time. Perhaps the telecommuter works at home on Monday, Wednesday, and Friday, coming in on Tuesday and Thursday or whenever an in-person meeting is called for. As to loss of productivity, the fact is, as in *any* work situation, either the jobs get done or they don't. If employers relinquish some control over the process of production, they still evaluate results.

Perhaps the more meaningful questions to ask about telecommuting concern yourself. Perhaps your first impulse is to exclaim, "Who *wouldn't* like to stay at home?"

Who wouldn't?

Anyone who needs the daily stimulation of leaving the house to go to work. Or the stimulation of working in a place that hums with activity. Anyone who needs a daily dose of camaraderie and faces familiar as well as new. Anyone who does not enjoy being alone for eight hours at a stretch.

Telecommuting takes discipline above all. If you are in an office away from home, it is quite a simple matter to separate the activities of home—the demands of children or spouse—from the demands of the job. If you are at home, it becomes more difficult, say, for you to convince your child that you are "at work" and cannot play. It is, let's face it, also true that the surroundings of home may make sustained concentration difficult. After all, doesn't the garden need weeding? And it's such a nice day! I'll just take the cordless phone outside with me. An hour or two won't hurt.

Finally, as the saying goes, "Out of sight, out of mind." It is possible that the telecommuting employee is at a disadvantage when it comes to office politics and that, therefore, his or her opportunities for growth and advancement are limited. Is this an inevitable tradeoff? It depends on what percentage of the office regularly telecommutes. It depends on how thoroughly management embraces the benefits of telecommuting. To minimize the negative political effects of telecommuting, however, it is prudent to ensure that you do regularly visit the office. Moreover, make certain that you are always "in the loop." That is, you should have electronic access to all memos and communications. These should be transmitted via e-mail and not on paper, lest only those physically present in the central office receive them on time.

Telecommuting is changing and will continue to transform the landscape of American employment. It offers new opportunities, the possibility of a better quality of life, and the potential for increased productivity. However, be aware of the pitfalls employers perceive and the personal pitfalls that really do exist for the would-be telecommuter. Emphasize your self-directness, your motivation, and, above all, your commitment to producing results. If telecommuting is a negotiable aspect of the job, consider easing into it, suggesting that you work from home only one or two days a week. Demonstrate a personal flexibility commensurate with that of the employer.

The Least You Need to Know

➤ Realistically assess your reasons for changing careers, and realistically assess the feasibility of the change you contemplate.

➤ Analyze your present as well as your prospective career by breaking each of them down into their nine constituent parts and comparing and contrasting the parts.

➤ Don't regard training programs or going back to school for a degree as a guarantee of breaking into the career you want.

➤ Always consider changing work styles as an alternative to the more difficult process of changing careers.

➤ Consider the assets and liabilities of telecommuting—the most dramatic vocational change you can make without necessarily moving into a brand-new career.

Chapter 6

Up the Mountain: Steps to a New Career

In This Chapter

➤ The informational interview

➤ Researching the present state and future prospects of a career or industry

➤ Industries and careers: what's hot and what's not

➤ Risk versus reward in growth industries

➤ Creative daydreaming and career sampling

Because you've turned to this chapter, I can only assume that you are at least thinking about a career change. You may already know *what* field you want to get into. Now you need to know *how* to go about getting into it. Or maybe you just know that you're dissatisfied with what you are doing now, and you feel the need to get into something else. Having read this far, you should have some notion of your transferable skills and areas of interest. If you've read the preceding chapter, you also know that the most successful career transitions are at least two-step processes, changing (in step one) *either* your job title *or* your field of knowledge, but not both in a single jump, then (in step two), moving into a job that completes the career transition by changing the element that had been left unchanged in step one.

But how, exactly, do you go about transforming your restless urge to change careers into a move—or set of moves—to a target company? This chapter leads the way.

What Next?

Most job-hunting manuals assume you know where you want to go. They propose to tell you how to get there. Or, perhaps, they provide guidelines for identifying areas of opportunity—hot industries, the "best" jobs, and so on. In fact, we'll get to that quite soon. But, look, the *Dictionary of Occupational Titles* (the *D.O.T.*), published by the U.S. Department of Labor's Bureau of Labor Statistics, lists approximately 20,000 different occupations. Yet 90 percent of the U.S. labor force are employed in just 300 job titles, and 50 percent are employed in fifty.

What's going on here?

Most of us fail to *choose* our careers. We enter into them, as it were, by default. We tend to "end up in" the same jobs as most everyone else.

The most profound life decisions are made with scarcely a thought. Tossing away the map, we just pick a direction and step on the gas. Strange thing is, with 20,000 different kinds of jobs out there, we end up just about where most everyone else does.

I SEE... **Case Study**

I knew a young man who was studying accounting in college. He dreaded going to class because he hated the idea of becoming an accountant. He told me that one hot, sunny summer day, he had finally had enough. He was going to change his major to liberal arts—even though he realized that doing so would—at least in the shortrun—present more of a challenge when it came time to find a job. Flushed with resolve, he strolled out into the summer air and walked along the bank of the river that flowed through the campus. Before him, on the sidewalk, something was glistening. He looked closer. What he saw were the shimmering trails of a number of snails that had ventured out of the cool grass and tried to cross the sidewalk, only to be baked by the blistering sun. With that, he turned on his heel, and the next day was back in accounting class.

Today, this young man—not so young anymore—is an accountant with a steady job and a middling salary.

He cordially hates the work he does.

The Informational Interview

In the next section of this chapter, "Upside Versus Down: Weighing the Potential Against the Problems," you will find some guidelines for evaluating potential career paths. But before I send you off in blind pursuit of what looks hot, I would like you to consider tempering whatever facts and figures and predictions you find with some face-to-face encounters. You see, you don't have to wait for someone to respond favorably to your résumé before you secure an interview. Assuming that you are employed and not desperate for a new job—just anxious to explore a new career—consider investing the time and effort necessary for an informational interview.

The informational interview is not an employment interview. It is an attempt to collect information about specific careers and companies. Identify a field in which you think you would like to work, then identify someone to talk with about it. Say you are interested in getting into business news writing. First, identify the companies that are producing business news: newspapers, business magazines, and industry magazines. Second, examine and evaluate their "product." Select the product—in this case, the writing—that most appeals to you. Third, identify folks who have some responsibility for producing the product. In the case of business writing, this is usually very easy; just look for a byline. Fourth, telephone as many of these people as you can. Get the company switchboard—or electronic call router—to connect you. Fifth, explain what you are about.

What *are* you about? You are most definitely *not* applying for a job. Even if, on some off chance, the person on the other end of the line asks, "Are you looking for a job?" or "Are you applying for a job here?" answer, "Not at the moment. I *am* very interested in [your industry], however. I'm interested in exploring careers in it, and I would greatly appreciate a few minutes to talk to you about it." If—as is more likely—the person you have called does *not* ask if you are applying for a job, simply proceed with your request: "My name is So-and-so. I am very interested in [your industry]. I'm not looking for a job at present, but I am thinking about a career in [your industry]. It would help me very much if I could spend a few minutes with you, getting your take on [your industry]."

If at all possible, especially if your callee is local, you should set up a face-to-face appointment rather than continue to discuss the matter on the phone. There are three reasons for this. The most important reason is that a "live" interview gives you the opportunity to see the work environment and to see the interviewee (*you* are the interviewer) *in situ*. Second, a face-to-face conversation lets you read the nonverbal, body-language clues that communicate a wealth of feeling and attitude. Finally, it is a good idea to get as much interview practice as possible, in preparation for eventual employment interviews. Of course, if the industry in which you are interested does not have local offices, conduct the interview on the phone.

The basic set of questions you want to ask is simple:

➤ How did you get started in this line of work?

➤ What do you like most about it?

➤ What do you dislike most about it?

➤ What are your views on the present state and future prospects of the industry?

➤ Can you recommend anyone else with whom I may speak?

Unless your interviewee extends the conversation, don't let this go on for more than ten minutes. When you leave, thank the person graciously. Ask for a business card, and give him or her yours, if you have one. Finally—and this is very important—send a thank-you note. This is more than common courtesy, though it is that as well. First, sending a note on this occasion will get you in the habit of sending a note after each and every job interview you may later have. Surprisingly, only about 2 percent of employment candidates send thank-you notes, so doing so will alone set you apart from the crowd. Second, the note will engrave your name in the memory of the interviewee. It may even get put in a file. Conduct more than a few informational interviews followed up by notes, and you will have broadcast your name to any number of companies in a particular industry—even before you have begun applying for jobs. You should send a note even after a telephone interview.

Upside Versus Down: Weighing the Potential Against the Problems

Either before, during, or after you conduct at least some of your informational interviews, you should begin researching your prospective new career in another way. Presumably you asked the interviewee for his or her views on the present state and future prospects of the industry. Flesh out this picture with some solo research.

BENJAMIN F. HOLLIDAY
2345 W. JACKSON AVENUE
SHANNON, NJ 01987
555-555-5555
FAX: 555-444-4444

August 4, 1995

Ms. Sheila Ralph
Systems Manager
Western International, Inc.
U.S. Highway 46
Schoolville, IL 60045

Dear Ms. Ralph:

I greatly enjoyed our conversation on Tuesday. It has really sharpened my thinking about making a move into the field. I remain enthusiastic--but my eyes are now wide open!

Thanks for sharing your time and knowledge.

Warmest regards,

Ben Holliday

Thank-you notes should be brief, but specific.

The thank-you note should not only convey courtesy, but also should let your correspondent know that you listened and learned.

MARY KAY SWANDER
███████████████

367 Elm Road
Ionia, Iowa 52243
555-555-5555

August 4, 1995

Peter Young
Director of Quality Control
Uriah Corporation
56 Sunset Boulevard
Kent, Iowa 52240

Dear Mr. Young:

Please let me thank you once again for sharing your time and expertise with me on Monday. Your insights have provided me with a truly helpful perspective on the industry.

Sincerely yours,

Mary Kay Swander

Anatomy of a New Career

Some general "outlook" books you should consult include:

Adams Jobs Almanac. Updated annually.

Jobs Rated Almanac, Third Edition.

Occupational Outlook Handbook for College Graduates (Washington, D.C.: Superintendent of Documents, U.S. Government Printing Office, updated frequently).

America's Fastest Growing Employers: The Complete Guide to Finding Jobs with Over 300 of America's Hottest Companies.

U.S. Department of Labor, *Occupational Outlook Handbook.* Updated frequently.

These are a good place to start. In addition to listing the names and addresses of some 10,000 employers, the *Adams Job Almanac* includes a close look at some forty careers and a forecast for the coming century. *America's Fastest Growing Employers* profiles some of today's leading companies, surveying industries in terms of hiring. Beyond these general resources, you should make it your business to follow the fortunes of your target industry in the general and business press. You should contact the publicity offices of as many firms in the industry as possible. Obtain copies of speeches by the CEO, and obtain industry-related press releases. At the library, use *The Reader's Guide to Periodical Literature* to find articles on the industry, the career, and on the relevant firms.

Jump Start
An important shortcut to this research comes with this book. It's time to load up the *Job Hunt 6-in-1* software. It includes an employment database with key names and numbers. See Chapter 24, "Using the Software That Comes with this Book," for instructions on getting started with *Job Hunt 6-in-1*.

Is all of this necessary? No, of course not. Instead, you can let yourself fall into a job through conversations like the one between "Jim" and "Fred." The statistics are on your side: Although most people are employed, few people devote much thought to their careers. It's up to you.

Where the Action Is

If you are fortunate, your heart's desire will coincide with a career that presents real employment opportunities. If, however, you really want to be a blacksmith, you will find your horizon severely constrained. Be honest with yourself as you evaluate, through informational interviews and solo research, the current state of your target career or industry. Be careful about interpreting how your sources define a "hot" industry. Does "hot" mean that everyone and his brother are competing for a handful of jobs? Or does "hot" mean that the industry offers a wealth of opportunities?

If you are eager to make a career move anytime soon, it will do you little good to long for a career in an industry with very few jobs. If you can live with a more protracted timeline, however, you may be able to afford the effort and the hours required to make the move into even a more or less "closed" industry. Just be aware that once you are in an industry with relatively few possibilities, your mobility is limited and you cannot meet unexpected contingencies as readily as you can in a career path with more branches.

Where the Growth Is (and the Action Will Be)

There is a great deal to be said for identifying the careers in a growth industry. It's a lot like investing in growth stocks. The savvy investor identifies companies whose stocks are currently undervalued, but which are likely to increase dramatically in value. The one thing a savvy investor does not do is lavish large sums on companies that have already grown—"mature" companies. Blue chip stocks have a relatively limited downside potential, but also a relatively limited upside, *and* they already come with blue chip prices. Similarly, you may find more career potential in a growth industry than in a mature industry. The trick—whether you are an investor or a job seeker—is to identify the growth areas.

Jump Start A "quick-and-dirty" gross measure of an industry's "buzz" can be made simply by counting the number of periodical or newspaper articles written about a particular industry during, say, a three-month period.

Jump Start One thing almost every job-hunting authority and employment commentator agrees on: The job market of the 1990s and 21st century is a volatile one. Like it or not, risk is a bigger part of the job scene than ever before. But all this movement within the job market also means opportunity—risk, yes, but risk with reward.

There is no magic formula, and there is no reliable substitute for research. Identify your own areas of interest, identify careers and industries and companies that jibe with your areas of interest, then set up informational interviews and pursue the solo research. Those books that promise to tell you where the job action is and will be are very good places to start. By all means, consult them. But, remember, they represent fairly superficial second-hand information. Look for current articles on cutting-edge industries. Try to pick up the "buzz" on predicted growth areas.

If your target career or industry produces something sold in retail stores, do plenty of window shopping. Look at the product(s) in question, and ask the store manager or assistant manager or the cash-register clerk how the merchandise has been moving and what people say about it. Finally, read the stock quotation pages in your daily newspaper. Look for companies with a pattern of upward movement in stock prices. Generally speaking, such a pattern suggests that a company is in a growth area—especially if the company is technology oriented or deals in an advanced service.

Should you deliberately seek out growth careers? As usual, the choice is up to you. You may do very well financially, and you may feel self-fulfilled in a career in a more mature industry. (You should think twice, however, about getting into a mature industry that is also shrinking.) Moreover, a growth industry—by definition, an immature industry—

might fail to grow. In business, failure to grow usually does *not* mean staying the same size. It means shrinking, retreating, cutting back, and laying off; therefore, seeking a career in a growth area has its risks. In the end, perhaps your most reliable motivator is how eager you are to work on the cutting edge of a field and how comfortable you are with risk.

Risk Management

Making the transition to a new career does not have to be a bungee jump. You have a range of options for easing the transition. These include:

➤ Extensive armchair adventuring

➤ Dipping a toe

➤ Finding a new career in your current company

➤ Finding a new career in your current industry

How to Be an Armchair Adventurer

I've mentioned that the business world has gone through many changes over the past few years. Traditionally, the good businessperson was viewed as hard-as-nails, with an enormous respect for facts and figures, and an absolute aversion to anything resembling daydreaming. Well, guess what? Business has learned to prize the daydreamers, those who can envision creative solutions to problems and whole new empires of profit.

Similarly, those who counsel others on the ins and outs of getting the job you want have usually been full of admonitions to "keep your feet on the ground" and "be realistic in your expectations." I'm here to tell you that, if you're serious about changing careers, that advice will keep you right where you are now. The more effective career-changing strategy? Dream on.

By using the informational interview and solo research techniques outlined earlier in this chapter, learn what you can about your target career or target industry. Then go home, settle into a comfortable chair or prop yourself up in bed on a couple of pillows. Don't doze off, but do start dreaming.

Imagine your work day in the new career. Start from the very beginning of the day. What time will you have to wake up? What will you have to wear? How far will you have to drive or take the train or bus? Where will you work? What kind of building will it be? What kind of office or work space will you have? With whom will you work? What will you talk about? How much time will you have to spend on the phone? What kinds of tasks will you handle each and every day? What will go right during the day and give you pleasure? What will go wrong and give you a royal pain? What is the pace of the work going to be like? How consistently interesting will the work be? Who calls the shots?

Imagine a conversation with some of your new subordinates. Imagine one with your new boss. Imagine talking to your new clients. Imagine performing some of the new tasks associated with the career.

Decide how you feel. If the result is a pleasurable daydream rather than a waking nightmare, chances are the prospective move is an idea with a future.

Dipping a Toe

Consider alternatives to jumping in with both feet. You may be able to sample a new career without quitting your current job. If your new career requires going back to school, you probably have a built-in toe-dipping opportunity. Unless you have accumulated a tidy nest egg, have generous relatives, or a very gainfully employed spouse/significant other, it is likely that you will attend classes while you are still employed. Your classroom experience should give you a preview of many aspects of your target career. It is possible that the most valuable thing you'll learn is that the career you thought would be great is just not right for you at all.

Pitfall
Make sure that you know your current company's policies concerning moonlighting and freelance work. Some organizations forbid it, making such outside employment grounds for dismissal. Few companies will bar you from charitable volunteer work done on your own time, but you'd have a hard time convincing your current employer that even an unpaid internship at a for-profit firm is charity.

If you already have the training to work in a new career area, consider taking on freelance assignments in that area. Work around your present job. Resist the temptation of resorting to the dangerous—and dishonest—practice of "stealing" time from your present employer to do work on the freelance projects.

An alternative to paid freelance work is volunteer work or a part-time internship. If you can manage the time, try volunteering your services. Identify someone at the target company who has the power to hire, and explain to him or her exactly what you are thinking: that you are contemplating a move into a career in so-and-so, and that you would like to see how an industry leader operates. You should outline your present position, putting emphasis on the transferable skills that you will, on an unpaid basis, put at the service of the target company. Make it clear that you are *not* looking for a job offer, but that you are seeking experience.

Finding a New Career in Your Current Company

Embarking on a new career need not be traumatic or overly dramatic. We've already seen, in the preceding chapter, how making the transition in two steps facilitates the transition. Another vocational shoehorn is changing careers without changing companies. You may find remarkably little resistance to your proposed career shift. In fact, large, diverse organizations often provide the institutional machinery to facilitate and encourage such moves. Do they do this out of the goodness of their corporate hearts? Don't bet on it.

During the 1970s, American automobiles, big, boxy, gas-guzzling dinosaurs, were being pushed off the road by sleek and sensible Japanese imports. After driving home in their Japanese cars, people switched on their Japanese television sets or cranked up the Japanese stereo. American industry fumed and fussed, asking the government for protection and even appealing to the patriotism of the American public, pleading with them to buy American—whether they liked it or not.

Then the thinking began. The "Japanese miracle" was in large part founded on one all-important resource: people. American companies had been accustomed to thinking of their assets as their cash, investments, patents and copyrights owned, buildings, machinery, and the like. From the Japanese, however, they learned that the greatest asset of all is human. And American companies began protecting as well as developing that asset. Hence, rather than lose a good asset, many firms instituted retraining and transition programs for employees who wanted to change careers.

Jump Start
In Chapter 3, "Same Ladder, Higher Rung: Upward Mobility within the Organization," I had some pretty harsh words about Human Resources departments, counseling anyone who wants to move from one department to another to avoid Human Resources, if possible. However, if you are looking to change careers—not just departments—and if your company offers any internal machinery to assist you in this, a trip to the Human Resources department is both necessary and potentially rewarding.

Even if your present company lacks the internal machinery to help you change careers, and even if you are working for a relatively small company, look to your present employer as your first resource. Learn from what all successful customer- and client-oriented businesses know: Your present "customer" is also your best potential "customer."

Finding a New Career in Your Current Industry

If you cannot change careers within your present company, explore the possibilities of a new career in a different target company within your present industry. This may take the form of a slight variation on the two-step career transition. You are presently an accountant working for Acme Widgets. You want to get into sales. You find a job in sales at Beta

Widgets. Same industry, same field (widgets), different company, different job title. Depending on the nature of the industry, however, both the field and the job title may be different. Still, if you keep your career move within the industry in which you have built a track record, the transition is likely to be easier for you, and, certainly, you will meet with less resistance from the target employer.

What Is This Thing Called Self-Fulfillment?

Wait a minute. Before I bring this chapter to an end, there is one final fuel that may propel a career change. In a word, it is *passion*. And you can't quantify or explain it in any book.

Now, I'm not saying that passion is a necessary ingredient for career changers. Remember number five of the "Five Attitudes Guaranteed to Fail" listed in Chapter 1, "Attitude 101." The fact is, you don't *have* to love your job, and waiting around for a job you love may earn you a semi-permanent niche in the unemployment line or, more likely, keep you underemployed, in a nowhere job, while you wait for passion to dawn. If you feel passionately about a career, however, that energy will overcome many obstacles, and it will tend to make your dreams reality.

To the degree that you are passionate about some career path, your choices become, if not easier, at least much clearer. In the absence of an overwhelming passion to drive your career choices, you may be tempted to turn to friends or to the books mentioned earlier in the chapter to identify the "hot" jobs. But be aware that a job isn't hot unless it is hot *for you*. By using a well-defined and reasonably objective set of criteria, the *Jobs Rated Almanac* for 1995 puts Actuary at the head of a list of 250 possible occupations, with Software Engineer second. These are both great jobs—if *you* want to do them. (At the *bottom* of the list? Dancer. And, below that, Lumberjack. But what if *you* want to be a dancer or a lumberjack? Or, for that matter, a dancing lumberjack?)

If you don't have a passion, make sure that you carefully consider what the following factors mean *to you* before you make a career move:

➤ Income

➤ Potential for growth (the job's *outlook*)

➤ Job security

➤ Physical work conditions associated with the target career: physical surroundings, environment; degree of confinement; the necessity of working in bad weather conditions; physical demands involved (lifting, crawling, bending, and so on); physical hazards and dangers

➤ Emotional environment: competitive pressures; performance pressures; emotional effect of job hazards; daily stress

➤ Time requirements: hours per day and per week; holidays and vacation time; deadline pressures; work load

➤ People: kinds of clients or customers; kinds of coworkers; kinds of supervisors; kinds of subordinates; busy office/workplace (much interaction with others) versus "lonely" office/workplace (little contact with the outside world)

➤ Status: what the world thinks of the career ("Be a clown! All the world loves a clown!")

➤ Travel required: depending on what you like, a demand or an opportunity

➤ Perks and amenities: wood-paneled office with a view; company car; company plane; vacation condo; free samples of products; discounts on desirable items; and so on

The Least You Need to Know

➤ Set yourself apart from the crowd by taking the time to research and evaluate your choice of careers.

➤ Combine solo research techniques with informational interviewing to discover career possibilities and to evaluate career paths that interest you.

➤ Manage the risk of moving into a new career through creative daydreaming as well as through career testing by taking freelance assignments or undertaking volunteer work and internships.

➤ Make use of career-development and career-change programs offered by your current employer.

➤ Weigh what others identify as "hot" careers against your own needs, desires, qualifications, and abilities.

oof, oof...

Chapter 7

Yet Another Move: To Another Region or a Different Country

In This Chapter

➤ Choosing a place to live and work

➤ Researching an area *before* you make a move

➤ The long distance job hunt

➤ Weighing the many costs of relocating

➤ Going rural or working overseas

It's no secret that Americans are movers. We regularly pull up stakes in one place and settle in another. Yet how many of us take the time and effort to identify a city or region in which we *really* want to live, then figure out a way to go and live there? The fact is, this major life decision, like that other one—*What will I do for a living?*—is often made by default. We live where we live because that's where we live. Maybe it's where we grew up. Maybe we came along with a spouse. Maybe it's where a job led us. Then again, many of us love—or learn to love—the place we live, and if opportunity beckons elsewhere, or has ceased to beckon at home, the decision to move becomes an especially hard one.

This chapter takes a look at how where you want to live affects what you want to be doing—your career choice.

Wanderlust—and What to Do with It

The reasons for moving to a new region are many, but two are most prevalent and pervasive. You decide that you can no longer stand the tired town in which you've been living, or you like it well enough, but you can't find any decent jobs there.

So, where do you go? For many of us, the move is to a place where we have family or friends—built-in emotional support and maybe even some financial help as well. For others, the destination is a place we know or believe we will love (I left my heart in Des Moines). For others still, the magnet is a job offer or, at least, the availability of employment opportunities. If you are moving to be closer to loved ones, if you are moving because you have found the city or region of your dreams, or if you've been offered a job somewhere, then you don't need any advice on choosing a place to live. If, however, you want—or need—to move, but aren't sure where you should go, it's time to do some homework.

Regions: The Hot and the Not

As with identifying the "hot careers" in the preceding chapter, deciding what regions are hot and what regions are not involves a combination of some more or less objective data with a consideration of your own needs and feelings. A good starting point for the objective data is a justly popular book by David Savageau and Richard Boyer called *Places Rated Almanac*. It weighs many factors relevant to 343 U.S. and Canadian metropolitan areas to rank them in what the book's subtitle calls a "Guide to Finding the Best Places to Live in North America." Unfortunately, the volume is not updated annually, and the most recent edition I've seen is already several years old. More up-to-date information can often be found in various popular magazines. *Time* annually rates the top five or ten cities, and other magazines, including *Entrepreneur*, *Fortune*, *Modern Maturity*, and others, regularly rate cities and regions for what they offer in terms of business opportunity, housing, and the assorted amenities of life.

Come with me for a moment back to 1993, when *Places Rated Almanac* put Cincinnati, Ohio, at the top of the list as, overall, the best place to live in North America, and deposited Yuba City, California, at the bottom. I've been to Cincinnati. I like Cincinnati. However, personally—and that is the key word—I wouldn't put it at the very top of my list of places to live, not in 1993 and not today. Maybe *you* would. Maybe *you* wouldn't. (Yuba City I've never visited and therefore can neither defend nor condemn.) The lesson here: Use "objective" data as a starting point for evaluation, but always bring to bear your own feelings, needs, and tastes. By definition, these cannot be wrong.

Identifying the Best Places to Live and Work

Besides *Places Rated Almanac* and the surveys you'll find in *Time* and other magazines, you'll find information about U.S. locales at the federal or state employment office in your current location. Either of these agencies can usually furnish up-to-date employment statistics for all 50 states and even for metropolitan regions within those states. Your local library may also have U.S. Labor Department publications with such statistics (just make sure that they are the most recent available).

Once you have identified states and metropolitan areas with low unemployment rates, contact the Chambers of Commerce in those locales. It is no great feat to track down the phone numbers for these organizations. Identify the appropriate area code, pick up the phone, dial Information, and ask for the numbers. Phone in a request for all the information they have—in printed form—concerning businesses in your trade or specialty. When you receive the material, send a thank-you note. This not only makes the world a more pleasant place in which to live, it also may smooth the way for further contact with the Chamber of Commerce as you zero in on a job. Finally, if your trade or career is tied to a particular industry or a particular set of companies, find out where the industry is centered and where the companies are located. That information may make your decision for you.

Objective sources for identifying places that offer the jobs you want are relatively easy to locate. More difficult are objective sources pertaining to the quality of life in a given locale or region. Beyond the Savageau and Boyer volume, you may try simply talking to people who live in your target location(s).

Whatever sources you consult, make sure that you consider the following factors in deciding what makes one locale livable, another desirable, and a third downright dreadful:

➤ **Cost of Living:** It varies widely from region to region, and you cannot make intelligent decisions about salary and lifestyle without considering it.

➤ **Jobs:** What and how many are available? If you take a job, move, buy a house, then hate your job (or your job hates you), can you find another one in this location before you starve?

➤ **Housing:** What's available and how much does it cost? Is it Rural? Urban? Suburban? How's the rental market?

➤ **Transportation:** Roads? Traffic problems? Public transportation? How about airports and bus lines? Does Amtrak grace the target locale with its presence?

➤ **Education:** Quality of the public school system? What about private schools—how good and at what price? Are colleges and universities important to you?

➤ **Health Care:** What's available?

➤ **Crime:** Increasingly a concern, this one is hard to pin down. Statistics for metropolitan areas tend to lump together "good" neighborhoods with "bad," making it hard to get a clear picture of the real risks. Once you have identified specific neighborhoods that appeal to you for aesthetic and/or practical reasons, talk to prospective neighbors and give the local police precinct a visit or call. Use your eyes. Are houses well maintained? Who's on the streets?

➤ **Arts and Culture:** What do you enjoy—music, theater, art museums, a good public library system? Check out the availability of these important amenities.

➤ **Recreation:** Parks, sports opportunities, scenic areas, camping, skiing, hiking—are these important to you?

➤ **Climate:** This will affect each day you spend in the target location.

➤ **Diversity:** It's hard to deny that America's greatness is built on ethnic and cultural variety. Who lives in your target location?

➤ **Food:** Do you enjoy good restaurants? Are there any good restaurants where you're going?

➤ **The Feel of the Place:** This is an intangible, but it is real. New York City "feels" very different from Iowa City.

➤ **Status:** This may be more important to you than you'd like to admit, even to yourself. Do you demand a Park Avenue address, or will any nice street in Secaucus do just fine?

The Depressed Area: Time to Move On?

Jimmy Stewart in the 1946 Frank Capra classic, *It's a Wonderful Life*, chafes under the confinement and limited opportunities of his hometown, Bedford Falls. Watching the film, many of us can sympathize. We, too, have felt those "little town blues," a perception that the future is limited where we live. But how do you distinguish your perception from the objective circumstances? You may feel like moving on, but does "reality" warrant this action?

If you've staked out for yourself a trade, specialty, or profession, and there is simply no demand for it where you live, the decision to move on is a pretty easy one. If, however, your opportunities seem more or less limited, but not nonexistent in your present location, you need to investigate some of the local economic indicators. How's business generally where you live? Are stores opening, closing, or is the retail climate (always a good indicator of a community's general economic health) steady? What firms—if any—

have recently relocated to your area? What firms—if any—have left? What about unemployment? Determine if the unemployment rate in your region is higher, lower, or the same as the national and regional averages. The local office of the federal or state department of labor will have this information, or you can check the newspaper files in your local library.

You may well discover that it is time to move on to greener pastures. Just do your homework before you pull up stakes. Make certain those distant pastures really are greener. Faced with fear and frustration, we all have a tendency to do something—*anything*—in the hope that doing something has to be better than doing nothing. Don't make a bad situation truly desperate by squandering precious resources on an ill-considered move.

Jump Start
The long trend away from a manufacturing economy and toward a service economy continues as the 21st century approaches. Regions heavily dependent on manufacturing are suffering and will likely continue to suffer.

Selling Yourself Long Distance

It's no secret that researching job openings and interviewing for positions is made more difficult by distance. Although it is feasible—and sometimes advisable—to make a walk-in application for a job when the trip involves nothing more than a bus ride downtown, it's hard to be so casual when you have to invest in an airline ticket and a hotel room. Planning is called for.

If you've already identified a target company headquartered in a different city from where you live, by far the best plan is to convince the potential employer to pay for your visit. In most upper-level positions, this is a matter of course. Getting to this point requires a persuasive letter (see Chapter 9, "Judged by Its Cover: How to Write Great Cover Letters" and Chapter 14, "How to Heat Things Up with a Cold Letter or a Cold Call"). Your inclination will also be to send a résumé. This is a dicey proposition, especially at long distance. Many employers welcome unsolicited résumés. Many, however, slice open their morning mail and automatically discard letters containing unsolicited résumés. The safest course is to send a cold letter *without* a résumé. Just summarize in the letter what you would have said in the résumé. The previsit stage may also involve a telephone interview, which I will discuss shortly.

Buzz Word
Face it: a *cold letter* is the employment equivalent of junk mail. It is an unsolicited application for a job that may or may not exist. Research beforehand will make the cold letter less of a shot in the dark.

If you have not identified a target company in the target location, then you will have to do some research. Usually, a trip is not required. Begin by obtaining copies of the target location's newspaper or newspapers. If possible, subscribe to the paper, even before you move. If you cannot subscribe, find a local store or newsstand that carries out-of-town papers. If the target location is a major metropolitan area, chances are the newspaper will be available at your local library. Do not confine yourself to the want ads, but look for news of companies that are expanding or opening in the target area. Also scope out the word on transfers, retirements, relocations, promotions, and, yes, deaths—all of which create vacancies that must be filled.

In addition to newspaper research, contact the local Chamber of Commerce and ask them for employment information in your field. You should contact the telephone company in the target location and request copies of the business white pages and the Yellow Pages. Explain that you are planning to relocate.

Finally, consider planning a vacation around a visit to the target location. Try to line up interviews—perhaps even informational interviews (see Chapter 10, "Reactive vs. Proactive Search Strategies")—for this period.

The Telephone Interview

You may receive a call in response to your letter of inquiry, or you may decide to forgo the letter and make a long-distance telephone call instead. Let's begin with the second scenario.

Once you have identified a target company and a person with the power to hire you (see Chapter 10), take a deep breath and dial. The objective of this call is to arrange a meeting, preferably one for which the target company will pay. Your fallback goal is to get the callee to *request* your résumé.

This is, in essence, a sales situation; specifically, it is a telemarketing sales situation. Now, experienced telemarketers always structure their telephone sales pitch on the so-called AIDA pattern. No, this isn't the brainchild of a Giuseppe Verdi fan, but of somebody (now lost in the mists of time) with a passion for acronyms. The first "A" in AIDA stands for *Attention*. The successful telemarketer knows that he or she has about two to four seconds to capture the callee's attention. Next comes the development of *Interest*, followed by *Desire*, and then a call to *Action*.

The very first sentence out of your mouth should be a pleasant greeting, using the callee's name: "Good afternoon, Ms. Johnson." Next, identify yourself by name. Both of these utterances are absolutely necessary, but they will cost you your first two seconds of phone time. You need to earn your first "A" *right now*. The best way is to state what you do—not what you'd like to do, not what you're interested in, and, above all, not that you are looking for a job. One thing you can be certain of, your *need* for a job will not command the attention of the callee. You must suggest—quickly—that you can do something for the callee, not that you want him or her to do something for you. So, here's your first "A": "I'm an experienced widget designer, specializing in innovative designs with a full spectrum of features."

It's one sentence, and there should be absolutely nothing spontaneous about it. Plan it. Write it out. Condense it. Pack into it as much unambiguous information as possible. It should have the clarity of the proverbial bolt from the blue. Balance specificity with vagueness, saying just enough to whet the callee's appetite, so that, instead of bidding you good afternoon, he or she will respond with, "Tell me a little about your experience" or, "Where are you working now?" Or something of the kind.

If such a question is not immediately forthcoming, continue with, "Have I called you at a good time?" Ask it just this way. It invites a "yes" response. In contrast, if you ask (as so many callers do), "Is this a bad time?" you will have planted the thought that, yes, indeed, this *is* a bad time, so *get off my phone!* On the other hand, it *is* important to confirm that this is a good time to talk. Why invite outright rejection by catching some-one in the middle of a crisis?

Proceed to the *Interest* phase. The way to develop this is to sell the callee on one or two of your specific accomplishments. Go ahead and review the first two chapters, which show you how to identify your specific accomplishments.

"I recently completed work on the Ultima Mark 3 widget. I was responsible for its deluxe repeating feature, which customer response surveys show as a key factor in making the purchase decision. Sales of the Mark 3 have been running 35 percent higher than sales of the Mark 2. In dollars, this represents $125,000 in new business for my present company."

I've said it before and, doubtless, I'll say it again. If you want to be heard by business, speak the language of business. And that language is dollars—dollars made or dollars saved. Nothing develops *Interest* more rapidly and certainly than the sound of money.

Next, develop *Desire* by expressing your interest in offering your services to the company: "I'm calling because I am looking for a new challenge and an opportunity to grow. I have researched your company rather thoroughly, and it seems to me there are a number of items that we can profitably discuss. Does the kind of experience I have and the level of my performance interest you?"

> **Winner**
> Warm up a cold call by seeking agreement whenever possible. Don't ask, "May I send you my résumé," but "I believe you will be interested in seeing what I have to offer, and I would like to send you my résumé. Is that something you would like to see?"
>
> YOU'RE HIRED!

The question should elicit a positive response. When it does, end with a call to *Action*: "I would very much like to meet with you. Can that be arranged?" From here, you may negotiate funding for your trip. If, however, you are planning to visit the area, say so: "I'm planning to visit your area during July, and I have July 2 and 3 open." Finally, your fallback position, should the callee not want to see you, is to ask if he or she would like to see a résumé. "Would it be worthwhile for me to send a résumé?" Don't ask for permission to send one. (Of course, you may send a résumé, if you want. And your target can toss it right in the circular file, if he or she wants.) Your object is to elicit an invitation to send the résumé, an action that will reduce the chances of its simply being thrown away.

Footloose Blues: Relocation Liabilities

Now that you've considered the benefits and some of the preliminary mechanics of job-related relocation, it's time for a reality check. Americans have a long history of trying to use geography to solve their problems. Your life stinks in the East? Go West, young man. Movement is in the American grain. But you'd better weigh the liabilities before you make any commitments.

Relocation Costs

Many employers, especially at the higher salary levels, will pay all or some of your relocation costs. At the very least, these should be a subject of negotiation. Such costs include:

➤ Interview travel and expenses

➤ Costs associated with selling your house in your present location

➤ Moving expenses

➤ Temporary accommodation costs (hotel, apartment, and so on) at your new location

➤ Furniture storage while you are in your temporary accommodations

These add up to a major expense. Moving the contents of a three-bedroom house and a four-member family five hundred miles costs in the neighborhood of $8,000 to $10,000. And this doesn't include the other expenses previously mentioned. At present, the Internal Revenue Service allows only a small percentage of these expenses to be deducted from your taxable income, so getting your new employer to foot some or all of your relocation expenses is a major compensation item.

There is another cost of relocation, less tangible than cash, but no less real. Psychologists say that only suffering the death of a loved one or losing a job exacts a greater emotional and physical toll than moving. This may be even more intense for children, who, without any say in the matter, are forced to leave a familiar place, a familiar school, and a host of friends.

Ways and Means: Compensation vs. Cost of Living

I have already mentioned cost of living as one of the factors you need to consider in evaluating a prospective place to live. It bears repeating here. The relative increase (or even decline) in salary entailed by your move is only part of the compensation story. What will your salary dollar buy—or fail to buy—in San Francisco as opposed to Kansas City? *Places Rated Almanac* is a good starting point for figuring this out, but be certain that you thoroughly investigate the cost of housing, local taxes, and utilities (especially in locations with extreme climates: long, hot summers or long, cold winters).

Cost of living is not the only economic factor that varies from region to region. So does level of compensation, so that a customer service representative for an insurance company based in New York City may be paid more than one based in Little Rock, Arkansas. Of course, it costs less to live in Little Rock than in New York City and environs. A big part of the reason is that people are generally paid less in Little Rock. The relationship between cost of living and levels of compensation is reciprocal. Reciprocal—but not all that simple. While salaries and costs may generally be lower in Little Rock versus New York, it is possible that, in certain cases, the law of supply and demand will partially cancel out or totally reverse this principle. If (and this is entirely hypothetical) very few advertising copywriters work out of Little Rock, the basic compensation for those who do may not be much less (or may actually be higher) than that for copywriters working in New York, where members of that profession abound.

The point is this. When considering a move, compare the following at your present location versus the target location:

➤ Cost of living

➤ General levels of compensation

➤ Compensation in your particular field or industry and for your particular position

Regional information on salaries is available through the U.S. Department of Labor and in *Jobs '95: By Career, By Industry, By Region*. The most accurate information, however, is likely to be found in the annual surveys published in journals devoted to a particular industry. Identify such a publication for your industry. If necessary, order a reprint of the most recent salary survey issue from the publisher.

Culture Shock

It's part of American folklore: the journey to the Big City to make one's fortune. During the past 30-some years, at least since the 1960s, a contrary move has been a much talked-about aspiration, if not always a commonplace actuality: the move into the country.

Special Risks of the Hinterlands

A desire for simplicity, a desire for room, a desire for clean air, for tranquillity, for (relative) freedom from crime—all of these may motivate you to move to the country. Anyone who has read Henry David Thoreau's *Walden* knows the benefits of country life. Just be sure that you understand all the risks before you chuck the urban for the rural.

Will you be able to *sustain* a living? The country life is ideal for writers and for others who can work from home and communicate via phone, fax, and computer, but, for others, opportunities can be limited and, worse, can suddenly and unexpectedly evaporate.

Are you sure that you really want to "return to a simpler time"? Whatever its many pressures and drawbacks, big cities also offer dazzling shopping opportunities, significant cultural opportunities, elegant troughs for wining and dining. In a word, they offer *stimulation.* Can you live happily without this—or with less than this—for more than four months?

Over There: The Upside and Downside of Overseas Employment

Between the wars—World Wars I and II, that is—a so-called "lost generation" of Americans packed up, went to live abroad, and sustained themselves overseas with a variety of jobs. Well, you can't do that anymore. I've tried to take a very positive, albeit realistic, approach in this book, and I hate to say *can't.* But that's the word for casual overseas employment. Most nations have stringent work-permit regulations, and many suffer from rates of unemployment that actively discourage foreign job seekers.

This said, the outlook for international careers is quite bright, *if* you approach your target position as a career. With the emergence of the European Community (EC), the development of the Pacific Rim (especially Japan, Korea, and China—and the likely development of Indochina and Vietnam in particular), the glorious revolution in South Africa, and the collapse of communism in Eastern Europe, political boundaries and obstacles to trade have yielded to a truly international economy. American businesses not only trade with foreign partners, but subcontract work abroad. By the same token, America, of course, is the principal market for many international businesses. Your best bet for getting a job abroad is not to find employment in a local London or Paris or Timbuktu shop, but to secure a position with an international company (that is, a company that does business internationally). Under the auspices of such a firm, you will not only have the opportunity for overseas employment, but (usually) assistance with getting settled, cutting through immigration red tape, and adapting to cultural differences.

> **I SEE...**
>
> ## Case Study
>
> Few people wake up one morning, decide to embark upon an international career, pursue a specific course of study in preparation for it, then move to some new part of the world. More typically, an international career develops from a combination of academic background, life interest, and the requirements of a given position, profession, or company at a certain time. Jane, a friend of mine, had an intense interest in literature. She thought of becoming an English major and, perhaps, teaching literature in high school or college. Then she began reading, in translation, the novels of Thomas Mann. This writer so intrigued her that she started poking around in the works of other 20th-century German writers. Soon, she had a hankering to read them in the original language and transfered from her major in the university's English Department to the German Department.
>
> After graduation, Jane needed to earn some money to help finance graduate study. Through the German Department's foreign-study office, she learned of a work-study secretarial position at Mercedes-Benz. Seeing an opportunity to improve her German among native speakers and earn some money, she applied for the job, obtained it, and set sail.
>
> Today, she is an executive assistant with the auto manufacturer and does most of her reading in German literature on frequent plane trips back and forth across the Atlantic.

The upside of an international career is twofold. First, such a career rides the crest of the social-political-technological wave of what former President Bush called the "new world order." Thinking beyond national borders extends not only one's philosophical horizons, but one's financial horizons as well. In general, salaries for middle to senior positions in international trade and in technical positions abroad exceed those for their domestic counterparts. For many who seek international careers, the cultural rewards outweigh even the financial: the opportunity to see a different world, to experience different cultures, to get a fresh perspective on life.

Is there a downside? Of course. International business is often riskier than domestic business. Monetary exchange rates and political instabilities are not the bedrock of strong business foundations. The frequent travel entailed by international business can be a burden as well as a blessing. Living in a strange country can be stimulating as well as frightening and unsettling, especially for families. Cultural differences are likewise both attractive and frustrating, often making it difficult to perform business functions taken for granted in a domestic context. Exotic locales and exotic foods can give you pleasure and can make you sick. Finally, ask anyone who has ever been homesick: It *is* a sickness, and it is no joke.

Here's an example of the kind of country information that you can access electronically; an official U.S. State Department travel advisory.

```
From 76702.1202@CompuServe.COM Fri Oct  9 20:38:54 1992
Newsgroups: wstd.travel.advisories
From: 76702.1202@CompuServe.COM (Charlie Smith)
Subject: *NEW* TRAVEL INFORMATION -- Belgium
Organization: The World @ Software Tool & Die
Distribution: wstd
Date: Fri, 9 Oct 1992 13:20:22 GMT

STATE DEPARTMENT TRAVEL INFORMATION - Belgium
==============================================================
Belgium - Consular Information Sheet
 October 7, 1992

Embassy Location:  The U.S. Embassy in Brussels is located at 27
Boulevard du Regent; telephone (32) (2) 513-3830.

Country Description:  Belgium is a highly developed and stable
democracy with a modern economy.  Tourist facilities are widely
available.

Travel Requirements:  A visa is not required of American citizens
for business or tourist stays up to 90 days.  For further
information concerning entry requirements for Belgium, travelers
can
contact the Embassy of Belgium at 3330 Garfield Street N.W.,
Washington DC 20008, tel (202) 333-6900, or the nearest Consulate
General in Atlanta, Chicago, Los Angeles, or New York.

Medical Information:  Medical facilities are widely available.
U.S. medical insurance is not always valid outside the United
States.  Travelers have found that in some cases, supplemental
medical insurance with specific overseas coverage has proved to be
useful.  Further information on health matters can be obtained from
the Centers for Disease Control's international Travelers hotline
on
(404) 332-4559.

Crime Information:  Belgium has a relatively low crime rate in most
regions.  However, U.S. citizens visiting major cities can become
targets for pickpockets and purse snatchers.  Areas around train
stations in both Brussels and Antwerp and the Rogier and De Brouker
metro stations in Brussels have a higher instance of crime than do
other areas within these cities.  U.S. citizens can refer to the
Department of State's pamphlet, "A Safe Trip Abroad" for ways to
promote a more trouble-free voyage.  The pamphlet is available from
the Superintendent of Documents, U.S. Government Printing Office,
Washington DC 20402.

Drug Penalties:  Penalties for possession, use, or dealing in
illegal drugs are strict, and convicted offenders can expect jail
sentences and fines.

Registration:  Americans who register in the Consular Section of
the U.S. Embassy can obtain updated information on travel and
security within the area.

No. 92-007
```

```
                         General Life

      Life in Hong Kong can be described as busy, competitive,
 dynamic and convenient.  People here work very hard.  Most
 people have to work at least 20 days a month, 8 hours a day.
 Almost all the shops open 12 hours a day, 7 days a week.
 Unlike in Europe or in America, people usually go shopping
 when they need something immediately instead of filling their
 refrigerator with trunk loads of food.  You can find goods
 from almost every corner of the world here, at reasonable
 price and with virtually no taxation.  That is why Hong Kong
 is also known as shopping paradise.  It is no surprise to see
 a Japanese tourist buying half a dozen made-in-Japan cameras
 in a shop in Mong Kok.

      Compared with other countries, Hong Kong is relatively a
 peaceful and safe place.  There are no religious and racial
 problems.  Jobs are plenty.  Tax is low (15% flat rate).  An
 average freshly graduated professional can earn US$13,000 a
 year after tax.  Inflation is around 10% per year.  The
 biggest problem for a normal Hong Konger may be housing.
 Real estate property prices soared recently.  People have to
 spend nearly half their monthly income for their flats, and
 the mortgage can last for 20 years.  As anywhere on earth,
 Hong Kong has its own social problems.  Many of the ones that
 have caught attention have much to do with the approaching
 1997 issue.  People have a confidence problem with their
 future, though it is being offset by the economic gain due to
 the tightening connection with China.  The wealth of the
 community is getting more and more unevenly distributed
 because of the expeculation activities in stock, foreign
 currency and real estate markets.  These somehow increase the
 social tension quite a bit, according to the social workers.
```

Thinking about relocating overseas? Explore the Internet. Here is a briefing about Hong Kong downloaded from an electronic forum maintained by an association of electrical engineers.

Here's something else to consider. Look around our own country. Japanese auto manufacturers, German chemical concerns, French tire manufacturers, and other off-shore companies have been opening plants not in the cultural capitals of New York, Chicago, and Los Angeles, but in the rural and small-town heartland. Well, the same is true of many American-based firms that do business abroad. Installations are being established not in Paris or London, but in smaller communities. It is also true that many major European firms who employ Americans are headquartered in places such as Clermont-Ferrand, France, with a population of 30,000 (Michelin Tire); Ludwigshafen, Germany, at 153,000 (BASF); and Ivrea, Italy, populated by 19,400 souls (Olivetti). Are you prepared to live abroad in the equivalent of Moline, Illinois, or Greenville, South Carolina? Consider, too, that the greatest *new* demand for international specialists will come in such non-European countries as Korea, China, Singapore, Brazil, India, Mexico, and Africa. Eastern Europe will also prove a growth area. The prospect of living in these places may or may not be exciting to you.

Finally, consider the preparation that may be required for an international career. Really, I am talking about a lifetime process, which encompasses cultural experiences as well as formal education. Traveling—not mere tourism—on your own is important, as is reading about different cultures. Your formal education should include a healthy dose of liberal arts as well as foreign language study. The liberal arts background will help to give you a strong cultural orientation, while languages will serve as the most basic and most essential tool of your trade.

The Least You Need to Know

➤ Use objective as well as subjective criteria to evaluate the pros and cons of a prospective move.

➤ Prepare the resources necessary to conduct your job hunt by long distance; the telephone interview is especially important.

➤ Realistically evaluate the costs of relocation, including the costs of the move itself and any increases or decreases in the cost of living relative to your original location.

➤ Understand how to evaluate the potential of an international career, including identifying the growth regions, coping with the special demands of a career based abroad, and acquiring the cultural and educational background for such a career.

Part 3
A Résumé Handbook

Here it is: the very thing many folks buy a job-hunting guide for—How To Write a Résumé.

Well, let me settle a major issue before I dive in. You don't write a résumé, you write a number of résumés—in fact, as many as necessary to tailor each comfortably to the needs of the target employer. The effective résumé isn't an eternal monument to yourself, it's a temporary scaffold built as required to put you into position to capture a specific interview for a specific job.

The "Handbook" that follows provides strategies for trimming and sewing your résumé to suit whatever employer comes your way.

Chapter 8

Looking Good on Paper

In This Chapter

➤ Limitations of the résumé as a job-hunting tool

➤ The importance of substituting *qualifications* for *experience*

➤ Focusing on the employer's needs rather than your own

➤ Structuring and designing a persuasive résumé

➤ Preparing a computer-friendly résumé

In her fascinating book about Europe's Dark Ages, *A Distant Mirror*, the late historian Barbara Tuchman describes a game popular among townsfolk in medieval France. It involved tying a cat to one's head and running headlong into a wall with the sole purpose of killing the cat before it scratched your eyes out.

Our own age of political correctness dictates a nonjudgmental attitude toward cultural values and activities that differ from our own, but this game of kill-the-cat, well, it just seems pretty cruel, stupid, and pointless, doesn't it?

Now, before we puff ourselves up with late 20th-century pride, think about what the Barbara Tuchman of some future age would say about one of our own cruel, stupid, and pointless popular obsessions: the résumé.

Guaranteed to Fail 1,469 Out of 1,470 Times

The author of one very popular job-hunting book mentions that he was on a radio call-in show. A caller complained that she had been unemployed for two years. The author asked her how many firms she had contacted. She replied that she had contacted 250. The author then asked her how many possible employers there were in her field. The reply was "about 3,000," whereupon the author said, "Next caller, please."

Virtually all job-hunting advisers tell us that we should contact every conceivable potential employer. That can be hard work. Now, by "contact," these advisers usually mean sending out a résumé. That makes the work not only hard, but also cruel, stupid, and pointless. Because the fact is that only 1 out of every 1,470 unsolicited résumés ever produces a job offer. The vast majority are immediately thrown away or, what may amount to virtually the same thing, *filed* away. Rarely do potential employers even acknowledge having received your résumé. And those relatively few who actually review unsolicited résumés do so with skepticism and distrust, assuming that much of what you've committed to paper as gospel is at best exaggeration and at worst total fabrication.

Yet job-hunt advisers continue to urge job hunters to write and mail résumés, and job hunters continue to heed that advice. Why is it so hard to kick the habit? I suppose that, next to the fact of unemployment (or unhappy employment), the worst aspect of looking for a job is getting rejected. In a twisted way, sending out résumés avoids rejection. If you call a target employer on the phone, or if you apply in person for a position, chances are you'll hear bad news. If you send a résumé, chances are you'll hear nothing. Of course, you won't get a job offer, either. At least, you'll feel like you are *doing* something. (You *are*. Mailing out one hundred—or even *three thousand*—résumés is hard, time-consuming work.)

Creating a Package for a Product (You!)

Parts 1 and 4 of this book suggest many *effective* alternatives to enriching the United States Postal Service by sending out mailbags full of unsolicited résumés. Here, in this chapter, I'll not abandon the résumé, but suggest ways of rethinking it.

Now, let's not kid ourselves. Your target employer does need summary information about you. Both you and the target employer have been led to believe that the résumé is the only way to present this information—even though that employer will automatically discard most of the résumés he or she receives.

It's decidedly time to rethink the résumé.

An overwhelming number of résumés "fail to do the job they're supposed to do in representing the person who wrote the résumé." Why? Because they describe *experience* instead of what an employer is really interested in: *qualifications*. "Experience" is merely what you've done in the past. "Qualifications" encompass not just what you have done, but what you have accomplished, and also include qualities, skills, and abilities that make (in the words of the third edition of *The American Heritage Dictionary of the English Language*) "a person suitable for a particular position or task." Let's take this to heart, then, and rethink the résumé in terms of qualifications rather than experience.

Pitfall
Avoid using "professional" résumé services. They tend to produce a canned product, which employers soon come to recognize. A bought résumé brands you as unoriginal and uncreative.

Qualifications for What?

Why, for the *job*, of course. Obvious, right? But it is precisely the requirements of the job—or, more to the point, the needs of the employer—that traditional résumés fail to address. As traditionally conceived, the résumé focuses on the needs of the applicant. If you rethink the résumé to address the needs of the employer, you can rest assured that the employer will read the résumé with heightened interest.

To accomplish this, you need to depart from the traditional résumé in three additional important ways:

➤ Whereas the traditional résumé inventories your duties, the "rethought" résumé describes abilities.

➤ The "rethought" résumé includes an indication of your level of performance—how well you do your job.

➤ The traditional résumé lists responsibilities. The "rethought" version presents accomplishments.

The Objective Case

I'll get to an example of a "rethought" résumé, embodying these principles, in a moment, but, before I leave my discussion of the elements of this new-style résumé, let me add one more essential: How do you begin?

It is most effective to start off with a statement of your career purpose, your "objective." Now, at first blush, it may be difficult to see how such a statement—by definition, a statement about yourself—can address the needs of the employer. But this, in fact, is the beauty of a carefully crafted objective statement: It seems miraculously to mesh what you want in your career with what the employer wants from the person who fills the position.

Many traditional-style résumés don't even begin with a statement of objective, and even those that do tend either to be too narrow or too broad, and they characteristically fail even to hint at how the applicant's objective will benefit the employer. Here's an example of a narrow objective:

OBJECTIVE: Quality Assurance Engineer

All this tells an employer is that the applicant wants a position—a fact that's self-evident, anyway. Furthermore, unless the employer has a position available with this precise title, it is not likely that he or she will pursue the applicant's candidacy. (The irony is that this employer may, in fact, have an opening for the equivalent of a "quality assurance engineer," but may identify that position with a different title and, therefore, pass up this applicant.) This kind of objective statement brings the candidate up to the plate with two big strikes already against him or her: What it says is both too specific, yet provides too little information.

Here is another losing objective statement:

OBJECTIVE: Seeking an opportunity to utilize my skills, education, and energy in a working environment that offers a good, solid career path.

Consciously or unconsciously, the employer will respond to this by asking, "What's in it for me?" Not only is this objective statement too broad (I mean, who *doesn't* want "a good, solid career path"?), it is entirely self-centered, offering the potential employer nothing.

Sir Isaac Newton proposed his First Law of Motion in 1687, declaring that a body at rest remains at rest and a body in motion remains in motion (at a constant velocity) *unless acted upon by outside forces.* This law of physics is just as valid in the realm of human behavior. The person who slices into the envelope containing your résumé is either inclined—so far as your application is concerned—to remain motionless or to keep right on going in the current speed and direction. Your task is to overcome this inertia. And that is precisely the function of the statement of objective. The rest of the résumé sustains, builds, and develops this initial burst of energy. The objective statements you've just looked at fail to overcome inertia. Now, here's one that almost works:

OBJECTIVE: To obtain a position where my 15 years of material, production, and inventory control experience will be a company asset.

This is a step in the right direction. The statement says something about what the applicant wants and what he or she brings to the employer's table. It would be better, though, if the applicant's *experience* were transformed into *qualifications*:

OBJECTIVE: To obtain a position where my 15 years of creating innovative and cost-effective systems for material, production, and inventory control will be a company asset.

The phrase "creating innovative and cost-effective systems" transforms passive experience into active—*proactive*—qualifications. Notice the use of the verb form ("creating"). Well-chosen verbs always energize a description of qualifications. They are your best shot at prompting the target employer to take his or her feet off the desk and act on what you have to offer.

Still, we can hone the statement yet more sharply:

OBJECTIVE: To be a member of a team that needs my 15 years of experience creating innovative and cost-effective systems for material, production, and inventory control.

> **Buzz Word**
> Remember, your *qualifications* are qualities, abilities, or accomplishments that suit you to a particular position or task, whereas *experience* is merely an event you've participated in or were present during. The first is active and creative; the second is passive and (at most) reactive.

The introduction of two powerful words, *team* and *needs*, sharply sets this résumé apart from the competition. The target employer is accustomed to such terms as *firm, company, employer, corporation,* and *organization. Team* will catch him or her off-guard, and that is just what you want to do. The feet come off the desk, and the word lingers in consciousness. "Yes," your target agrees, "That's just what we are: a *team.*" The word *needs,* of course, shifts the focus from you to the employer. Suddenly, your target employer is no longer reading a job application, but an answer to what his or her *team needs.*

Rethought and Reborn

Is the résumé dead? No. The *résumé* is not dead, but the vast majority of *résumés* are. It's time they were rethought and reborn. Following are two examples of résumés that incorporate the features I've just discussed.

> **Jump Start**
> The objective statement can begin with a noun—the name of the position sought—or it can begin with an infinitive verb: "To be an office assistant...." The infinitive is most effective when you don't begin by mentioning a specific job, as in "To be a member of team...."

103

An attractive and effective résumé for someone just starting out. The "Objective" is clear: to satisfy the employer.

SARALEE GOLDSTEIN

677 Howard Drive, NW • Cornice, GA 30355 • 555-555-5555

OBJECTIVE

Office assistant, where typing skills, mastery of all major word-processing software, absolute commitment to deadlines, a strong sense of responsibility, detail-orientation, energy, and a positive attitude are required.

EDUCATION

GRADUATED IN TOP 25 % FROM ANDREW JOHNSON HIGH SCHOOL IN JUNE 1995. My best grades were in English and foreign language (German). I also excelled in general science. I learned to type 50+ wpm--with maximum accuracy. I speak and read German.

SUMMER EMPLOYMENT

CLERK, ADAMS DRUGS
During summers from 1993 to 1995, I worked as a checkout clerk and had responsibility for maintaining general stock. I reported directly to Mr. Charles Adams, owner of the store, who was always complimentary about the efficiency and accuracy of my work. He relied on me to create small in-store displays of special sales items.

RELATED EXPERIENCE

I was a reporter for the *Andrew Johnson Leader,* our high school newspaper. I never missed a deadline. I also participated in student government as a Student Council representative. My classmates elected me each time I ran.

AIMS AND ASSETS

I am a fast learner and a self-starter. I enjoy taking on new responsibilities and going the extra mile. I have always made friends, especially among those who have worked with me. I plan on continuing my education in evening school, as work permits.

BENJAMIN TYLER

RR 2 ▪ Eastwood, NY 14568 ▪ 555-555-5555
Fax: 555-555-4444

OBJECTIVE

Project/Design Engineer in an organization that requires strong, efficient, cost-effective management of projects from conceptualization through implementation of final design.

EMPLOYMENT

DELEM CORPORATION, PENNYPACKER, NEW YORK
Manufacturing/Project Engineer, 1987-89
I was responsible for all projects pertaining to assigned customers, which included Westinghouse, Pratt & Whitney, and Lycoming. The scope of work ranged from the production of gas and turbine components to the manufacture of orthopedic implants used in biomedical engineering.

o My cost estimates were critical to the company-wide cost-savings initiative. Between 1987 and 1989, I reduced fabrication costs an average of 8 percent.

o I initiated and chaired concept meetings for new programs, including our Customer Education program, which (according to Sales Department estimates) increased sales by 5-9 percent in 1988-89.

o I acted as liaison between the Engineering Department and our customers.

o I performed extensive troubleshooting and completed a Total Quality Assurance Program, which resulted in significant cost reductions for the company.

SEMPLE, INC., GARNER, NEW JERSEY
Tooling Supervisor, 1985-87
I was in charge of in-house tooling, and I supervised tool room personnel.

o I conceived, planned, and organized the total structure of a new department, customizing the shop layout to achieve increased flexibility of production and to save money. My design was credited with reducing product turn-around time by 3-5 percent.

o I designed injection molds for an aerospace product line--a task that required familiarity with military specifications and a complete understanding of engineering drawings.

EDUCATION

HERMAN J. GAW UNIVERSITY SCHOOL OF ENGINEERING, NEW CALEDONIA, NEW YORK
B.S., Mechanical Engineering, 1987
I was editor of the *Mech Eng Bulletin* from 1985 to 1987. I graduated with high honors.

SKILLS SUMMARY

o Strong technical experience
o Absolute understanding of complex engineering drawings
o Complete familiarity with manufacturing processes and supporting tool designs
o Communicate clearly with customers and subcontractors

An effective résumé is clean, functional, and specific. All elements should add up to a single point: I will create satisfaction.

Generic Box vs. Custom Pack: A Different Résumé for Every Target?

Over the years, I've talked to many job seekers. At some point in the conversation comes a statement made in hushed, almost reverential tones. Shhh. Listen.

"I am working on my résumé."

May as well have said, "I am working on the *Magna Carta*."

As I hope this chapter succeeds in conveying, much thought (or "rethought") should go into your résumé. But the résumé is hardly a sacred document. In fact, you shouldn't think of it as *a* document or *the* résumé. A résumé is like a suit, but a very special kind of suit. The suit you wear to work has to fit you and you alone. The "suit" that is your résumé has to fit you *and* your target employer. Unless your spasms of passion for cheesecake and cannoli are followed by sieges of monastic fasting, you can count on your dimensions remaining relatively constant, and you don't have to keep altering your suit. But in the case of your résumé, while you may stay pretty much the same, the target—the other "body" this "suit" must fit—changes.

To some folks, tailoring your résumé to fit the needs of a specific employer seems a trifle sneaky. That's because the traditional résumé was intended to represent who you *are*, your being and your character. But the "rethought" résumé does not simply represent who you are. Instead, it shows how you will satisfy the needs of the target employer. If the target changes, so should the résumé.

Another objection to creating custom résumés for each employer is that doing so makes more work for you. That's right. But would you rather do the work of identifying and researching your targets, creating umpteen cover letters, addressing a gazillion envelopes, taking out a second mortgage to pay the postage, and renting a truck to haul the mail to the P.O. only to have your generic résumé tossed into corporate wastebaskets throughout our great republic? I mean, isn't the object to create documents that will get you the job you want? Besides, word processing makes creating custom résumés much easier than it was in the days of the typewriter.

In *those* days, it really was a royal pain. Today, you can create a basic, master résumé, then cut, paste, and edit—electronically—to make it fit each target employer. Of course, you still have to do the kind of research discussed in Part 4 of this book; that's how you can assess just what it is that the target employer needs. And, yes, it is easier to skip all that and just send out a load of résumés. But, for that matter, it's even easier to do absolutely nothing and wait for someone to call you with an offer. Either way, you almost certainly won't get a job.

The Tried and the (Apparently) True

From my lofty philosophical perch, I have advised you to break with the past and think anew. Let's return to planet earth for a moment to consider a few résumé nuts and bolts.

How Long?

There is a classic story about a neophyte Hollywood screenwriter who asked his seasoned and cynical agent how long the summary of his script (Hollywood types call the summary a "treatment") should be. The agent answered, "No more than ten pages. Any longer, and the producer's lips get tired."

It's my guess that most people who volunteer to tell you how to write a résumé feel about business folk the way this agent felt about Hollywood producers. Repeatedly, you encounter the commandment, *Thou shalt not write more than a page.*

"A foolish consistency," Ralph Waldo Emerson said, "is the hobgoblin of little minds." As a *general* rule, be brief. Focus on qualifications and abilities. Don't allow your résumé to become a rambling laundry list. If, however, your qualifications and abilities cannot be encompassed within a single page, go on to another.

> **Jump Start**
> A rule of thumb: If you've worked fewer than ten years, a single page will probably be sufficient. Ten or more years of work experience will likely require a second page.

Put This Stuff In

In addition to a strong statement of your objective, the résumé should include the following headings:

> **EMPLOYMENT:** Avoid the passive word *experience*.
>
> **EDUCATION:** Begin with your most advanced degree, then work backward chronologically.
>
> **SKILLS, SKILL SUMMARY,** or **QUALIFICATIONS:** This is a summary statement of your special skills expressed in a way that tailors them to the needs of the target employer.

It is always best to list EMPLOYMENT immediately after OBJECTIVE. If the position you are aiming at requires special educational background, list that heading next. If, however, skills are most important, put the SKILLS heading next, followed by EDUCATION.

Leave This Junk Out

This is not intended as an invitation to write a multipage document. Eliminate the following dross from your résumé:

➤ Detailed descriptions of jobs held more than ten years ago (mention the jobs, but keep the descriptions to a single line each).

➤ Reasons for leaving previous jobs.

➤ Salary history and pay desired. Try never to be the first to bring up salary (see Chapter 22, "Negotiating Salary and Other Matters"). Even if you are answering a want ad that requests "salary history," do not include it in your résumé or cover letter.

➤ Your personal biography.

➤ Date of availability. Address this in the cover letter, if you feel it necessary. However, it is more appropriately addressed in the interview.

➤ Social Security number.

➤ Names of references. Employers assume that you have references available. This being the case, you can also safely eliminate the pro forma line about "references available on request."

➤ Canned quotations from official job descriptions.

➤ Certain backup information may be included with the résumé, if appropriate; for example: a bibliography of professional articles you've written or contributed to, a list of special courses you've taken, a listing of technical equipment with which you have competence, a client list, and so on. However, you should eliminate:

> A title page or cover sheet for your résumé
>
> Official documents
>
> Letters of recommendation

Does the last item-to-omit surprise you? Letters of recommendation should be sent by your recommender directly to the target employer. They should not come from you. Moreover, these letters should be individually addressed to the specific target. Avoid "boilerplate" letters addressed "To whom it may concern." Avoid photocopied letters. If the recommender does not think highly enough of you to write individual letters, tap someone else for a recommendation.

Design Basics

Three *don'ts*:

➤ Don't be sloppy.

➤ Don't be flashy.

➤ Don't let a "professional" résumé-writing house make your résumé look as if it has been churned out by a "professional" résumé-writing house. (Employers have seen a gazillion of these.)

What *should* you do?

➤ Use the examples in this chapter as models for a neat, conservative, functional, and pleasant page layout. Do not labor to achieve a beautiful design. To the extent that the target employer takes conscious note of the design of your résumé, his or her focus will shift from the content of the document.

➤ Keep paragraphs short. Double-space between them.

➤ Keep margins ample: 1 1/2 inches, left, right, top, bottom.

➤ Make *judicious* use of highlighting devices: marginal descriptions, underlining (or italics, or boldface type—but not all three).

➤ Use centered headlines to stress positions held and achievements achieved.

➤ Choose a conservative, readable typeface. In the days before word processing, all you had to worry about was having a fresh and clean typewriter ribbon. Nowadays you must give thought to fonts and point size. A sans-serif face (such as Helvetica, Optima, or the equivalent) conveys streamlined functionalism. A serif face (such as Times Roman, Schoolbook, and so on) conveys traditional solidity. In general, don't mix the two—except that you may want to use a sans-serif face for your centered headlines and a serif face for your text. Avoid eccentric typefaces, including script faces that mimic handwriting. In general, use 12-point type for the body text of your résumé. You may want to use 14-point type for centered headings.

Pitfall
Federal law prohibits employers from discriminating on account of race, gender, age, or physical disabilities. The law notwithstanding, if you believe that a photograph will suggest anything about yourself that may discourage an employer, omit the photograph. On the other hand, if you see your physical appearance as an asset, use it.

You may include a photograph of yourself. This is a personal decision. However, this should *not* be a casual snapshot. Supply an informal portrait in appropriate business attire (not a vacation snap of you lolling on the beach of St. Tropez). Smile and relax. You want to appear friendly, competent, and self-assured.

Daring and Different

There are at least three major alternatives to the paper résumé. One of these, the on-line résumé, is gradually entering into the mainstream, and I will discus it in a moment. The other two alternatives are putting your résumé on audio or video tape. For most positions, these unconventional approaches are inappropriate and counterproductive. Exceptions—where such résumés may well prove effective—are public-contact positions, including (for example) telemarketing, public relations, spokesperson positions, and the like. If you do opt for these approaches, your tape should be accompanied by a paper cover letter and a paper résumé.

The Computer-Friendly Résumé: On-Ramps to the Information Superhighway

There is a lot of buzz these days about an "electronic job search revolution," and I discuss the potential and techniques of computer-driven job hunting in Chapter 13, "Cruising the Infobahn." At this point in time, such resources as CompuServe, America Online, Prodigy, and the Internet are more useful as a means of obtaining information about particular firms and industries than they are as anything resembling employment clearinghouses. You have observed at the beginning of this chapter that sending out unsolicited résumés is not an effective job-hunting tactic, and that truth does not change just because you post your résumé electronically. However, an increasing number of firms are requesting that you submit your résumé via e-mail, while other firms now make it a practice to scan paper résumés and file them electronically. Therefore, it is worth your time and effort to learn how to make your résumé computer friendly.

Putting Your Résumé Online

Chapter 13 gives you the basics of getting online in the first place and some books that offer more detailed help. One you should be certain to consult is Joyce Lain Kennedy and Thomas J. Morrow's *The Electronic Résumé Revolution*.

The first principle to observe in preparing an on-line résumé is to confine yourself to ASCII text—plain, pure, nondocument text, which has not been laced with word-processing software formatting codes. It's not pretty, but ASCII text will ensure that anyone with any kind of software will be able to download and read your résumé. Among the limitations of ASCII text are the inability to provide underlining, boldface, or italics. Use paired asterisks (*like this*) to indicate italics, and use a lowercase "o" (letter, not numeral) wherever a graphic "bullet" is called for.

Set your margins carefully. A safe setting is 0 for the right-hand and 65 for the left. Even if your monitor displays 80 characters across the screen and your printer is set to print 80 characters across the width of the paper, setting 0 and 65 will ensure that none of your lines will be truncated if the target employer's computer display or printer are set up differently from yours.

Jump Start
You don't need special word-processing software to produce ASCII text. All of the major word-processing software packages, whether for DOS, Windows, or the Macintosh, allow you to save your work in ASCII. Consult your software manual.

Employers who look for or solicit on-line résumés are also likely to use software programmed to search for certain keywords in résumés. These keywords (in theory, at least) allow the employer to zero in on applicants with certain qualifications. Include at the very top of your on-line résumé a heading for "Keywords." Then list all the keywords that you think apply to the target position.

Beyond these considerations, the on-line résumé should resemble the paper résumé.

Life Beyond ASCII?

Of course, it is technically possible to incorporate attractive type, graphics, even a photograph into your on-line résumé. *U.S. News and World Report* (October 31, 1994) even published an article about creating a *multimedia résumé*, complete with sound and graphics, which you could send either on disk or via e-mail.

In a few very special circumstances, such techniques can be useful—especially if you are applying for positions in graphic design or in computer graphic design. Generally, however, few employers have the hardware, software, or—most importantly—the time to monkey with fancy multimedia presentations. Better stick with ASCII.

Tailoring Hard Copy to the Scanner

Even if you have no intention of putting your résumé online, it is possible that it will end up on somebody's computer. A growing number of employers make it a practice to scan the paper résumés they receive, converting them to digital form by using optical character recognition (OCR) software. Once digitized, the résumés can be filed and searched electronically. It behooves you, then, to make your paper résumé scanner friendly. Avoid the following:

➤ Fancy typefaces, graphics, and any hand lettering or handwriting

➤ Colored or patterned papers

➤ Folding the résumé

Do use high-quality 8 1/2 × 11 white paper, preferably 24-pound stock, and be certain to include your e-mail address (if you have one) along with your street address, phone, and fax. Print the résumé by using a high-quality laser printer.

Because the scanned résumé will be a digitized document (just as if you *had* posted it online), it is likely that the target employer will use a keyword-seeking search program on it. Make certain that you include likely keywords within the body of the résumé. Alternatively, you can phone the target employer's human resources department to ask them if they scan résumés. If the answer is yes, then include a keyword heading either at the top or end of the résumé.

The Least You Need to Know

➤ Despite tradition and received wisdom, do not rely on the résumé as your only job-hunting tool. Understand its limitations.

➤ The effective résumé does not simply present your job-related experience, but shows how your qualifications and abilities will satisfy the needs of the prospective employer.

➤ Customize your résumé for each target employer at whom you take aim.

➤ Make your résumé computer friendly so that you can post it on-line or transmit it by e-mail; paper résumés should be easy to scan.

Chapter 9

Judged by Its Cover: How to Write Great Cover Letters

In This Chapter

➤ The purpose of a cover letter

➤ Focusing on what the employer needs

➤ Building a persuasive cover letter

➤ Selling your qualifications and abilities

Just as few job hunters question the conventions of the résumé, few give much thought to the cover letter that accompanies it. It's pro forma, right? I mean, you can't send a résumé—*naked*.

There is more than a grain of truth to this. Business etiquette—common courtesy, even—dictates the inclusion of a cover letter: a voice, if you will, that announces your presence and states your purpose in sending the accompanying résumé.

Well, most cover letters succeed in being polite enough. But that's not much of an accomplishment. A cover letter is an opportunity to communicate with a prospective employer; you should regard each of these opportunities as infinitely precious. Don't squander it on mere courtesy. Seize the opportunity and make the most of it.

But I'm getting ahead of myself. The fact is, most cover letters don't just squander opportunity. They actually kill it. Let's begin with that awful truth.

Dear Sirs, Throw Me Out

Please consider the following letter:

> Dear Sirs:
>
> My current position no longer challenges me, and I am looking to move on.
>
> I am currently the assistant manager of customer service for Acme Widgets, and I would like to be considered for a similar position with your firm. I want to go to work for a firm that offers excellent opportunities for advancement.
>
> Obviously, I've heard very good things about your organization. I'm sure I would be happy working for you, and I can assure you that you would be pleased with my work.
>
> Please find my résumé enclosed.
>
> I look forward to hearing from you.
>
> Sincerely,
>
>
> Joseph Blow

The best thing about Mr. Blow's letter is its brevity. From there, unfortunately, it's all downhill. Let's take a closer look.

It's bad. Few readers will get past the salutation before balling up the letter, accompanying résumé, envelope, and all, taking aim at the wastebasket, and executing a very nice lay-up. The surest way to be ignored is to fail to address a person by name. The surest way to offend is to force your reader into an unwanted gender transformation. The reader of this letter—let's call her Jennifer Smith—will not appreciate being addressed as a "Sir." Before you write, identify someone to write to—preferably someone with the power to hire you. Take the time to research this. Sending out a blind letter—even if you have the foresight to begin it with "Dear Sir *or* Madam"—is entirely futile.

We could pick apart the body of the letter in some detail. For example, this fella begins by implying that he is tired of his job. Starting off with a negative is almost never a good way to sell anything, and it is a particularly bad way to "sell" somebody on the notion of considering you for a job. In this case, Mr. Blow makes matters worse by asking to be considered for a position "similar" to the one with which he is apparently bored. Finally, the letter says nothing concrete beyond the following:

➤ I'm bored with my current job.

➤ My current job is assistant customer service manager.

➤ I want a similar job.

➤ Your company will do.

➤ My résumé is enclosed.

Not much to go on here, and, worst of all, the most specific statement is negative.

But the letter is even worse than what I've just described. There are 98 words in the body of this letter. Of these, nine (10 percent of the letter) are some form of "I." Most cover letters—this one included—talk a lot about "I": to wit, what *I* want. Just imagine a car salesperson who made a pitch like this: "I want you to buy this car, because I'm carrying a heavy mortgage, and I have to put a son and daughter through college." The pitch might work if you have a profoundly charitable nature. But if you are interested in what the automobile can do for *you* and how much it will cost *you,* rather than what *your* purchase will do for the salesperson, the pitch will fall very flat. The same holds true for a cover letter. Your reader wants to know what you will do for him or her, not what his or her hiring you will do for you. The cover letter should immediately shift from your needs to those of the target employer.

> **Jump Start**
> If you are responding to a "blind ad" (one that gives no name), you may have no alternative to "Dear Sir or Madam." Likewise, if an ad directs you to respond to "Sales Manager" (without supplying a personal name), "Dear Sir or Madam" is acceptable. However, even in such cases, consider going the extra mile by doing some basic research to obtain the name of the appropriate human being to address. If you can find a name, use it. This simple action will set your response apart from dozens, perhaps hundreds of others.

Why a Cover Letter?

Now we're ready to answer this question. If you take a pessimistic view, the purpose of the cover letter is to keep your reader from throwing out your résumé. If you are more optimistically inclined, you may see it as a sales letter that tells the target employer what hiring you will do for him or her. Conceived this way, the cover letter supports the résumé, in which you demonstrate in detail just what you can do for the employer.

> **Jump Start**
> Many employers tend automatically to discard any correspondence containing a résumé. They don't bother to read the résumé or the cover letter. If you are making a "cold" inquiry rather than responding to an ad or even acting on information that the employer *might* have an opening, think about sending a letter without a résumé. (See Chapter 14, "How to Heat Things Up with a Cold Letter or a Cold Call.")

Productive vs. Pro Forma

There are a half dozen ingredients that set a productive cover letter apart from a pro forma one:

➤ A strong opening

➤ An appeal to the *employer's* self-interest

➤ Facts that highlight your qualifications and accomplishments

➤ Challenging issues

➤ Introduction to your résumé

➤ Interview opportunity offer

Let's explore them in detail.

Opening Strong

The most compelling opening says nothing about yourself except in the context of what you can do for the target employer. Ideally, the first sentence should set up an equation between you and the target employer's well-being, success, and prosperity. But this is no place for generalities. "I am a terrific assistant customer service manager, who will make a real difference to your operation" is too vague to capture and hold the reader's attention. It asserts, rather than demonstrates. Instead of relying on assertions, which are built on the shifting sands of adjectives, look into your own experience and find some verbs and nouns: "As assistant manager of customer service at Acme Widgets, I have developed techniques for upselling, which I believe will interest you." An even more effective opening speaks forthrightly the language of business—that is, dollars and cents: "As assistant manager of customer service at Acme Widgets, I developed upselling techniques that were responsible for $48,900 in revenue last quarter. I'd like to talk with you about this as well as some other revenue-generating ideas I believe will be of interest to you."

The guiding principle is very simple. Begin by addressing your reader's needs rather than describing your own. Talk to a person about him or herself, and you will be heard.

Develop the Appeal to Self-Interest

This should be accomplished in the first paragraph, following up on your strong opening. Explain some valuable aspect of your experience in terms of how it can benefit your employer:

> As assistant manager of customer service at Acme Widgets, I developed upselling techniques that were responsible for $48,900 in revenue last quarter. I'd like to talk

with you about this as well as some other revenue-generating ideas I believe will be of interest to you. I discovered that Acme, like most other firms, was under-utilizing its customer service operation, looking at it exclusively as a support department rather than another center of profit. With surprisingly minor changes, I introduced upselling as a major customer service function.

The secret is to be specific, but brief. Think of this opening paragraph as announcing a discovery, based on your experience, that will benefit anyone who learns of it. The best part is: *you are willing to share your revelation.*

But what if you don't have years of experience on the job? What if you are just getting out of school? Or what if you are changing careers?

The answer is to draw creatively on whatever experience you do have. Did you create an important project as part of your course work? Is your thesis or dissertation relevant to the needs of a target employer? Did you have a special experience as an intern or in a work-study program? Did you do significant volunteer work? Did you take an active role in student government? Summon up such experiences, and present them as valuable to the employer.

> **Winner**
> If you are fresh out of school, don't forget to emphasize extracurricular activities that demonstrate leadership and self-motivation: committee work, part-time employment, charitable work, student government work, and the like.

Q & A

This doesn't stand for question and answer, but qualifications and accomplishments. If you want to keep the letter brief, tightly integrate the Q & A into the first paragraph, as part of your appeal to the target employer's self-interest. If your qualifications and accomplishments are extensive or if you are sending the cover letter without an accompanying résumé, you will want to develop this section further.

The key to creating an effective Q & A section is selectivity. Your selectivity "filter" should contain two elements:

➤ The qualifications and accomplishments you discuss must appeal to the self-interest of the target employer.

➤ Make sure that you discuss your "experience" in terms of qualifications and accomplishments. (See Chapter 8, "Looking Good on Paper," for more on this.)

Let's return to Joe Blow. Here's the first paragraph again:

> As assistant manager of customer service at Acme Widgets, I developed upselling techniques that were responsible for $48,900 in revenue last quarter. I'd like to talk with you about this as well as some other revenue-generating ideas I believe will be of interest to you. I discovered that Acme, like most other firms, was under-utilizing its customer service operation, looking at it exclusively as a support department rather than another center of profit. With surprisingly minor changes, I introduced upselling as a major customer service function.

Begin the next paragraph with another appeal to the employer's self-interest: "You may also be interested in some of the cost-saving procedures I have implemented." Then continue the paragraph:

> These include supervising the installation of a customer-friendly automated call director and participation in redesigning our customer service database. I estimate the quarterly overhead savings of these innovations to be in the neighborhood of $10,000.

Creating Desire

In Chapter 7, "Yet Another Move: To Another Region or a Different Country," you made the acquaintance of the AIDA acronym, which, you may recall, stands for Attention, Interest, Desire, Action—the four-part formula that structures most successful sales pitches. Your cover letter is, in essence, a sales pitch. Now, we've already seen how beginning with an appeal to the target employer's self-interest commands Attention, while developing that theme arouses Interest. The next paragraph should take that interest to the more visceral level of Desire. This is accomplished by suggesting that the great things you've outlined in the opening two paragraphs are—quite possibly—within the reach of the target employer:

> I made these innovations during the four years I spent with Acme. You will find this experience detailed in the résumé I have enclosed. Certainly, the experience has given me a keen appreciation of the problems and potential of customer service, and it has provided an opportunity for creating profitable solutions. I would greatly enjoy sharing some of my ideas with you.

ELIZABETH JOAN HENROTIN
4334 S. ELSWORTH STREET
LAGRANGE, IL 60054
555-555-5555
FAX: 555-555-4444

August 4, 1995

Mr. Patrick Intourist
Director of Operations
International Development Corporation
2300 E. 12th Street
Chicago, IL 60644

Dear Mr. Intourist:

In view of International's major new initiative in the area of TQM, I think that you will be interested in the following experience:

Successful establishment of a TQM program for a major industrial engineering firm . . . created initiatives in SPC, process improvement, quality system development, statistical techniques, auditing, root cause analysis, quality training . . . spearheaded the implementation of the ISO 9002 program, which has resulted in my current firm's eligibility for top-level aerospace contracts

My resume, which details my abilities and qualifications, is enclosed.

Whether or not you are currently hiring, I do hope to have the opportunity to meet with you. I would like to share with you the latest developments in the ISO 9002 program, which will impact any new implementations.

I will call you during the week of August 14 to learn when a meeting can be arranged.

Sincerely,

Elizabeth Joan Henrotin

You must engage your correspondent with the very first words of the letter. Talk about what your correspondent needs—not what you want.

Action!

All that remains is a call to Action, and, believe it or not, this is the easiest part of the letter. All you have to do is make it possible for the target employer to act. By far, the most desirable action to provoke is a call for an interview. But you don't even have to ask your reader for that. Just lay the foundation:

I will call you during the week of September 5 to learn when we might get together. If you will not be available during that week, please call me.

If you are writing to an out-of-town firm, tell your correspondent when you will be available for an interview:

I will be in New York on September 5, 6, and 7. I will call you before then to learn when we might get together. If you will not be available during that period, please call me.

Who says flattery will get you nowhere? Just combine it with research to make it convincing. Note the use of a bullet list, which invites thoughtful skimming.

Glenda M. Doheny
645 Franklin Square
Yardley, PA 19067
555-555-5555

August 5, 1995

Pamela Barnett
Human Resources Director
RH Company, Inc.
Wilmington, DE 19810

Dear Ms. Barnett:

I enjoyed reading your interview in *Trends in the Trade* and was excited to learn that RH Company is developing a new firm-wide human resources policy manual. As you well know, it is one thing to develop policy and quite another task to implement it. I believe you would be interested in discussing my experience in policy implementation during the past eight years as Assistant then Associate Human Relations Coordinator at IWOOD Corporation.

I worked closely with the Human Resources Director and the directors and managers of all company departments to implement policy on

- employee relations
- labor relations
- staffing
- training and development
- government compliance
- compensation issues
- benefits (including pension plans)
- HRIS

My intensive program of research resulted in a modification of policy that has made IWOOD's employee relations program not only effective, but highly cost effective. I have been credited with improving product quality and finding highly workable solutions to manufacturing and customer service issues.

Doubtless, you will encounter many of the same problems, obstacles, and difficulties I encountered and overcame at IWOOD. I would welcome discussing these with you and will be calling by the end of next week to learn when we can conveniently set up a meeting. In the meantime, I have enclosed my resume, which details my major qualifications, abilities, and achievements in human resources policy implementation.

Sincerely yours,

Glenda M. Doheny

Glenda M. Doheny

The Essential Triad

I'm not here to tell you that what I've presented is the only effective way to write a cover letter. In fact, I urge you to avoid following my advice—or anyone else's—slavishly. What I do hope is that this chapter will inspire you to rethink the cover letters you do write, radically refocusing them on the needs of your target employer.

This said, there is a particular formula that is worth not only memorizing, but, in fact, following. I call it the *essential triad*, and you will find it invaluable for structuring how you present your qualifications and abilities, not only in cover letters, but in interview conversations as well (see Chapters 20, "To Give the Right Answers, Get the Right Questions," and 21, "Asking Questions and Making the Sale").

It's simple, really. Express as much of your cover letter as you possibly can in terms of a *problem*, a *solution*, and an *outcome*: the essential triad. Let this pattern control what you say in the letter. If you've done the exercises in Chapter 2, you should already have a list of problem-solution-outcome events.

Let's revisit Joe Blow's letter yet again. Here is a problem he presents: "I discovered that Acme, like most other firms, was under-utilizing its customer service operation, looking at it exclusively as a support department rather than another center of profit." Here is Joe's solution: "With surprisingly minor changes, I introduced upselling as a major customer service function." After alluding to a few other miracles he has performed, Mr. Blow wraps it all up in a statement of outcome: "I estimate the quarterly overhead savings of these innovations to be in the neighborhood of $10,000." Whenever possible, state the outcome in dollars earned or dollars saved.

The Least You Need to Know

➤ Always address your cover letter to a specific individual—preferably one you have identified as a person with the power to hire you.

➤ Focus your letter on issues related to the employer's self-interest and how you possess the qualifications and abilities to provide what the employer needs.

➤ Use the AIDA formula to structure your letter as a persuasive "sales" document.

➤ Always try to elicit a request for an interview.

➤ Ensure that the "essential triad" (problem-solution-outcome) appears throughout your letter.

Part 4
The Search and Interview

Maybe you were like me. When I was a kid, I loved to take apart old wind-up clocks. Trouble was, after I took one apart, I couldn't put it back together again, and what had been an efficient machine—a system—was now a random pile of gears, springs, and screws. Unfortunately, our nation's so-called job-hunting "system" bears a far closer resemblance to the clock after I got through with it than it does to the happily ticking machine.

Despite the appearance of order and system—want ads, employment agencies, human resources departments, communication via e-mail and Internet—the universe of employment opportunities is pretty much a random pile of gears, springs, and screws.

Now that's not your fault, but it is your problem. It's up to you to put all the elements together to identify and get the job you want.

The chapters in this section will show you how to make effective use of want ads and employment agencies and the other apparatus that can help you find a job, but, even more important, these chapters suggest key strategies for moving beyond such apparatus—because ads, agencies, and the rest are hardly ever all that you need to get the job you want.

Chapter 10

Reactive vs. Proactive Search Strategies

In This Chapter

➤ Tapping the "hidden job market"

➤ Proactive—innovative—job hunt methods

➤ Reaching the person with the power to hire you

➤ Advantages of applying to a small company

➤ Turning rejection into opportunity

Maybe you've seen it up close. Maybe you've been to the visitors' gallery. Maybe you've seen it on TV or in the movies. The New York Stock Exchange (NYSE). Billions of dollars change hands each and every day through something that resembles a street riot rather than a sober financial process. Traders shout, scream, and gesticulate on the floor of the Exchange, jockeying for position, straining to be heard above the racket. With uncharacteristic directness, the financial community calls this the "open outcry system" of trading.

The funny thing is that all this seeming chaos is really quite orderly. It works so well that the NYSE has long resisted replacing open outcry with a more sedate computer system to register offers and trades. Noisy and hectic, the NYSE is nevertheless a genuine marketplace, where goods and cash are efficiently exchanged.

Unfortunately, I think that if we could somehow visualize what we call the national "job market," we would behold a seething monster far more chaotic than the floor of the NYSE. Worse, what we saw is exactly what we would get. Whereas the noisy stock market is actually a genuine *market*, subject to rules, supervised by government regulations, and wired with advanced communication systems, the so-called "job market" lacks any real organization and is governed by no regulations. As to communication, it's strictly catch as catch can.

The good news is that, each and every month, at least two million jobs are open and available in this country. The bad news is, plentiful though they are, our chaotic job market can nevertheless make them pretty hard to find.

Reactive Strategies and Other Oxymorons

We blissfully delude ourselves into believing that there is a method to this job-hunting madness. After all, there are want ads to scour, employment agencies to visit, professional and trade journals to peruse, and the U.S. Postal Service, which will cheerfully accept all the cold letters and blind résumés we can stuff into its gaping jaws. Finally—wonder of wonders—there are various "registers" and "job banks," many of them now posted electronically, which let you simply "sign up for" a job.

Let's stop now and face an important fact: Fewer than 10 percent of job hunters who use these "tried-and-true" job-hunting methods get a job through them. Let's put it another way: If 100 job hunters relied exclusively on ads, trade journal postings, agencies, shotgun résumé mailings, electronic job-bank postings, fewer than 10 (probably no more than 5) would get jobs.

The point is not to reject these traditional job-hunting methods. Just don't rely on them as your only approaches to getting the job you want.

Want Ads

Many people fool themselves into believing that the want ads in the daily paper are the "official" tickets to a job—as if some law obliges those with jobs to offer to post them here. In fact, in terms of percentages, relatively few responses to ads result in jobs. However, our world is virtually buried in want ads, so that, while the "hit rate" is small as a percentage, it is large as a gross number. Unreliable as they are, want ads do yield jobs. Because the ads are ubiquitous, we'll discuss them in their own chapter, Chapter 11, "Trekking the Want Ad Jungle."

Trade-Journal Postings

Trade-journal postings are want ads that are not in newspapers, but in specialized journals devoted to your field of interest. Generally, you can expect a better hit rate if you answer these ads rather than devote yourself exclusively to the newspaper. Chapter 11 explores them in detail.

Electronic Job Bank Postings

Information is gold—unless everyone has it. These days, you still have an edge on access to information if you make it your business to cruise the electronic superhighway. As more and more people discover the Internet and other online connections, however, that edge is rapidly becoming blunt. Read Chapter 13, "Cruising the Infobahn," for tips on using electronic resources to help you in your job hunt.

Jump Start
There is nothing magical about electronic job postings. As with print postings, expect no more than a 5 percent hit rate; therefore, as with the other reactive search strategies discussed here, combine your electronic wanderings with other job-hunting methods.

Agencies

Chapter 4, "Up Another Ladder: Moving to Another Employer in a Company Similar to Yours," briefly discussed employment agencies and headhunters, and you will examine them in detail in Chapter 15, "Agencies and Headhunters." For now, a word about adjusting expectations. Our country is a nation of people who make a habit of "putting themselves in the hands of experts." We visit doctors for this or that complaint. We consult interior decorators to make our homes look good. We hire tax accountants to fill out volumes of government forms. And we go to employment agencies, hoping to relieve ourselves of any further responsibility in finding a job.

By all means, gentle reader, use employment agencies. It is particularly useful to register with any and all of those that specialize in your field. However, bear in mind that they find jobs for, perhaps, 5 percent of their clients. As an adjunct to other job-search methods, that 5 percent is a welcome *little* edge. But if you look on an agency as your primary job-hunting method, that edge just becomes a long shot.

Mailings

Chapter 8, "Looking Good on Paper," already touched on the fallacy of mass-mailing and mass-produced résumés, but it is worth mentioning here again because a great many so-called employment experts recommend that you simply flood your field with résumés. At one time, this was truly a demanding task. You had to type all those cover letters! Depending on the number of prospects in your chosen field, the typing chore alone could give you carpal tunnel syndrome—and make you eligible not so much for a job, but for disability payments. Nowadays, however, the personal computer and printer have made the task much easier.

Jump Start
The software included with this book makes it so painless to do a mass-mailing, that you will be sorely tempted. Instead, use its employer database feature as a starting point for researching and selecting companies to approach.

Easier. But no more effective.

If generic, mass-produced, mass-mailed résumés actually worked, I'd say type away, and the drudgery be damned. But they don't work. It is far better to research prospective employers by using the methods and resources discussed in Chapters 9, 12, 13, and 14, then go through the process discussed in the rest of this chapter.

Proactive=Creative

The "tried-and-true" job-hunting methods are reactive. These methods allow you only to react to whatever circumstances may develop: an ad, a job posting, a possible response to a cold letter. Don't get me wrong, reacting is important. But to devote yourself entirely to reaction is, to paraphrase Tennessee Williams' Blanche Dubois, to rely on the kindness of strangers. It is more effective to develop, alongside your reactive strategies, a set of proactive ones as well. With these, you can identify opportunities *before* they are advertised or, better yet, *before* your target employers even realize they have opportunities to offer. You can tap into what some job-hunting advisers call the "hidden job market."

Buzz Word
Proactive is a term already used several times in the course of this book, and it's one of the most frequently heard business buzz words of the last two decades. It means, simply, to act in advance. To be proactive is to *anticipate* problems as well as opportunities rather than to react to them *after* they emerge.

The truth is, just about all real opportunities, in any field of endeavor, are "hidden." The growth stock—Xerox, when everybody was still using carbon paper, or Microsoft at the moment IBM brought out its first PC—is a growth stock as long as it is a hidden opportunity. After everyone and his brother jumps on the bandwagon, much of the opportunity is gone, and there is little chance of making a killing. The same is true of jobs. After a position is advertised, competition for it dramatically increases, and your chances of landing the position proportionally decrease. Proactive job hunting gives you a jump on the competition by finding—and even creating— opportunities that have yet to be publicly exposed.

Buzz Word
Reactive is effectively the opposite of *proactive*. It means to act in response to events or circumstances. Obviously, we are obliged to *react* all the time. (We wouldn't stay alive very long if we didn't.) However, in business, leaders strive to act as frequently as possible in advance of events and circumstances in order to gain a competitive edge.

Know Thyself (Or Just Read Chapter 2)

Here's something writers often do to keep their books moving: They put words in the reader's mouth. Open wide, please, and make way for some of my words:

But what you're talking about is "inside information." I don't have access to that! Other people do. But I don't.

This much is true. The bad news is that you are not Bill Gates's favorite nephew. The good news is that you *can* become an insider nevertheless. (And the additional good news is that, in contrast to the stock market, where acting on "inside information" is usually illegal, exploiting whatever you know to get a job is perfectly kosher.)

The first items of "inside information" to gather are found inside yourself. Be certain that you have surveyed, assessed, and come to understand your interests, your talents, your abilities, and your qualifications at *least* to the degree that is discussed in Chapter 2, "Where Do You Want to Be (and Should You Really Go There)?". Then make certain that you really *use* this information, that you fully appreciate and are prepared creatively to exploit all the interests, talents, abilities, and qualifications that you find. Be especially attentive to your *transferable skills*—those skills that are portable and can be used across a wide range of particular positions and professions.

Jump Start

Maybe waking up one day to discover that you really *are* the favorite nephew of Microsoft's founder and CEO isn't the great news you think it would be. True, the U.S. Department of Labor recently determined that almost one-third of the job force found their jobs through friends and relatives, but this means that more than 70 percent found theirs entirely through their own efforts.

Identify the Employers That Interest You

Look at this heading very carefully. It's not "Identify the Employers Who May Be Interested in You." Remember, getting a job is an equation. You may say that Employer X hired you. But, really, you also hired Employer X. An important piece of "inside information" is to know which employers are most likely to hire you. The really wonderful thing is that the most effective way of discovering this information is to identify those employers who interest you. If an employer interests you—*you*, defined as the sum of your abilities, qualifications, and transferable skills—it is a safe bet that you will interest the employer.

Seek the Bearers of Clout

People worry about running out of things: running out of money, running out of ideas, running out of orange marmalade at breakfast time, and so on. If you are ever worried about running out of mean thoughts or deadly sins, just pay attention to your feelings when your best friend tells you something like, "I just got an interview with Supreme Widgets International."

Your lips say, "Hey, wow! That's really great! Way to go!" But, inside, you're thinking, *Lucky stiff. How did he do it? I'm smarter. I'm better. I deserve the job. Maybe I could sneak into his house, rewire his alarm clock, push it back a few hours, make him miss the interview. Naw. This is just silly. It would be easier to put sugar in his gas tank and….*

Supreme Widgets International is a powerhouse and monolith of a company. Tremendous profits. Colossal opportunity. Huge office building with receptionists, security guards, an army of executive assistants (even the assistants have assistants), and flak catchers. How do you break into a club like that? How do you go about getting the coveted *Interview with Supreme Widgets International*?

You don't.

Nor do you get an interview with General Motors, or AT&T, or Kraft Foods, or Microsoft. What you get is an interview with a human being, a person, an individual associated with the organization. You'd better make sure, then, that it's the right person. And who, out of 5,000 or 10,000 or more people, is the *right* person? That's easy. The right person is the one who has the authority, the power, and the clout to hire you.

Now, we all know some time-tested ways of *avoiding* the person with the clout to hire you. You can go to a convention or job fair. That's one place where you may be able to avoid a person with the power or authority to hire you. You will almost certainly meet someone who has the authority to screen you out but *may* pass on your name to a person with the power to hire you.

I'm not saying that you should avoid job fairs and the like. Just don't rely on them, because, chances are, they will not produce a job.

Okay, what about sending a cover letter and résumé directly to the company that interests you? I've talked about this in Chapters 8, "Looking Good On Paper," and 9,

> **Buzz Word**
> Larger employers are inundated by job applications. Because of the sheer volume of applications received, most big firms begin not by trying to identify qualified applicants, but by screening out those who do not match a set of specifications or qualifications for whatever openings are available. Even in companies that are careful about listing the desired qualifications, screening is in large measure a judgment call. That's why it's always best to avoid going through the screening process.

"Judged by Its Cover: How to Write Great Cover Letters." This can be a fairly effective method or an almost totally ineffective one. The choice is yours. Research your target, identify the guardian of the clout, and then mail out a résumé and cover letter (or a letter *without* a résumé; see Chapter 14, "How to Heat Things Up with a Cold Letter or a Cold Call") carefully crafted to address the needs of that particular target employer. This will give your inquiry the best possible chance of actually producing an interview. If you prefer, however, you can just send out a shotgun-mailing of copies of a form letter and your "standard" résumé to "Dear Sir or Madam" at a gazillion firms and be pretty much assured of getting no interviews, let alone a job offer.

> **Buzz Word**
> A *contact* is anyone you know who might connect you (either directly or through other contacts) with the guardian of the clout in a specific company or industry.

So much for avoiding an encounter with the person who can actually give you a job. Let's talk about how to make contact with him or her. First, how do you go about identifying him or her? And, second, having identified the person, how do you get through?

Research your field and the particular companies that interest you. Often, this research will turn up the names of the individuals you need to reach. In addition, cultivate as many contacts as possible. "Contacts" can be just about everyone you know. Ask any and all of them to help you identify the guardian of the clout.

If nobody you know can tell you who has the power to hire you at Such and Sucha Corporation, try another question: "Do you know anybody who works at Such and Sucha—or who used to work there?" Get a phone number from your contact and ask permission to use his or her name: "May I tell So-and-so that you recommended I call?" Then make the call. Explain that you are interested in working for Such and Sucha Corporation, take the opportunity to ask questions about the company, and then ask the key question: "Who would I contact who has the authority to hire me for a *whatever* position?"

> **Buzz Word**
> The systematic acquisition of contacts is called *networking*. The subject is discussed in Chapter 12, "Making Networking Work for You."

And then there are those job fairs and conventions. Don't spend too much time with "recruiters." Instead, listen to the talk and to the speeches. Likely, you'll start to hear about key individuals. Also pay a visit to exhibitor's booths; highly placed individuals are sometimes present.

Back home, there's the public library, which offers a host of resources that list key individuals in various large organizations. Key publications include:

Daniel Starer, *Who Knows What: The Essential Business Resource Book.*

Contacts Influential: Commerce and Industry Directory (San Francisco: Contacts Influential, Market Research and Development Services, updated frequently).

Standard and Poor's Register of Corporations, Directors and Executives.

What Now?

When you've identified the person who can hire you, what do you do with him or her? The most effective strategy is to make a phone call, followed up with an in-person interview, if possible. If you do secure an interview, bring a copy of your résumé—customized for this particular target employer. The second most effective strategy is to send a customized letter and résumé without calling first. Within the cover letter (see Chapter 9), bid for an interview.

If you obtained the person's name from one of your contacts, speak to the contact first. Ask permission to use his or her name. You may even ask your contact to call ahead on your behalf. If you obtained the name through your own research, let that be your lead-off point: "Ms. Smith, my name is Grant Helm. I've been doing quite a bit of reading about your company, and, in just about everything I've read, your name appears prominently."

Where do you go next? If you're on the phone, don't ask for an interview. In fact, don't *ask* for anything. Instead, make an offer. It may be something like this: "I am a data analyst with Acme Widgets, where I've been involved in upgrading data-collection methods. I've been able to cut collection turnaround time by 30 percent here, and I would be grateful for the opportunity to discuss with you how what I've learned at Acme may benefit Such and Sucha." Pack into your opening statement the kind of appeal to the target employer's self-interest that I have discussed in Chapter 9 and will discuss further in Chapter 14. Appealing to your target's self-interest is a far more effective way to begin the conversation than telling him or her what *you* want.

At this point, the person on the other end of the line may ask if you are trying to sell something or if you are looking for a job. Respond like this: "No, I'm not selling anything, but I would like to suggest a discussion about what I could do for Acme." If the callee shows interest, set up the interview. Make it simple for the target to act by telling him or her when you are available. Of course, you may be available just about *any* time, but leaving things wide open like that not only invites your target to return a vague response that puts the interview on the back burner, it also suggests that you are either desperate or very little in demand. Better to offer a range of limited choices: "I will be available on Wednesday and Friday of next week. Can we set up a time on one of these days?" Or: "I will be in your city from December 10th through the 14th. Can we set something up for one of those days?"

Immediately after you hang up the telephone, write a note to the target employer, confirming the interview. Keep it friendly and informal; however, do type it rather than handwrite it:

Dear Ms. Howard:

I enjoyed speaking with you this morning, and I very much look forward to meeting with you on December 11 at 10 a.m. to discuss how my experience in data analysis can benefit Such and Sucha.

Sincerely,

Grant Helm

But what if your target turns you down? "Mr. Helm, we just aren't hiring now. I don't really have the time to see you at present."

Make no mistake, you *will* be turned down—maybe more often than you will connect. Yet all is not lost. You have at least made contact with the person who has the power to hire you. Reply politely: "I understand. Circumstances do change, of course, so may I send you my résumé?"

Unless the callee says no, do send the résumé along with a thank-you note as part of a cover letter. You may have been turned down for an interview, but by saying thank you, you refuse to confirm the target employer's impression that you have been rejected. The Thank You is evidence of contact, and it may, when circumstances do indeed change, serve as the basis of future contact.

A positive, polite, and practical thank-you note following a telephone conversation that resulted in a turndown.

Maria Schneider
6111 Elm Street
Pilot, SD 54322
555-555-5555
Fax: 555-444-4444

August 14, 1995

Mr. Barry Digby
Director of Financial Projection
H.W. Slide Company
5 Slide Pavilion
Watertown, S.D. 54321

Dear Mr. Slide:

I enjoyed our telephone conversation Thursday, for which I thank you very much. As you suggested, I have enclosed my resume.

If experience is any indication, as H.W. Slide continues to grow, you will need additional financial projection specialists who are familiar with the industry. I have developed projection strategies for my present firm, Mead & Co., that have resulted in dramatically increased accuracy of resource allocation. I invite you to see this detailed in my resume.

If you have any questions, please don't hesitate to call.

Sincerely,

Maria Schneider

Maria Schneider

Small Firms, Big Opportunities

Most job hunters start off going after the big game: corporations sized large to mega-large. But think about this for a moment. If the key objective of the job hunt is to identify and reach the individual with enough clout to hire you, don't you have a better shot if you approach a firm with, say, 50 employees as opposed to one with 5,000 or more?

The answer is a resounding *yup*.

The easiest way to get to a person with the power to hire you is to call a company with fewer than 50 employees and ask for the name of the boss. Then write a letter to that person. If you prefer, you may cut to the chase by making the call and asking to speak to the boss.

Do not fail to target small firms in your job search. You'll have an easier time reaching the person with real power, and you probably won't stumble over someone or some department whose job it is to screen you out. Just as important, by going after smaller employers, you are actually more likely to find a company with a job to offer. Since 1970, firms with 100 employees or-fewer have created two out of every three jobs.

I SEE... **Case Study**

Let's call her Ellen Dudley. Like many young people about to graduate from college with a degree in English, Ellen thought she was destined for a career in teaching—something she had decided that she really didn't want to do. Then one of her professors suggested that she look into a career in publishing.

Ellen spent months answering ads and writing letters to the nation's major publishers. The entry-level positions were not only few and far between, but not very appealing. For the most part, they were clerical jobs and variations on secretarial positions. At one interview, it was explained to her that the publishing industry was very hierarchical, that you started at the bottom and tried to work your way through from editorial assistant, to copy editor, to assistant editor, to associate editor, to editor, and maybe, something more.

Ellen was discouraged by the prospects of such slow and limited advancement. However, another interviewer suggested that she investigate some of the small—very small—companies that furnish subcontract and freelance labor to publishers, principally editorial, proofreading, indexing, and other services. Ellen learned that the bible of the publishing industry is a book called *The LMP* (which stands for *Literary Market Place*), an industrywide directory. She looked up all the freelance editorial services she could find in her region and secured interviews with some of them.

Today, Ellen is a full partner in one such company—which consists of only five people—and she feels that she is far happier and has more opportunity in this environment than she would if she were working for a corporate giant.

A Downside?

It used to be that the biggest risk in working for a small firm was that, compared to a big corporation, the small company offered less stability and perhaps less opportunity for individual advancement. In some industries, this may still be the case. However, following the epidemic of mergers and acquisitions that plagued the 1980s and (to a lesser degree) broke out anew in the 1990s, a large segment of the American workforce learned that there is precious little security in working for a big firm. Come the merger, positions dissolve and—suddenly—there are a good many more spaces available in the company parking lot.

This is not the world of your parents and grandparents, who could reasonably expect to join a big firm, work up through the ranks, and retire with a generous pension. Like it or not, you must expect to be more mobile. Indeed, these days, you may actually have *more* control over your professional fate in a smaller firm than in a large one.

Ultimately, the only significant downside to employment in small firms is the extra work it takes to identify the target companies. Your best sources are trade journals and professional directories. But don't overlook the Yellow Pages—both the local phone book and books for whatever cities you'd consider moving to.

The Least You Need to Know

➤ Use the passive traditional ("reactive") job hunting methods as adjuncts to the more creative and innovative ("proactive") strategies.

➤ Identify the employers that interest you so that you can identify the employers likely to be interested in you.

➤ Identify the person within the target organization who has the power to hire you; then approach that person.

➤ Always consider applying to small firms—companies with 50 employees or fewer.

➤ Identify, focus on, and appeal to the target employer's self-interest.

➤ Every employer contact is an opportunity; exploit positive responses as well as rejections.

Chapter 11

Trekking the Want Ad Jungle

In This Chapter

➤ Effectiveness of want ads

➤ "Fake ad" traps

➤ Agency ads vs. employer ads

➤ Interpreting the language of want ads and responding effectively

➤ Using want ads in trade journals and specialized magazines

Mom, apple pie, and the want ads. What could be more wholesome? What could be more American? Here, in the Land of Opportunity, the streets may not be paved with gold, but all you have to do is buy a newspaper, and you have access to a wealth of jobs! I mean, the ads are published every day. Employers pay for them. Job hunters read them. No wonder Communism's dead.

Dear Reader, please raise your hand if the following is true for you: I got my most recent job through a want ad.

Well, I can't see you, but I can *imagine* you all out there. And what my mind's eye perceives is anything but a sea of upraised arms and waving hands. Getting a job through the want ads is not exactly something to write Ripley about, but it's not as common an occurrence as you'd think.

The Awful Truth About Want Ads

A U.S. Department of Labor survey reported that five out of every one hundred job holders got their positions through newspaper want ads. Other surveys have placed this figure even lower, at two out of every hundred. Had these surveys been limited to holders of upper-level positions, the numbers would have faded into true insignificance. Most want ads are for entry-level or lower intermediate-level positions. Your copy of the *Pine Bluff Daily Disappointment* is unlikely to carry ads for "general manager" or "vice president." The exception to this may be certain public-sector positions. Federal, state, and local laws often require public agencies to advertise *all* available positions. These laws, however, do not require the agencies to *act* on applications generated by such ads.

Pitfall
A survey conducted by the Olympus Research Corporation back in 1973 in San Francisco and Salt Lake City revealed that 85 percent of San Francisco employers and 75 percent of those in Salt Lake City did *not* hire any employees through want ads that year. Limiting your job search to answering want ads may cut you off from more than three-fourths of employers.

Is this depressing or what?

Only if you *rely exclusively* on want ads. If, instead, you use them as merely one of many portals into the job market, the ads are not inherently evil and, in fact, are quite useful. After all, it is a good thing to add 2 to 5 percent to your chances of getting the job you want. And, in the case of want ads placed in special-interest, professional, and trade publications, your "hit rate" should be higher—and the jobs more attractive.

Fake!

But here's something else to worry about—just in case you were afraid you'd run short of anxiety. A certain number of ads, particularly those found in daily and Sunday newspapers, are fakes.

Now, who would place a fake ad—and why?

The biggest culprits are employment agencies. They run fake ads—often for real jobs, which, however, have already been filled—in order to get you to sign up with their agency: "Oh, Ms. Kline, I'm sorry. I see that that *particular* position has just been filled. However, we have a number of similar or even more attractive opportunities, which we haven't advertised yet. Please come in...."

Is this so bad? Perhaps not—as long as the agency is not thoroughly crooked and doesn't try to charge *you* a fee. After all, registering with any number of employment agencies gives you that much more access to the job market. Yet, do you want to have a business relationship with an outfit that uses a fundamentally dishonest practice? Probably not. But, then, it's almost impossible to tell if an agency is deliberately using such bait-and-switch ploys. After all, advertised jobs *do* get filled. You could, of course, conduct a study, answering this agency's ads over a certain period. But, hey, you have neither the time nor the inclination to do that. You are looking for a job. Here are the two best defenses against bait-and-switch:

➤ Don't restrict yourself to registering with a single agency.

➤ Don't rely on agencies as your only job-hunting strategy.

Some fake ads are more sinister than agency bait-and-switches. *Employers* have been known to run fake ads in order to test the "loyalty" of their employees. These ads always list a box number for replies, not an address or even a company name.

Most sinister of all are the out-and-out swindles. Never answer a "want ad" that lists a "900" number for you to call. You will be charged—who knows what—for the call, and no real employer would ever list a "900" number. Never answer an ad that requests your Social Security number or asks for the number of your driver's license. Scammers can do untold evil with such numbers.

How to Read a Want Ad

You've already been warned about ads that invite a reply to a box number *without* identifying the company by name. (There is nothing wrong with being asked to reply to a P.O. box, as long as the firm placing the ad has identified itself.) You should also read the ad carefully to note if you are being asked to respond directly to a firm or to an employment agency. It's okay to respond to either kind of ad, but just be aware that you have far less of a chance of

Buzz Word
Ever hear of a *reverse ad*? They're often called "situation wanted" ads. You advertise your qualifications in the hope that some employer, desperately scouring the classifieds, will jump at what you have to offer. Now that you're familiar with the term, don't bother to place a reverse ad. "Situation wanted" ads are worthless.

Buzz Word
A *blind ad* advertises a job without listing the name of the advertiser. Usually, applicants are invited to respond to a box number.

Pitfall
The majority of ads that list only a box number are not employer-set booby traps. However, you should avoid replying to anonymous ads. Avoiding them will not only keep you from being duped by a psychopathic boss's loyalty test, it will also keep you out of the clutches of an employer who, for whatever reason, cannot summon up sufficient forthrightness to tell prospective employees who he or she is.

being called for an interview, much less hired, if you have to go through an employment agency. Adjust your expectations accordingly.

Beyond these basics, there are a few additional things you should know about reading want ads. You see, they often use the English language in a way that's reminiscent of, say, the U.S. Department of Defense during the Vietnam War or Richard Nixon's staff caught red-handed during Watergate. Those of us who lived through these events remember how uniformed spokespeople referred to napalm bombing raids as the "vertical deployment of antipersonnel devices" or how the president's men, grilled on the witness stand, would try to erase a Watergate lie by declaring "that statement is no longer operative." So be on the lookout for some of this "want ad-ese":

➤ *Great opportunity:* TRANSLATION—The salary is unconscionably low, so you'll need to convince yourself that this job will open doors… sometime, somewhere, somehow.

➤ *Varied responsibilities:* TRANSLATION—You'll be the "utility person," go wherever you're kicked, and learn to like it.

➤ *A valuable management-training position:* TRANSLATION—You'll get the assignments even a high-school-age intern would balk at doing.

➤ *Self-starter wanted:* TRANSLATION—Much of your salary will come from commissions.

➤ *Detail-oriented:* TRANSLATION—The job is almost unendurably tedious, and your colleagues will think of you as a myopic grind without a future.

➤ *High-energy environment:* TRANSLATION—We'll run you ragged.

➤ *Good organizational skills:* TRANSLATION—You'll do the filing.

➤ *A growth position:* TRANSLATION—Hey, there's no way to go but up (or out).

➤ *A people-oriented job:* TRANSLATION—You handle the phones. You make cold calls. You deal with those the others shun.

➤ *An investment in your future:* TRANSLATION—This is a franchise or a pyramid scheme. You pay us, we don't pay you.

➤ *Planning and coordinating:* TRANSLATION—You make the boss's travel, lunch, and dinner arrangements.

➤ *Traffic the department's work:* TRANSLATION—You sort the mail.

Responding: How to Turn a Screen into a Net

With most newspaper ads, time is of the essence. Firms expect and usually get a quick response. The bulk of résumés will reach the employer's desk within 96 hours of the ad's hitting the streets. Day three tends to be the peak. By day four or day five, the employer will start going through his or her pile in earnest.

There is a basic misunderstanding, both on the part of the employer and the applicant, about the purpose of want ads. The employer believes he or she is casting a net, and the applicant believes he or she is grabbing hold of a lifeline leading to gainful employment. This is partially true. But that net is also a screen. Employers don't sift through the 20, 50, 100, or 1000 résumés they've been sent with an eye toward discovering the most wonderful candidate. Instead, their first objective is to screen out those they find unsuitable. Usually, this screening process discards 95 (or more) résumés out of every 100 received. This being the case, *your* object in responding to a want ad is not—as you probably believe—to get hired. It is, first and foremost, to avoid getting screened out and, second, to secure an interview.

ENGINEERING

STRUCTURAL DESIGNER

John Wellman Homes, a nationally recognized Home Builder, is looking for a talented Structural Designer, 2+ yrs exp w/ residential construction exp including the design & drafting of framing plans, value engineering & CAD. Related degree preferred. Growth opportunities w/exc compensation & bonus program. Send resume to: JWH, ATTN; Architect, P.O. Box 8054, Wilmington, DE 23456.

A typical daily newspaper want ad. A responding cover letter follows in the next illustration.

The cover letter, meant to accompany a résumé, precisely echoes the specs given in the want ad—no more and no less.

Sarah Howard
55 Peale Drive
Ardmore, PA 54321
555-555-5555
Fax: 555-444-4444

August 15, 1995

JWH
ATTN: Architect
P.O. Box 8054
Wilmington, DE 23456

To whom it may concern:

I am a talented structural designer, who has worked for Peterson Home Builders for three years, specializing in the design and drafting of framing plans, with an emphasis on all phases of value engineering. My expertise with CAD programs is such that I also served as the firm's CAD "guru" and troubleshooter.

I hold a B.S. (1989) in Structural Engineering from Piedmont University, from which I graduated with honors.

My resume is enclosed, and I look forward to hearing from you.

Sincerely,

Sarah Howard

Sarah Howard

To escape the screen, take the following steps:

➤ Keep your response brief. The cover letter should be short and to the point.

➤ When responding to specific ads, quote (or paraphrase) the specifications asked for in the ad, then confine your response to those specifications. This is a tough one.

Your natural tendency will be to give the employer something extra or to try to follow the advice given in Chapter 10, "Reactive vs. Proactive Search Strategies," about emphasizing the benefits you offer an employer. When you answer a want ad, resist the urge to supply anything beyond what the ad asks for. Seeing that "something extra," the target employer may quickly decide that you don't quite fit in, and you'll end up as rejection number 95.

➤ Don't put your qualifications into a narrative paragraph; instead, list them, highlighting each with a bullet. The letter must "sell" you *at a glance*. If you make the reader "work" to find out who you are, you're likely to get screened.

➤ Do not ignore specifications you don't meet. Figure out a way to address them. For example, if an ad asks for "experience with database programs," and you lack such experience, respond that you are "interested in database programs."

A special area of concern is responding to salary requests in ads. This causes a great deal of alarm— not only among job applicants, but among job-hunting advisers as well. What do you do when an ad requests—or even demands—your salary requirements?

The first thing you should do is remember that this is really a request (or demand) that you furnish the

> **Jump Start**
> If you are not asked to state your salary requirements, don't. There is no advantage to you in furnishing this information.

employer a *good reason* to screen you out. If a position has been budgeted at $25,000 a year, and you say you want $30,000, it is highly unlikely that the employer is going to say, "This person is so impressive, that we'd better meet for an interview. Maybe we can come up, or she can come down." Almost always, asking for a salary outside of the range budgeted will get you screened without an interview. And this is also true if you ask for too little. If your salary requirement seems inappropriately low, the employer will not think, "Golly! This guy's a bargain." Instead, you'll be viewed as inexperienced, and you will be screened out.

Difficult as it may be when you are striving to appear cooperative and responsive, it is probably safest to ignore the request or demand. Don't even mention salary in your response.

If failing to respond to the salary question will cause you to lose sleep, then try one of these compromises:

➤ Don't mention a figure, but simply allude to the subject of salary: "As I have moved upward from position to position, my salary has increased commensurately."

➤ If you feel you absolutely must give a figure, don't pin it down, but provide a range. If you want $30,000, but will settle for $25,000, set your range at $25,000-$35,000. For good measure, add the phrase "depending on the scope of my responsibilities."

Neither Rain, Nor Snow, Nor Gloom of Night

Your target employer may well be buried in responses to his or her ad. How can you set yours apart from the crowd?

➤ Try to time your mailing so that your letter will arrive on Tuesday, Wednesday, or Thursday rather than on Monday or Friday.

➤ Consider sending your reply via overnight mail, courier, or two-day Priority Mail.

Most upsides have a down. Some authorities caution that sending a want ad reply in an envelope marked "Personal and Confidential" will merely irritate the employer. This is a possibility. As for using expedited delivery service, there is absolutely nothing wrong with that—except the cost to you. Remember, responding to a want ad has about a 2 percent chance of success. Can you afford to invest in special delivery for every ad to which you respond?

Want Ads Not in Newspapers

The employment ads found in specialized publications devoted to your field of interest are generally more useful than newspaper ads. To begin with, they are likely to be more directly relevant to what you do. More important, the fact that the advertiser chooses to place the ad in an appropriate publication suggests a level of discrimination, professionalism, and good sense that's not always easy to find, but that is highly desirable in an employer.

Trade and Professional Journals and Bulletins

Employment ads in these publications are useful and likely to be more productive than newspaper ads; therefore, one of the first objectives of your pre-job-hunt research should be identifying any publications relevant to your area of interest. Monitor these regularly, and respond promptly to any ads that interest you. *The Encyclopedia of Associations* (Detroit: Gale Research, annual) is a convenient means of locating publications relevant to your field.

Special-Interest Magazines

If you peruse any good bookstore that also carries a wide variety of magazines, you will notice how many specialized periodicals are generally available. There are magazines for people interested in almost any field—electronics, computers, automobiles, fashion, aviation, communications, history, literature, psychology, advertising, marketing, and so on. While these are not strictly professional or vocational publications, they often contain classified employment ads. Generally speaking, the ads in these publications are a notch below those in trade and professional journals in terms of real usefulness to the job hunter, but they are still likely to be more productive than ads found in a newspaper. Make it your business to know the special-interest periodicals relevant to your areas of interest.

Pitfall
Beware. Special-interest publications tend to have more than their share of questionable franchise offers and other "opportunities" that require you to "invest."

Electronic Ads

These come in two varieties: those found in various "electronic job banks," which are accessible via the Internet and such commercial on-line services as CompuServe, America Online, Prodigy, and others, and those posted by individual businesses. It is the latter that have the greater potential. Some businesses take the Internet seriously enough to have developed "home pages" entirely devoted to employment. Chapter 13 "Cruising the Infobahn" covers the range of ads you're likely to find and how to respond to them.

A Fine Vintage

Despite all that I've said here about realistically adjusting your expectations when it comes to want ads, I'll admit that there is something hopeful and exciting about a fresh and freshly purchased newspaper, with its column upon column of classified want ads, each one suggesting opportunity. Yet how quickly that freshness fades! A week-old want ad section, let alone one that is several weeks old or more, is a forlorn object, a dead letter.

Or is it?

At least two prominent and frequently published job-hunting advisers counsel candidates to look through back issues of newspapers and professional and trade journals as old as 18 months. When you write or call, do *not* respond to the ad:"I'm just now getting around to responding to the ad you placed in my yellowing copy of *The Daily Disappointment* eight months ago." Instead, respond as if you heard "through the grapevine" that the company is looking for a person to fill such-and-such a position or, even better, that you have been "highly interested" in the So-and-So Company, and that you have the following skills, abilities, and qualifications to offer.

Why is this strategy worthwhile? A significant percentage of advertised jobs do not get filled right away. If an ad is not immediately successful, many employers simply give up on the ad. Or, oftentimes, the person hired as a result of the original ad fails, for one reason or another, to work out. Whatever the reason, combing older ads is one way to find companies that are interested in acquiring what you have to offer.

The Least You Need to Know

➤ Want ads are less effective than most people think, especially for obtaining the higher-level positions.

➤ Learn how to avoid "fake ads" and how to interpret the language of legitimate ones.

➤ Want ads function both as a *net* and a *screen*; learn how to avoid getting screened out.

➤ Avoid responding to requests (or demands) for your "salary requirements."

➤ Respond to the ad and nothing but the ad; avoid including "extras" in your response.

➤ Consider strategies—including timing and using expedited mail—that set your response apart from the crowd.

➤ Selectively follow up on outdated want ads.

Chapter 12

Making Networking Work for You

In This Chapter

➤ Identifying and making contacts

➤ Networking pitfalls

➤ Structuring the networking meeting

➤ Asking the right questions

➤ Finding or starting support groups

Networking was a buzz word of the early 1980s and has been heard ever since. There's a lot of mystique surrounding it, and, you do have to admit, it sounds like something pretty wonderful: quietly, secretly, efficiently building up a kind of underground communications and power structure through which information travels with the speed of light and influence is felt where it really counts—in getting you the plum job. It's like a secret society, isn't it? If you could only get in....

The fact is, you already *are* in. More or less, at least—because networking is nothing more or less than how the world *really* works. We all operate through networks, both professionally and personally. They are the sum total of all our contacts and relationships. When you ask your neighbor to recommend a good dry cleaner, you're networking.

How the World Really Works?

I'm tempted to say, "It's just that simple." But, alas, it's not. For networking to be more than a word that covers casual encounters and random relationships, you have to work at transforming your interpersonal contacts into a kind of systematic structure on which you can rely for:

➤ Information

➤ Exposure

➤ Referrals to expand the network

Information

The information you acquire should help you focus on your job search. It should alert you to trends, events, and other factors relevant to your job search. Finally, if your network is really operating up to speed, it should be the means of informing you about job openings.

Exposure

Anybody who has ever tried to sell anything—merchandise or a service—knows that the very best advertising cannot be bought at any price. It is word of mouth.

The problem is getting the right mouth to speak into the right ear. Networking multiplies mouths and ears, giving you as much meaningful exposure in the job market as possible.

Expanding the Network

The third and last function of the systematized network is expansion. A successful network grows so that it can be effective and continue to grow. It's like a living organism or, if you're feeling in a less expansive mood, it's like a chain letter. The more the network grows—yet remains a cohesive network—the more information and exposure it will generate.

Jump Start
You gotta give a little to get a little. Networking is a set of *mutual* relationships. If you just pump your contacts, they (quite rightly) will resent it. Be prepared to be helpful to them, too.

Reality Check

In the 1970s and 1980s, networking became a kind of mantra, with some experts claiming that 80 percent of jobs are secured through it. But, beginning in the 1990s, dissenting voices made themselves heard. In the November 22, 1994 edition of the *Wall Street Journal*, William J. Morin, chairman of the Drake Beam Morin outplacement firm, proclaimed that "Networking is dead!" He identified a "backlash" against networking, because "it's been so overworked." Other contributors to the article called networking a "bankrupt concept," and David B. Opton, associated with Exec-U-Net (a networking cooperative for senior executives), remarked that "You get a call at work that feels like networking, and you want to throw up."

Pitfall
I have to warn you: Networking doesn't always work. It's time for a reality check. Please read the following section carefully.

Skip to the next chapter, then?

I wouldn't. Networking should never have been regarded as a panacea, let alone a kind of religion. It has proven itself a useful tool—no more and no less—and for that reason it should not be rejected out of hand because some authorities have grown tired of it. The lesson to be learned here is to tread softly. You may discover many individuals who are highly receptive to your networking attempts. You may find others who are turned off by them. Don't push these people!

It is likely that you will find plenty of helpful folks to network with. However, you must face the possibility that, in your particular industry or geographical area, a networking phone call really does induce vomiting. If your attempts at making network contacts repeatedly fail, do not emulate that Little Engine Who Could (*I-think-I-can-I-think-I-can*). Instead, hang up the phone, sigh once, and—yes—turn to the next chapter.

Do You Need Friends in High Places?

Who do you want in your network? If you have the proverbial friends in high places, by all means start with them. But all you really need is anyone who can serve as an antenna, a set of eyes and ears to alert you to what's going on in your industry. Does this mean that you should restrict your network to professional colleagues? No, but you might well begin with them as your core group.

Stop now and make a quick list of all your professional colleagues—everyone you know in your industry or field, including your clients and customers.

Make up a form like this one and keep it at your desk for jotting down networking contacts. It's better than trying to keep track of a lot of little scraps of paper.

Networking Rolodex

People I Intend to Contact

Name	Phone Number/Address
1. _____	_____
2. _____	_____
3. _____	_____
4. _____	_____
5. _____	_____
6. _____	_____
7. _____	_____
8. _____	_____
9. _____	_____
10. _____	_____
11. _____	_____
12. _____	_____
13. _____	_____
14. _____	_____
15. _____	_____
16. _____	_____
17. _____	_____
18. _____	_____
19. _____	_____
20. _____	_____

Now let's move on to what may be considered a secondary core: The people you know in your particular organization. Of course, this will likely include many of your professional contacts, but it will also include coworkers outside your field.

Finally, don't forget your personal friends and acquaintances.

Yes, the fact is that just about everybody you know can be a part of your network. However, it is best to concentrate on professional and organizational contacts for the purpose of transforming your informal circle of acquaintances into a more systematic and cohesive group.

Help!

Fine. So what do you do, go up to the folks on your list and say, "Do you want to be part of my network?" No. What you do is ask for help.

Now, there are ways to ask for help that will invite resentment, anger, and resistance, and there are ways to ask for help that really don't so much *ask* for a favor as they *offer* a wonderful opportunity: the chance to derive a great feeling of satisfaction from having aided a fellow being. That feeling is at the heart of the networking idea.

Uh, lemme be a little philosophical for a minute here, okay?

Those of us who have been raised in the Judeo-Christian tradition think that helping another person makes us feel good because "it is more blessed to give than to receive"—or words to that effect. We have been taught that self-sacrifice is virtuous and good for the soul.

Maybe so, maybe so.

But let's look at another tradition of belief. The Buddhists think that doing good deeds, including apparent self-sacrifice, creates good "karma" for both the doer and the beneficiary of the deed. To put it more simply, what goes around comes around. Actually, you don't have to look far in our more familiar Western religious traditions to find something similar. The Gospel asks us to cast our bread upon the waters.

You don't need a Sunday school lesson. You need a job. All I'm trying to say is that, if you do a little digging, you'll find that the world's most "popular" religions teach that doing good creates good. And that is the great and powerful engine that will drive your request for help. For at some level of awareness, the person who agrees to help you, feels that by doing so, he or she is creating a "good" that will come back to help him or her. And this, too, is the glue that holds together any network. "Self-interest" sounds ugly, I know, but I don't mean it cynically. It is self-interest that will get folks to help you.

Make no mistake, though, there are at least four ways to screw up this wonderful phenomenon of human nature.

1. **Ask for help—but not too much.** "I want to invade your office, push aside any deadlines you may have, and force you to think about *my* life. I'm going to bore you with a lengthy recitation of my career history, and I'll expect you to generate an analysis of it, complete with recommendations for the next decade."

2. **Ask for help—but not for participation in your impossible dream.** "I don't know what to do with my life. Please tell me."

3. **Ask for help—don't insist on it.** "I'm coming in at 5:00 on Friday. Don't make any plans."

4. **Ask for help—but don't lie about what you want.** "Look, this will only take about five minutes."

First, What Do You Want?

To avoid screwing up a good thing, begin by deciding what you want from the person you are about to approach. Are you looking primarily for referrals, names of those "people in high places"—that is, the folks with the power to hire you? Or are you looking for a more general discussion about the industry or profession? Or is the person you are about to approach the guardian of the clout?

Let's begin by assuming that your network, at this point, does not include the guardian of the clout, and that you want your professional colleague, Hank Wellborn, to point you in his or her direction.

Keep it low-key. Pick up the phone and start talking:

"Hank? Hi. I'm calling to ask you for a little help. Everywhere I turn here at Acme Widgets, I've been hearing about cutbacks. I don't think I'm in any immediate danger here, but, I can tell you, opportunities are getting pretty few and far between, and I thought it was about time to start testing the waters—while I still have options. Trouble is, I haven't hunted up a job in a good ten years, and I really don't want to take the plunge into the job market—well, uh—naked."

Personal Networking Log

Person Contacted	Date	Referred By	Follow-up Date	Response
_____	_____	_____	_____	_____
_____	_____	_____	_____	_____
_____	_____	_____	_____	_____
_____	_____	_____	_____	_____
_____	_____	_____	_____	_____
_____	_____	_____	_____	_____
_____	_____	_____	_____	_____
_____	_____	_____	_____	_____
_____	_____	_____	_____	_____
_____	_____	_____	_____	_____
_____	_____	_____	_____	_____
_____	_____	_____	_____	_____
_____	_____	_____	_____	_____
_____	_____	_____	_____	_____
_____	_____	_____	_____	_____
_____	_____	_____	_____	_____
_____	_____	_____	_____	_____
_____	_____	_____	_____	_____
_____	_____	_____	_____	_____
_____	_____	_____	_____	_____
_____	_____	_____	_____	_____

When building a network, you may call upon many people. Keep a record of your calls to help you identify your most productive contacts and prevent the embarrassment of calling the same person twice with the same request.

"I was wondering if I could sit down with you for 45 minutes or so to have what, for lack of a better word, I'd call a networking meeting. Don't get me wrong. I'm not going to hit you up for a job. I just want to talk to you about who's who at your shop and anywhere else you might know about—who I should see—and I want to talk to you about the outlook for the industry in general."

"I can drop by your office at your convenience—but I would like to make it to *your* office, since I'm not eager for anyone here to know that I'm 'looking around.'"

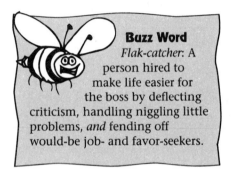

Buzz Word
Flak-catcher: A person hired to make life easier for the boss by deflecting criticism, handling niggling little problems, *and* fending off would-be job- and favor-seekers.

Hank may or may not get you closer to the person with the power to hire you, but, chances are, whatever information you do get from the conversation will be of value. Let's assume that, through Hank or another one of your contacts—or through someone Hank tells you about—you do succeed in identifying the wielder of clout. You should secure your contact's permission to use his or her name in order to get an *informational* interview. Then, armed with this, prepare to penetrate the flak-catcher.

Most highly placed people employ an assistant for the express purpose of deflecting the kind of call you are about to make. Use your referral to get by this obstacle. If the contact's name fails to perform the Open Sesame, arrange a specific time for *you* to call back. Make certain that the flak-catcher concurs on the time and agrees that you should call back. Before hanging up, ask for the assistant's name. When you call back—at the agreed-upon time—use his or her name, and transform *your* attempt to make contact with the boss into a *team* effort:

"Good afternoon, Ms. Johnson. It's Art Taylor again. How are we doing on getting through to Mr. Grosse?"

When you do get through, state the purpose of your call, beginning with the fact that Hank Wellborn suggested it:

"Mr. Grosse, Hank Wellborn suggested I call you about getting a little informal advice. Hank is very familiar with your expertise in marketing widgets, particularly in the direct mail area. He tells me that you know all the major players."

"I've been with Acme Widgets for five years. I'm the associate sales manager, but I've been looking to move into marketing. There's some sense of urgency to my move. As you are probably quite well aware—since you're quite well aware of most everything in this industry—Acme is beginning a downsizing program. I don't see myself being in immediate danger personally, but I know my department is going to shrink—along with opportunities generally."

"I am hoping that we could sit down for a few minutes—at your convenience—to discuss direct mail approaches to widget marketing. I'd love to get your take on where the industry is going and who the folks are that I should contact. I'd also be grateful for any feedback you may have to offer on my own background and experience."

Conclude by pushing—gently—for a specific meeting time. Reiterate that the meeting, which will last for a half to three-quarters of an hour, can be entirely at Mr. Grosse's convenience, but then suggest a time, if Mr. Grosse fails to. A meeting during the course of the regular work day is best, but breakfast may be convenient. Lunch is also a possibility.

Talking

The actual face-to-face is informal—and should be—but that does not mean it is unstructured. Begin by thanking Mr. Grosse, reiterating who recommended you, and reminding him of the reason for your visit. This reminder should consist of a quick review of your current situation and the verbal equivalent of a bulleted list of what you want Mr. Grosse to help you with: "I'd like to pick your brain about industry trends, growth areas, and specific people I should talk to."

Now that Mr. Grosse understands what you want, proceed to a thumbnail sketch of your background. This should consume two or three minutes, and it should be prepared beforehand. It should consist of

Jump Start
You may face renewed resistance if Mr. Grosse thinks you are just trying to get a foot in *his* door. Fend this off with extra assurance: "I am not here to hit you up for a job. At this point in my job search, I'm just surveying the marketplace. Of course, if you know of any specific opportunities, I'd appreciate hearing about them."

the kind of material about yourself that you include in a cover letter (see Chapter 9, "Judged by Its Cover: How to Write Great Cover Letters"). Practicing at these informational networking interviews will have the additional benefit of letting you hone your "verbal résumé" for full-blown job interview situations (see Chapters 20–22).

Having presented your verbal résumé, proceed to the questions you have.

The questions you have?

Just what you ask depends on whether you are pursuing a more-or-less linear career path—climbing the ladder within your industry—or changing careers. For those pursuing a linear path, the questions fall roughly into three areas:

➤ About yourself

➤ About the marketplace

➤ About specific job leads

For career changers, the areas are sharply different:

➤ About the person with whom you are talking

➤ About the industry/career

➤ About how you can fit into the picture

Questions for Climbers

Let's begin with some questions about yourself. Think of yourself as a "product" you are offering to the job market. Ask Mr. Grosse the following questions:

➤ Is my background clear to you?

➤ Are my objectives clear?

➤ Are my objectives feasible?

➤ What skills and credentials don't I have now that I will need to acquire?

➤ Do you see any problem areas for me, given my background?

➤ Do you see anything in my background that is particularly strong or appealing to employers?

Next, ask about the marketplace:

➤ What trends—especially employment trends—do you see in the industry?

➤ Who are the industry leaders?

➤ What sort and size of company would find my qualifications most attractive?

➤ What level of compensation can I expect?

➤ What is my realistic outlook for advancement in the industry?

➤ What is the outlook for my particular field?

➤ Where should I look for further information? Any periodicals or directories I should consult? Anybody I should talk to? (May I tell him or her that you suggested a meeting?)

Conclude with questions about specific job leads:

➤ Do you know of any openings available right now?

➤ Are you personally familiar with any employers who may want to see me?

➤ Have you learned of any developments that may suggest a particular company would be interested in a person like me?

➤ Where's the best "listening post" to hear about job openings?

If Mr. Grosse suggests a particular company or two, you may follow up with some questions concerning the nature of the company: its market share, its reputation, the kind of corporate culture for which it's known.

Questions for Changers

If you are networking to learn about the potential of a new career, begin, reasonably enough, by asking Mr. Grosse how he got into the field and why:

➤ How did you get into this field?

➤ What motivated your decision?

➤ What kind of training, qualifications, background, and other credentials were required and/or helpful?

➤ What do you do in a typical day?

➤ What *don't* you like about what you do?

➤ What's the usual pattern of career progression in this field?

Next, some questions about the industry or career itself:

➤ Where is the industry centered geographically?

➤ Are there *essential* prerequisites for getting into the field?

➤ What are the *desired* skills, abilities, and qualifications for this field?

➤ What's the job market like? What's the demand for people in this field?

➤ What kind of compensation can I expect?

➤ How receptive is this field to career changers like me?

➤ What trends do you see in the industry—positive and negative?

➤ What kinds of problems confront the industry?

➤ Where should I go to learn more? What books and periodicals should I consult? What other people should I talk with? (And can I tell them you suggested a meeting?)

Finally, address the issue of just how you might fit into the picture:

➤ From what I've told you about myself, what are my chances of getting into this field?

➤ What hurdles will I face?

➤ What additional training or credentials do I *need*?

➤ What additional training or credentials would be *helpful*?

➤ How would you suggest I go about getting work in this field?

➤ Are there specific employers I should target now?

Wrapping It Up

End the session by making certain that you have gotten down on paper any names that may have been dropped. "You mentioned someone over at Ajax Widgets, in marketing. What was her name?"

Then make sure that you have permission to contact each of the people mentioned, using Mr. Grosse's name as an Open Sesame.

When it comes time to leave, thank Mr. Grosse, underscoring how very helpful he has been. Ask permission to call back with a specific question or two, in case something has slipped your mind. Then, *ask* if you should leave a résumé behind: "Could you use one of my résumés?" Remember, you do *not* want to leave the interview with Mr. Grosse thinking that all of this was nothing more than an attempt to get a foot into *his* door. But, after all, he is a potential employer, and it is also possible that he may want to pass your résumé on to someone else.

A Little Help from Your Friends

The most directly effective form of networking begins with peers and coworkers and moves up to those folks with the power to hire you. Another aspect of networking, however, centers directly on your peers.

Hunting Up Job-Hunting Groups

Investigate the job-hunting support groups that may exist in your community or in your field. You may find information about these at your local church or synagogue, Chamber of Commerce, or adult education center. Often, community colleges (or community-oriented colleges) offer adult-education classes in job hunting, which serve as de facto support groups. The *National Business Employment Weekly*, generally available at larger newsstands, offers a "Calendar of Career Events," which includes a listing of various support groups. (You can reach the *National Business Employment Weekly* at 1-800-JOB-HUNT.)

Starting a Job-Hunting Group

You may consider starting a job-hunting group yourself. You can run an ad in the local newspaper, announcing that you are currently job hunting and that you would like to meet with other job-hunters for "mutual support and networking." Another alternative is the Internet. Check out Chapter 13, "Cruising the Infobahn," and log on. Use any of the Internet-searching software available to look for employment-related Internet sites. Try "jobs" as a keyword. Then follow up on the sites that turn up. Alternatively, try one of the commercial on-line services. Here you may find a Special Interest Group ("SIG") or news group with vocational interests in your field, or some SIGs that are appropriate places for you to post a message calling for a gathering of job hunters, such as yourself, searching for networking and support.

The Least You Need to Know

➤ Use your network to gather information, gain exposure, and continually expand your contact base.

➤ Making contacts: Know when to be persistent—and, just as important, when to back off.

➤ Develop realistic expectations and clear goals for your networking campaign.

➤ Use your contacts to reach the person with the power to hire you.

➤ Structure the networking meeting with prepared questions, but keep it loose and never press for answers.

➤ The networking strategies you choose depend on whether you are climbing the ladder within your field or changing careers.

LET'S GO CRUISING!!

Chapter 13

Cruising the Infobahn

In This Chapter

➤ Range of on-line resources available

➤ Internet vs. commercial services vs. private BBSs

➤ Research vs. job hunting online

➤ On-line databases not available through the Internet

➤ Posting your résumé online

I could begin by pontificating about what a revolution in information gathering and information processing personal computers have wrought upon the world. Doing so would make this the 4,005,876th book to proclaim the computer/information highway revolution. Thank *you*, Paul Revere!

I could also begin by rounding up the usual statistics: 25 million U.S. households have personal computers, of which at least 4 million are connected via modems to a host of on-line services, including CompuServe, America Online, Prodigy, GEnie Information Exchange, Delphi, eWorld, The WELL, and the Microsoft Network (MSN), as well as any of some 45,000 local bulletin board systems (BBS) and the Mother of All Networks, the Internet. Now, those are just computers in households. Add businesses and other organizations into the picture, and it is estimated that *at least* 25 million computers have access to the Internet alone, which has been described as a "virtual community" electronically superimposed over the geopolitical world. Whatever metaphysical qualities you want to ascribe to it, the Internet links up about 32,400 computer networks in 135 countries.

Buzz Word
Modem stands for MOdulator/ DEModulator. Why? Because, on the transmitting end, a modem modulates (converts) digital electrical impulses generated by a computer into sounds that can be transmitted as analog signals over a phone line and, on the receiving end, demodulates those analog signals into digital electrical impulses the computer can use.

I could begin this way. Indeed, I *have* begun this way. Trouble is, the statistics will be outdated by the time you read them. More importantly, they are misleading for the job hunter. Look, anything as vast as the information superhighway has *got* to be important. But do you *need* it in order to get the job you want? Almost certainly not. Can you get the job you want without ever "going online"? Almost certainly yes.

So why read this chapter? Because getting "connected" is one more way of—well—getting connected. The more you know about your industry, your current field of interest, and other potential fields of interest, the better chance you'll have of getting the job you want. Just don't expect miracles, and, more importantly, don't be seduced into tapping endlessly on a keyboard while munching a granola bar and guzzling Jolt Cola, thinking that what you're doing is looking for a job.

Easier Than a Trip to the Library

With your expectations properly tuned to reality, become aware that your personal computer and modem *can* make the job search easier, faster, and more comprehensive. It can do this in at least five ways:

➤ By providing access to places to post your résumé

➤ By providing access to places for employers to list vacancies (which you can find)

➤ By providing access to opportunities for job-hunting help and career counseling

➤ By providing access to contacts

➤ By providing access to information about companies and industries

The keyword here is *access*. The computer will not process the information or decide which information is useful to you and which is not. It will, however, provide a means of getting at the information.

Getting Started

If you already have a computer and a modem and know how to use them, move on to "Where to Look." If you need more help getting started, check out Alfred and Emily Glossbrenner's *Finding a Job on the Internet*, which is specifically directed at the job hunter, but which contains enough of the general basics to get you started. If you want more, consult *The Complete Idiot's Guide to Modems & Online Services* and *The Complete Idiot's Guide to the Internet.*

And Where to Go

Once armed with a PC (or Mac or Mac clone) and modem, your next task is to decide where to let them take you. *The Complete Idiot's Guide to the Internet* is useful for identifying Internet sites, and the Glossbrenner volume contains a wealth of suggestions for logging on to specifically job-related sites. You can supplement any or all of these books with one of the several Internet "Yellow Pages" now available.

In addition to the major commercial on-line providers and the Internet, you might want to survey the thousands of electronic bulletin board systems (BBSs) around the nation and the world. BBSs are born and die daily. For up-to-date listings, consult *BoardWatch Magazine* (call 800-933-6038 for information). *Computer Shopper,* another magazine, publishes a list of BBS numbers monthly—or, rather, publishes half the list one month and the other half the next, so that, in effect, it publishes updated lists six times a year.

Jump Start
How useful is a BBS? The answer is: probably not as useful as a large commercial service or the Internet. Few corporate recruiters post jobs on BBSs. Use local BBSs for getting information about local places.

Use any or all of these sources to identify commercial, Internet, and BBS sites that appear to be relevant to employment in general and to your field or industry in particular. However, when you're using a commercial service or the Internet, there is no substitute for actually getting online and doing a live search yourself.

Commercial services such as CompuServe and America Online are quite well organized and, with a little practice, easy to search using keywords (such as "jobs" and "employment" or words related to your industry or field, for example "aerospace"). Such searches will yield job- and career-related sites for you to explore. The Internet, which can potentially put you in touch with a much greater segment of the job-related world than any commercial service, is more challenging.

Begin by understanding two essential facts about the Internet:

➤ The Internet is *not* a company, an institution, an organization, or a system. Hopeful types like to call it a community. Maybe. All that's definite, though, is that the Internet is a huge number of computers and computer networks linked and interlinked without supervision.

➤ The Internet is pulled in opposite directions by two powerful forces: an imperative to gather, organize, and make accessible everything known to humankind versus an equally strong urge to achieve and maintain absolute anarchy.

Understand and accept these two facts, then pick and choose among the following Internet features or tools: World-Wide Web (WWW), Archie, e-mail, news groups, mailing lists, FTP, Telnet, Gopher, Veronica (and Jughead), and Wide Area Information Server (WAIS). The job hunter need only be concerned with the following:

➤ World-Wide Web (WWW): This is the feature that is bringing the Internet into the mainstream. In contrast to other aspects of the Internet, which often accept cryptic commands and issue commensurately cryptic output, the World-Wide Web transforms your computer screen into a highly graphic electronic magazine page. WWW software (such as SPRY's MOSAIC program) offers a variety of tools—called "Web browsers"—for searching specific WWW sites. Type in a keyword or phrase ("widget marketing"), and the software will list relevant sites. Even more exciting is the concept of hypertext. Each WWW site has a "home page," a kind of interactive table of contents for that site. Certain words and phrases are highlighted. Click on one of these with your mouse, and you will be transported to a related site.

➤ E-mail: This is the service you use to communicate electronically with target employers. You will need two things: the electronic address of your correspondent and your own e-mail address. If you use one of the commercial services (CompuServe, America Online, and so on), an e-mail address will be assigned to you. If you subscribe directly to the Internet via a SLIP/PPP account, you will be able to establish a so-called "domain name" address. Consult any of the Internet books mentioned in this chapter for the details.

➤ News groups: Some folks consider this the heart of the Internet. It is a vast array of sites devoted to "articles" on specific subjects. Despite the name "news groups," the articles "posted" are not so much news as they are notes and comments from people interested in the particular news group topic. Topics range from *Star Trek* to coin collecting to permutations of so-called cybersex to employment-related issues. News groups are places to exchange information, and, for the job hunter, can serve as a virtual grapevine. The list of available news groups changes frequently. For updates, FTP to **ftp.uu.net** and follow the path: **/usenet/news.answers/alt-hierarchies/** and also **/usenet/news.answers/active-newsgroups/**. What's "FTP"? Read on.

➤ FTP: It stands for "file-transfer protocol," and is a means of downloading (transferring) files from the Internet into your computer. You will find many sites on the Internet that allow you to access files via "anonymous FTP"; that is, you will be able to download material without using a password, but just by invoking the user ID "anonymous." Various guides, including (for example) Harley Hahn and Rick Stout's The Internet Yellow Pages, provide the addresses of many important FTP-accessible sites. Some commercial services (for example, CompuServe) provide an FTP gateway to the Internet, which makes it easy to jump to any FTP-accessible site.

➤ Mailing lists: The Internet is clogged with cryptic terms, but *mailing list* is just what the name implies. Add your name to one of these lists, and messages relevant to the list will appear in your electronic mailbox—automatically. Mailing lists are a great way to "get into the loop." Of course, the key is to identify lists relevant to the industries and topics of interest to you. The two most important lists of mailing lists are the SRI List (to obtain, send an e-mail request to **mail-server@sri.com**) and Publicly Accessible Mailing Lists (PAML), which is posted at **news.lists** and at **news.answers**.

➤ Telnet: Some Internet sites are accessible directly through the Telnet program. Addresses accessible in this way are usually identified by an instruction telling you to "telnet to" such-and-such a site.

➤ Gophers: A "gopher" is an animal that burrows. A "gopher"—go-fer—is also slang for a person who "goes for" things (like getting the boss a cup of coffee and a danish). The Internet equivalent is a little of both. Many Internet sites confront the cybertraveler with a bewildering array of files labeled in a way that no mere mortal could ever hope to understand. But, access a Gopher site, and all you have to do is tell the Gopher what you want ("marketing jobs in Chicago"). The Gopher will then locate as well as retrieve ("go fer") any relevant items it finds.

Jump Start
But how do I get connected in the first place? Most commercial on-line services now provide an easy gateway into the Internet. Another simple leg up into the Internet is to obtain software through your local computer store that lets you sign on to the Internet and establish an account.

Using any of these sites and services takes practice, and it will also take time to search out the sites that are truly useful to you. By far the easiest Internet service to use is the colorful World-Wide Web. Why go anywhere else, then? First, WWW sites represent only a fraction of what is available on the Internet. Second, the intensive use of graphics makes heavy demands on your modem and computer. Even with a fast modem, a fast microprocessor, and a fast video board, waiting for Web images to unfold on your monitor screen can try your patience. If your computer and modem are a bit long in the tooth and not so swift, you will find the Web unusable.

Researching Careers, Industries, and Companies Online

Using the tools you have just reviewed, you can research almost any subject, including careers, industries, and specific companies, on the Internet. Just pick a tool, type in keywords or choose commands from a menu, and start exploring. If you want to narrow your focus to a handful of highly useful research tools, try some of the following resources.

If you have a fast computer and a fast modem, make it easy on yourself and begin with the World-Wide Web. Use Web browser software and a particular search engine to identify and retrieve relevant sites. Try using the names of specific companies as keywords. More and more Internet service provider companies are creating "home pages" with links to relevant information and search engines.

Buzz Word
A *home page* is an Internet site created by an individual or organization; it contains "hypertext links" to data relevant to the individual or organization. It is roughly equivalent to an electronic table of contents.

Use a Gopher server, such as the RiceInfo Gopher, which presents Internet resources by subject area. You can get to the RiceInfo Gopher through the Web (**http://riceinfo.rice-edu**) or by gophering to **riceinfo.rice.edu**. You can type in a specific industry or field of interest, and you will find a wealth of specific information, including material directly related to employment.

Another subject-oriented resource is the Clearinghouse for Subject-Oriented Internet Resource Guides (from the University of Michigan's University Library and School of Information and Library Sciences). You can reach this through anonymous ftp (**una.hh.lib.umich.edu**) or Gopher (**gopher.lib.umich.edu**) or Telnet (**una.hh.lib.umich.edu.70**) or the Web (**http://www.lib.umich.edu/chhome.html** or **http://http2.sils.umich.edu/~lou/chhome.html**).

The Gopher Jewels—yes, that's what it's called—takes the menus from the Internet's major Gopher sites and classifies them by subject. The result is the closest thing you're likely to find to a subject index of the Internet. Get to the Gopher Jewels via the Web (**http://galaxy.einet.net/gopher/gopher.html** or **http://galaxy.einet.net/GJ/index.html**) or Gopher to **cwis.usc.edu**.

Employment Opportunities and Resume Postings

- Academic Positions
  - ACADEME THIS WEEK (Chronicle of Higher Education) (Job Listings)
  - Academic Physician and Scientist (Job Listings)
  - Academic Position Network
  - Columbia University Experimental Gopher (Job Listings)
  - HoodInfo CWIS (Hood College, Frederick, MD) (Job Listings)
  - Mississippi State University (Job Listings)
  - MIT Personnel Office (Job Listings)
  - North Dakota State University (Job Listings)
  - Northwestern State University (Job Listings)
  - Ohio State University (Job Listings)
  - Purdue University (Job Listings)
  - Saint Louis University (Job Listings)
  - Southern Illinois University (Job Listings)
  - Syracuse University CWIS (Job Listings)
  - Texas A&M, Central Gopher (Job Listings)
  - Univ of California, Riverside (Job Listings)
  - Univ of Pennsylvania, Gopher-Penninfo (Job Listings)
  - Univ of Southern California (Job Listings)
  - Univ. of California - Santa Cruz, InfoSlug System (Job Listings)
  - University of Arizona (Job Listings)
  - University of Chicago (Job Listings)
  - University of Hawaii (Job Listings)
  - University of Maryland (Job Listings)
  - University of Minnesota (Job Listings)
  - University of Missouri-Kansas City (Job Listings)
  - University of North Dakota (Job Listings)
  - University of Southern Maine (Job Listings)
  - University of Utah (Job Listings)
  - University of Wisconsin, Madison (Job Listings)
  - USCgopher (University of Southern California) (Job Listings)
  - Yale (Job Listings)
- American Physiological Society (Job Listings)
- ArtJob: Jobs & Opportunities in the Arts - The Meta Network
- Attorney Job listings, U.S. Department of Justice
- BIONET Employment
- Career Advice - The Princeton Review Gopher
- Dartmouth College (Job Openings in the Federal Government)
- Defense Nuclear Facilities Safety Board (Job Listings)

The opening of the "Employment Opportunities and Resume Postings" page from "The Gopher Jewels" World-Wide Web Internet site.

No reasonable discussion of information access would fail to mention the United States Library of Congress, one of the greatest information resources in the world. The Library maintains a service called LC MARVEL, which is another subject-oriented view of the Internet. You can reach MARVEL via Gopher (**marvel.loc.gov**) or Telnet (**locis.loc.gov**) or the World-Wide Web (**http://lcweb.loc.gov/homepage/lchp.html**).

Alternatives to the Internet

Vast as it is, the Internet does not encompass all of the employment-related information you may find useful. At latest count, there are more than 5,000 electronic databases available on more than 800 systems *outside* of the Internet. How do you know where to turn among these? If you are very serious about gaining access to the freshest, most thorough information relating to your particular career area or industry, you will have to pay. The major business-related databases are found on such services as Dialog, Nexis, Dow Jones News/Retrieval, and Newsnet, all of which charge substantial subscription premiums. The mainstream commercial providers—America Online, CompuServe, and so on—also provide some company profiles. America Online features "Employer Contacts Databases," a collection of brief profiles of some 60,000 companies, and an Occupational Profiles Database, which contains job and career descriptions.

And you may want to pay even more. Instead of floundering in a sea of data, consider hiring an information broker. These are professionals who will find and deliver whatever information you specify. The best of them will conduct a "reference interview" with you in order to help you determine just what data you should be going after. For a directory of reputable information brokers (these are folks who hold Master of Library Science—MLS—degrees and the like) check out *The Burwell Directory of Information Brokers* (Houston: Burwell Enterprises, updated frequently), which may be available in your local library or by calling 713-537-8344.

Winner

Want to see the future? Check out *The Occupational Outlook Handbook*, which you can purchase in print form (see Chapter 26) or access on the Internet by gophering to **umslvma.umsl.edu**. It is your window onto present conditions and trends discernible through the latest statistics compiled by the U.S. Department of Labor's Bureau of Labor Statistics.

Searching for Vacancies (with Career Counseling to Boot)

Here we are, at the three-quarters milepost in this chapter, and we're just getting to the meat, right? I mean, this is where I tell you how to use the on-line electronic want ads. Well, the ads *are* here. But searching them is not the most effective way to cruise the infobahn for jobs. Electronic want ads are no more effective than want ads posted anywhere else (for a discussion of want-ad effectiveness, see Chapter 11, "Trekking the Want Ad Jungle"). The best use you can make of the Internet, the major commercial services, and the myriad specialized business databases available on-line is to research your career, your field, your industry, and particular companies you have targeted. The second best use is to drop in on news groups (on the Internet) and forums or SIGs (special interest groups—on commercial services) related to your field; there, you can pick up on trends and trench-level industry news.

The Commercial Services

Enough said. Now let's review the want ads. Here, some of the commercial providers are particularly strong. America Online provides a "Career Center," which includes want ads as well as a career counseling service (offered by James C. Gonyea of Gonyea and Associates). In addition, you will find the Federal Employment Service (providing help locating federal government jobs), a Career Resources Library, an Employment Agency Database, an Employer Contacts Database, and a Job Listings Database. The latter consists of Help Wanted-USA, the E-Span Employment Database, a Classifieds Bulletin Board, and the *Chicago Tribune Help Wanted.*

CompuServe, though bigger and deeper than America Online, does not offer as much in the way of employment features. The most important sources here are the classifieds and the E-Span Online Job Listing, but typing appropriate keywords should yield more. Prodigy's offerings are slimmer than CompuServe's. Here you'll find the Prodigy Classifieds and the Career Bulletin Board.

Back to the Net

Let's return to the Internet. The two principal employment-related Internet sites are the Online Career Center (OCC) and an E-Span offering: the E-Span Interactive Employment Network, which is a richer version of what is available on CompuServe. OCC can be reached by Gopher at **occ.com** or on the World-Wide Web at **http://www.occ.com/occ/**. OCC offers many want ads. E-Span Interactive Employment Network is primarily accessible via the Web at **http://www.espan.com/**. However, you can also go to the news group **misc.jobs.offered** to access the job listings only. Getting to E-Span via the Web not only makes the search through the classifieds easier, it also gives you access to a variety of career-related reference tools. With either OCC or E-Span, typing in a keyword ("medical secretary") will yield want ads or job postings related to that area.

On the commercial services as well as the Internet, there are other places to explore for job postings. Use keywords to search for specific firms, some of which may post employment opportunities at their own sites. The Internet also offers an array of sites with postings for academic positions, federal jobs, careers in science and technology, and health care positions.

I SEE...

Case Study

An electrical engineer acquaintance of mine—we'll call him Pete—found himself out of a job when his company was acquired by another. Being a technically-minded guy, he naturally turned to the Internet and some commercial on-line services to jump start his job search.

He soon discovered that the on-line world produced no more attractive job leads than the want ads. It did produce an offer or two, but the salary levels were well below what he'd been used to. However, with the needle of his money meter dipping below the halfway point, Pete steeled himself to take the next offer he got, reasoning that some cash flow was better than none.

He had a working spouse, but he also had two children, two cars (with lease payments), and a "comfortable" house (with a mortgage that had become anything but comfortable). He thought about taking a lower-paying job in his field, then making up his salary shortfall with some kind of part-time work. It would be hard, but, he decided, he had no choice—at least for the time being.

That's when it hit him. Working the Internet and the on-line services in search of leads and want ads *was* the equivalent of a part-time job. The only difference: it didn't pay. At least, not yet.

In the three months that Pete had been scouring the on-line universe, he had become an old hand at navigating the job-related sites and databases. Now it hit him: He could sell this expertise to others. Pete took out a classified ad in one local paper, under "Job Search Services," and he used the HTML editor (which had come with the new word-processing software package he had bought shortly before he was laid off) to construct his own World-Wide Web homepage for the Internet, offering his services as an electronic job hunter for hire.

Pete hasn't grown wealthy from this enterprise. But it does provide the salary supplement he needs. Unfortunately, the EE (electrical engineering) job he's taken does pay less than the one he had. But, by working at home after hours, helping others search for jobs on the Infobahn, he more than makes up the shortfall. This has given him the anxiety-free time he needs to find fully satisfying and fully remunerative work in his field.

The Groves of Academe

For academic positions, try searching for particular colleges and universities. Many of these institutions post jobs electronically. More centralized sources include the on-line version of *The Chronicle of Higher Education* (Gopher to **chronicle.merit.edu** or crawl the Web to **http://chronicle.merit.edu/.ads/.links.html**) and the Academic Position Network (APN), a growing clearinghouse of employment opportunities (Gopher to **wcni.cis.umn.edu 11111** or use a Web browser to reach **gopher://wcni.cis.umn.edu 11111/**). More specialized is Academic Physician and Scientist (Gopher to **aps.acad-phy-sci.com**). Finally, Texas A&M University offers a clearinghouse site on the Web at **http://agenifo.tamu.edu/jobs.html#otherorgs**); Rice University offers one at **gopher://riceinfo.rice.edu:70/11/Subject/Jobs** or directly by Gopher at **riceinfo.rice.edu**; and the University of Minnesota College of Education offers another at **rodent.cis.umn.edu 11119** (via Gopher) or **gopher://rodent.cis.umn.edu:11119/** (via Web). Whereas most of the sites mentioned post positions in colleges and universities, the Minnesota site is specifically for elementary, middle school, and junior and senior high school positions.

Federal Cases

Jobs with the federal government are accessible using the Dartmouth College Gopher (at **dartcms1.dartmouth.edu** or via the Web at **gopher://DARTCMS1.DARTMOUTH. EDU:70/11/fedjobs**—be sure to type this one with the upper- and lowercase letters indicated here) and through FedWorld, a database prepared by the National Technical Information Service of the U.S. Department of Commerce. You can Telnet to **fedworld.gov**, FTP to **ftp.fedworld.gov**, or take the Web to **http://www.fedworld.gov**. If you prefer, you may just dial up FedWorld's BBS directly at 703-321-8020 (set your communications software to 9600 bps, 8/N/1).

The top screen announcing FedWorld's home page on the World-Wide Web.

FedWorld Information Network

Last revised on September 14, 1995

 What is the NTIS/FedWorld Information Network?

● General Information Services

U.S. Government Information Servers *(Internet)*
- List of web servers, ftp, gopher, and telnet sites, organized by NTIS subject categories.

National Technical Information Service *(NTIS)*
- Scientific, technical and business-related titles, including reports, databases, and software.

Recent U.S. Government Reports *(All Agencies)*
- Search abstracts of recent government reports, studies and information products sent to NTIS within the past 30 days and order free catalogs.

Commerce Information Locator Service
- Search abstracts that describe information products available from the U.S. Department of Commerce.

● FedWorld Services and Files

FedWorld FTP Site *(Government information, documents and files)*

Sci/Tech

For positions in science and technology, try CareerMosaic on the World-Wide Web at **http://www.careermosaic.com/**. Not only will you find job postings here, you can also download a variety of profiles of high-tech corporations. Another relevant Web site is the Monster Board at **http://www.monster.com**. Of course, be certain also to search for specific companies and fields.

Health care professionals will want to explore MedSearch America (via the Web at **http://www.medsearch.com** or via Gopher at **gopher.medsearch.com**) in addition to using keywords for finding specific firms and institutions.

Posting Your Résumé

Many of the sites and services just discussed offer not only employer-generated classifieds, but areas for you to post your résumé. See Chapter 8, ""Looking Good on Paper" for guidance on how to make your résumé computer friendly. It is particularly important that you heed the advice in that chapter on restricting yourself to ASCII text and ensuring that you provide appropriate keywords, since it is by keyword that your résumé will be retrieved by a prospective employer.

But *will* it be retrieved?

The chances, quite frankly, are not great—although they are certainly better than if you posted a "situation wanted" or "position wanted" ad in a newspaper or even in most trade or professional journals. Because most of the sites and services offer the résumé-posting service without charge, it certainly cannot hurt to avail yourself of this additional exposure.

The Least You Need to Know

➤ Tapping into job-related resources on the Internet and other on-line services requires practice, patience, and a good guidebook.

➤ Exploit the Internet features that are most useful to the job hunter: World-Wide Web (WWW), e-mail, news groups, mailing lists, FTP, Telnet, and Gopher.

➤ While the Internet and commercial on-line services offer electronic want ads, the on-line connection is most useful as a means of obtaining information on prospective employers.

➤ Posting your résumé electronically is easy, but not very effective.

Chapter 14

How to Heat Things Up with a Cold Letter or a Cold Call

In This Chapter

➤ Using background research to "warm up" the cold letter or cold call

➤ Identifying the person with the power to hire you

➤ Writing effective cold letters

➤ Reducing cold call anxiety

➤ Combining cold calls with cold letters

If you read Chapter 9, "Judged By Its Cover: How to Write Great Cover Letters," you already know that one of the main purposes of a cover letter is to stop the target employer from routinely, reflexively, and automatically tossing your unsolicited résumé in the wastebasket. It's a real problem.

Many potential employers treat unsolicited résumés the way we mere mortals habitually treat articles of "junk mail" received at home. They throw them away unread. Now, as I briefly suggested in Chapter 9, there is a simple solution: Instead of trying to write a great cover letter to preserve your résumé from instant oblivion, don't send the résumé. Just send a letter, and make it do all the work. Or, instead of a letter, make a phone call. This chapter shows you how to do both effectively.

Yeah, It's a Crap Shoot (So Load the Dice)

I'd like to be able to tell you one way or the other: *Send a résumé* or *Don't send a résumé*. I'd like to, but I can't, because it's anybody's guess as to which tactic is better. It is a fact that the sight, smell, or feel of an unsolicited résumé stuffed into an envelope seems to trigger the release of some as-yet undiscovered hormone in many employers. Under the influence of this substance, the hand moves unthinkingly from the desk to the wastebasket, hovering there a moment before the fingers loosen their grip and the hopeful résumé disappears forever.

Just when you've convinced yourself of the inevitability of this scenario—and you've therefore resolved to send a letter without a résumé—the thought occurs to you that it is foolish to withhold information from a prospective employer, that you should give it your best shot, that the target employer will open your letter, read it, and remark to him- or herself, *"Gee, I should call this guy and get his résumé."* And then, in the crush of daily business, forget about the whole thing.

You're not paranoid. It really can be a case of "damned if you do and damned if you don't." Here's all the advice I can reasonably share with you. It consists of two items: my personal preference and what you might call a "Rule of Thumb (Sort Of)."

As someone who has been in positions with the authority to hire people, I personally paid more attention to convincingly written cold letters unaccompanied by résumés than to unsolicited résumés accompanied by cover letters. (By the way, the résumés that came without cover letters I almost always pitched into the wastebasket.) There's my preference. Take it or leave it.

Now, for the Rule of Thumb (Sort Of). If you are sending unsolicited correspondence to a large organization (more than 500 employees) or an organization that you know has a human resources department, send a great cold letter only, without a résumé. Why? Because, if an unsolicited résumé doesn't end up in the wastebasket, it may end up in the next-worst place: a human resources file. I have said it elsewhere, and I will say it again in just a few moments. Identify the person with the power to hire you, then communicate with him or her rather than with the human resources department. But, even if you do take the trouble to do this, by stuffing a résumé into an envelope, you run the risk that a secretary (who may open, screen, and route the busy boss's mail) or the addressee will automatically forward the document—unread—to Human Resources. There it shall be duly filed. Maybe you'll get a letter acknowledging receipt of the document, but, chances are, that will be the last correspondence you receive from the company.

In contrast, if you are sending unsolicited correspondence to a smaller organization (under 500 employees) or one you know lacks a human resources department, consider sending a résumé accompanied by a great cover letter. Maybe it will end up in the wastebasket—that's a possibility—but it will not automatically be filed away in a department remote from your target.

Be Prepared

From the perspective of your target, cold letters and cold calls come "out of the blue." Now, most chance occurrences lead to nothing more. They occur, they're over with, and that's the end. But wouldn't it be wonderful—for you and your target—if the addressee opened your unsolicited letter, read it, then remarked, *"This is incredible! I've been looking for someone like this!"*?

Dumb luck? Fat chance?

Not quite so dumb or quite so improbable *if* you load the dice before rolling them. That means doing the kind of homework discussed in Chapters 8, 9, and 10, identifying the needs of your target employers, then creating letters that address those needs rather than present your own.

> **Buzz Word**
> *Cold letters* and *cold calls* are unsolicited applications. Your target employer doesn't know you and hasn't asked for you. Cold letters can be sent in random mass mailings, and cold calls can be made from the Yellow Pages. However, you will greatly increase your chances of making a meaningful connection if you warm up your cold inquiries through research.

Personnel? Human Resources? Walk on By

Perhaps you are intimidated by the thought of all that is riding on a cold letter or a cold call. After all, this single action can lead either to a job, a dream job, a challenging and profitable career, or....

You need not be intimidated. The cold inquiry does have an important mission, but it is a less ambitious one than getting you a job. Its more immediate and more modest purpose is not so much to get you *in* as it is to *not* get you screened out. A cold letter or call is successful if it gets you a single step beyond where you are now (which, vis-a-vis the target employer, is nowhere). It stands to reason, therefore, to avoid addressing your cold inquiry to the part of the organization whose job it is to screen people out.

At their best, personnel or human resources departments consist of specialists trained to recognize talent and special ability. The key phrase, however, is "at their best." Unfortunately, in all too many firms, the principal recruitment function of Human Resources is not finding talent, but eliminating unsuitable candidates from the pool of applicants. When you apply to a firm, there is no way of knowing how its particular human resources department functions. Does it actively seek talent? Or does it passively screen applicants? Who knows? Maybe you won't be screened out. But why run that risk? Unless your diligent research has utterly failed to turn up a contact within the department or division in which you are seeking employment, avoid sending a cold letter or making a cold call to Human Resources. Go directly to a person with power to hire you.

Find the Clout

In Chapter 10, "Reactive vs. Proactive Search Strategies," I stressed the importance of identifying the person with the power to hire you and then targeting your job hunt efforts on that person. But what if all of your Chapter 10 homework fails to turn up that individual? In this case, use Human Resources creatively.

Call—do not write—the firm's human resources department and ask not for a job or even a job application, but, rather, for some help. Explain that you are researching careers in the X field and that you would like to talk to a senior staff member in the X department. "Could you give me the name of that person?" Emphasize that you are not applying for a job, but only seeking information. Once you have the name of the contact person, you can start with a request for an informational interview, as discussed in Chapter 6, "Up the Mountain: Steps to a New Career," and in Chapter 12, "Making Networking Work for You." Just tell the contact that "your human resources department recommended I speak with you." Or you may want to proceed directly to the cold inquiry, which you may warm up a bit by mentioning, as with the request for an informational interview, that "your Human Resources people suggested I contact you." To avoid being dishonest, however, frame your cold inquiry as a request for an informational interview rather than a full-speed-ahead bid for a job. There is a thin line separating out-and-out deception from the "creative" use of Human Resources.

Pitfall
Is it okay to "trick" someone into giving you information you need? The answer is no—and not just because deception is morally distasteful. If the target employer feels deceived, you're certain not to get the job. What's worse, failing to get the job or having the employer discover your deception *after* he or she hires you?

The Art of the Cold Letter

Writing an effective cold letter is quite similar to writing a persuasive cover letter to accompany a résumé (see Chapter 9, "Judged by Its Cover: How to Write Great Cover Letters"), except that, in the absence of a résumé, the letter itself should incorporate *some* of the information that would normally be included in a résumé. Bear in mind, though, the big problem with the traditional résumé. To wit, the traditional résumé says a lot about you—which is important to you—but says nothing about what most concerns the target employer: his or her needs. In Chapter 8, "Looking Good on Paper," I suggested strategies for refocusing your résumé away from your needs and onto those of the target employer. Similarly, make certain that your cold letter comes across less as an announcement of what you want than it does as the good news an anxious employer has been waiting for.

An Assortment of Hooks

The world of business is populated by many creative and imaginative people. Just don't *count* on your letter reaching one of them. The majority of cold letters, however, place absolute faith in the creative imagination of the reader. The typical letter introduces the writer and lays out his or her experience and background, as if to say, *"Here I am. Here's what I do and have done. Now, you figure out how you can use me."* It's as if most of us operate with a belief that we'll be "discovered," like Lana Turner in Schwab's Drugstore on Hollywood and Vine. All we've got to do is lay out the pieces of who we are, and some great good soul will pick them up, put them together, and grant us a life of fulfilling employment.

It doesn't work that way. And that being the unalterable truth, you'd better write a cold letter that leaves nothing to the imagination—except for prompting the target employer to imagine how much more productive and profitable his or her life will be with you on board.

Writers of sales letters know that they've got at most a single phrase or sentence to "hook" the reader and keep his or her hand from flipping the document, 99 percent unread, into the trash. That hook should not only pull the reader in, it should also guide his or her thoughts through the body of the letter.

The one characteristic all successful hooks share is that they are not about you. They are about your correspondent. A letter that begins, "My name is Joe Blow, and I'm looking for a job" is a letter without a

Winner
Almost all books on "business correspondence" admonish you to use plain white stationery and plain white envelopes. For the purposes of the cold letter, consider an envelope with a splash of color—a bright stripe, a simple design—which you can carry over onto the stationery inside. No flowers, hearts, or smiley faces, but a dash of ink to capture just one more fraction of your target's interest.

YOU'RE HIRED!

hook. It provides no motive for the recipient to read on, but furnishes a fine motive for him or her to throw the letter away. Now, a letter beginning with credentials—"As a widget wonker with six years of experience in the field, I am writing to inquire about the availability of a position with your firm"—is somewhat better. It is possible that the letter may find a reader who is in need of an experienced widget wonker, and, if they are in short supply, he or she may well contact the letter writer. But that's a big "if."

This opening sentence is a hook, but a weak one, because it still is about what the "I" wants, not what the target employer needs. If widget wonkers are not all that hard to come by, and a competing wonker writes a letter beginning something like, "Now that you are expanding your widget operations into the Toledo area, you will need the most creative and qualified widget wonkers you can get," the writer of the first letter is sure to lose.

But, you protest, this isn't fair. Wonker #2 had some kind of inside information—he or she *knew* that the company was expanding into Toledo.

That's just the point. A good hook begins with an understanding of what your target needs. Before you sit down to write a letter, do your homework, then come up with something like the following examples, in which you put into words what the target employer needs. Opening statements such as these are powerful hooks:

➤ Expansion creates a need for a proactive approach to public affairs.

➤ "Personnel operations require policies and procedures to assure higher productivity with lower costs and turnover." I read those words in an interview you gave to *Human Resources Week*. It was like reading my own thoughts.

➤ Scope and depth are the qualities you need in program development.

➤ The new government regulations have created a climate of crisis. I see them as a challenge and an opportunity.

➤ In your business, you can't afford to hold the line. In a highly competitive industry, you know that you have to expand your markets, and, to do that, you also know that you need people in marketing research who can deliver the data necessary to develop new marketing concepts, products, and services—now.

➤ While serving as assistant international shipping manager for Postmark Industries, I discovered information about customs processing that, I believe, will be of great interest to you.

➤ Extensive experience in all aspects of quality control has taught me some remarkable ways of streamlining quality assurance protocols while increasing their effectiveness.

For some positions, a recommendation is a *required* hook: "Jane Doe, sales manager of Postmark Industries, strongly suggested that I contact you." Or: "Your client, Peter Prentiss, urged me to contact you." Then proceed to a hook similar to one of the examples, a hook that catches the target employer's self-interest.

Create Interest

Follow up the hook by developing the target's interest in *you* as a means of providing what he or she needs. Whereas the cover letter accompanying a résumé (see Chapter 9) highlights abilities and qualifications listed in the résumé, the cold letter must stand in for the résumé. An effective tactic is to develop a bit more narrative following the hook, then list your most relevant abilities and qualifications set off with bullets.

Jump Start
Emphasize *qualifications* and *abilities* over *experience.* The first two say what you can and will do, whereas the last merely says what you have done. For a fuller discussion of this important distinction, see Chapter 9.

The new government regulations have created a climate of crisis. I see them as a challenge and an opportunity. As Assistant to the Director of Regulation Compliance at Techworld, Inc., I have been instrumental not only in achieving cost-effective compliance, but also in making compliance a bottom-line asset by:

➤ *Developing* energy-efficient fabrication procedures

➤ *Combining* internal quality assurance with regulatory compliance

➤ *Communicating* the end-user benefits of compliance to the consumer

Evoke Desire

After developing the target employer's interest by detailing your abilities and qualifications, evoke desire by suggesting that all you have to offer can be acquired: You are for hire. Let's continue with the regulatory compliance expert's letter:

"I would welcome the opportunity to discuss these and other strategies with you, and, in particular, how I can best work with your organization to turn compliance into opportunity."

Prompt Action

End by *telling* the target employer what to do next—or, better yet, act *for* him or her:

"I will call next week to learn when we can get together."

And the Cold Call

As much as most of us crave instant gratification, we also dread instant rejection. And that is why the cold call is both appealing and threatening. There are two ways to psych yourself for the call:

➤ Convince yourself that you are not asking for a job, but that you are offering fulfillment of the target employer's needs and solutions to his or her problems. The callee will be grateful for this.

➤ Whether or not you succeed in convincing yourself of the foregoing, just make the call. Anxiety will vanish if you *just make the call*.

The strategies that follow will also reduce your anxiety—and make the call more effective.

Set Goals

Go into the call with a distinct set of goals. If you think the goal of the call is to get a job, you're mistaken. That's an unrealistic objective for one little phone call. Here's your primary goal: *To arrange a meeting.* Here's your first fallback goal: *To arrange a time to talk further on the phone.* Finally, a second fallback: *To secure a lead on a job possibility elsewhere or to seek information on future prospects for employment at the target company.*

If you keep your goals firmly in mind, you are less likely to blank out when the voice answers on the other end of the line. A feeling of drift or directionlessness is a prime cause of "phone fright."

Beware the Voice of Fear

In stressful situations, many people feel betrayed by their voice. They don't want to sound scared, but the voice comes out thin, tight, quavering, high, and utterly unpersuasive. Worse, with each word you utter, you realize more powerfully just how anxious you are. And, as you become more anxious, the voice gets tighter, higher, and thinner. Soon, listening to yourself, all you hear is fear. Your concentration slips, you lose focus, and you've blown the call.

I won't kid you. It can happen. How do you avoid the voice of fear? The great American psychologist William James once said, "We do not run because we are afraid. We are afraid because we run." Much of the anxiety of a cold call is a product of listening to the voice of fear. We sound scared. Therefore, we get scared. And, therefore, we sound even more scared. And so on, in a vicious cycle.

A big part of cold call anxiety, then, is physical, and it will at least partly yield to a physical solution. Anyone who has been through natural childbirth training—either as a mother, father, or "birthing partner," is all too familiar with the emphasis placed on breathing exercises and routines. Maybe a doctor or nurse explained that it is very important to keep oxygen flowing to the baby, right? True enough, but the more direct function of the breathing exercises is to give the mother something to concentrate on. If you are breathing in a regular, self-conscious way, you're less likely to scream. If you don't hear yourself screaming, well, then things can't be all that bad, can they? I mean, if you were in real pain and terror, you'd be screaming your head off.

Just as regular breathing does not radically alter the process of childbirth, but focuses attention away from pain, concentrating on your voice, rather than your fears, will help you "walk around" your cold call anxiety. Focus on pushing your voice to a lower pitch than what comes naturally. This applies equally whether you are a man or a woman. A low-pitched voice conveys more authority and self-assurance than a high-pitched one. Concentrate on achieving a resonant pitch, and slow the pace of your speech to match it. Follow the example of all good singers: open your mouth and give weight to each word. One last thing: smile. It may sound silly—you're on the phone, after all—but a smile is heard as well as seen.

Winner

YOU'RE HIRED!

Do you have "call waiting" service? It can be very useful, but also very distracting if your cold call is interrupted by an insistent signal from another caller trying to get through. Usually, you can temporarily disable call waiting by dialing *70 before you dial the rest of the number (for example, *70-555-5555). This will ensure that your call will not be interrupted. Call waiting will be restored when you hang up.

Stamp Out Spontaneity

No law dictates that a telephone conversation has to be spontaneous. You would probably not attempt to "wing" a major presentation. Assigned to report on the current market for the latest computer chip, for instance, you would at least take the time to gather the relevant facts and figures. Indeed, you would probably do quite a bit more. Why not do the same for this very important presentation—for a presentation in which the subject, the "product" is yourself?

The safest course is actually to create a script for the call, using the same strategy—and, in fact, the same material—as what you would write in a cold letter. Just make it a bit more conversational—and don't go immediately into your hook. You *must* begin by greeting the callee and identifying yourself. If you are calling on the recommendation of someone, make this the third thing you say: "Good morning, Mr. Galsworthy. My name is Sandra Burns. Your client Ed Goodrich strongly recommended that I give you a call." Then launch into your script. I've adapted this one from a cold letter:

"As you know, the new government regulations have created a climate of crisis. But, Mr. Galsworthy, I see them as a challenge and an opportunity. I'm Assistant to the Director of Regulation Compliance at Techworld, Inc. And I've been part of a team that's not only been achieving cost-effective compliance, but has been making compliance a bottom-line asset by developing energy-efficient fabrication procedures, combining internal quality assurance with regulatory compliance and effectively communicating to our customers the benefits—*to them*—of our compliance program. We've made compliance a product benefit."

"Mr. Galsworthy, I'd really welcome an opportunity to sit down with you and share some of the strategies I've been a part of, and I'd like to explore how my work in this field might benefit your firm."

Where Do We Go from Here?

Depending on Mr. Galsworthy's response, you would continue the cold call by further discussion, by fielding questions, by securing an interview date, or by arranging a time for further phone conversation. If Mr. Galsworthy tells you that he has no positions available, you have two options.

> **Jump Start**
> Try to frame your requests as offers of opportunity for the target employer or someone associated with him or her. Not "Do you know anybody who can give me a job?" but "Do you know anybody who *could benefit from....*"

You can ask to arrange an informational interview: "I understand. But would it be possible for me to speak with you about your likely future needs in the compliance area?"

Or:

You can ask for a referral to other job leads: "I understand, Mr. Galsworthy. But may I take this opportunity to ask if you have any recommendations about anyone else I may contact who could benefit from a compliance specialist?"

The Letter-Call Strategy

Cold letter versus cold call is not an either/or proposition. An effective strategy is to combine the two, generally beginning with a cold letter and following up with a cold call, which underscores the points made in the letter and has as its ultimate goal setting up a face-to-face interview. Another twist on this strategy is to begin with a cold call and follow up with a letter. This is especially useful if there will be a significant time lag between the call and the interview—say, two or more weeks. In this case, send a letter thanking the callee for agreeing to the interview, underscoring how much you are looking forward to it, and briefly recapitulating the *target employer* benefits you outlined on the phone. If the original call resulted in a turndown—no interview—consider sending the kind of thank-you letter discussed in Chapter 10.

The Least You Need to Know

➤ Consider sending a cover letter with a résumé when you write to a small business (500 employees or fewer), but a cold letter without a résumé when you write directly to the person with the power to hire you.

➤ Identify the person with the power to hire you and address him or her.

➤ Your cold letters and cold calls will be far more productive if you prepare by researching the needs of the target organization.

➤ The cold letter combines persuasive salespersonship with the kind of information usually supplied in a résumé.

➤ Begin with an irresistible "hook" to excite and direct the imagination of the target employer.

➤ Prepare for a cold call by setting realistic goals for that call.

➤ Develop a confident telephone voice and persuasive phone presence.

➤ Prepare a script for each cold call you make.

Chapter 15

Agencies and Headhunters

In This Chapter

➤ What agencies can and cannot do to get you the job you want

➤ Who pays and who calls the shots?

➤ Responding to a headhunter

➤ Using public employment agencies

➤ Evaluating a private agency

If you've reached this chapter having read much of what's come before, you realize how chaotic our job-hunting "system" is. Rising above the sea of chaos, like a lighthouse, stands the majestic employment agency, prepared, valiantly, vigilantly, and selflessly, to guide you to the safe harbor of vocational fulfillment. Right?

Right?

Right...?

Don't Get Too Comfortable

Judging from the number of employment agencies out there, the industry must be a successful one. The agencies come in three basic varieties: private; those retained by employers to fill specific, usually higher-level, positions (these are popularly called head hunters); and public (run by the federal or state government). Within the private category are many agencies that specialize in serving particular industries. Some supply accoun-

Jump Start
On average, for every 100 hopefuls who walk in the agency's door, 5 get a job through the agency.

tants, some furnish sales and marketing staffs, others find nannies for beleaguered parents, and so on. Some of these agencies further concentrate on placing temporary employees, while others fill permanent vacancies, and still others do both.

You would think that, with all the specialized agencies available, there would be a lid for every pot, that all anyone would ever have to do to get a good job is register with the right agency and let them do the rest. Not quite.

What an Agency Is—and Isn't

You are most likely to deal with a private agency that functions not as your "agent," but as the agent of the employer. That's one of the reasons the agency idea seems so great: The employer picks up the tab. *You*, the job hunter, don't pay a thing (usually). But the downside of this arrangement is that *you* are not the client, and *you* don't call the shots. Even if the nice person you talk with at the agency assures you that his or her firm is interested equally in the satisfaction of the employer and the job hunter, be aware of the fact that the agency is working for the employer.

Because of this, the agency acts as both a talent scout and a screening service. The agency is pulled in two directions. To the degree that it wants to create long-term satisfaction for—and repeat business from—its clients, it will try to screen out anyone it deems a dud. Expressed more positively, the agency will make an effort to match the job hunter's qualifications and abilities with the demands of the job. However, to the degree that the agency wants to collect a fee here and now, its recruiter may be motivated to talk the job hunter into a position he or she isn't particularly well suited for. The point is that the interests of the job hunter and the employment agency do not always coincide.

You should also not make the mistake of thinking of the employment agency as a career counselor. Agencies survive on volume, which means that rapid turnover is essential. Process a candidate, match him or her to a job, collect a fee, and go on to the next candidate. Little time can be devoted to individual job hunters, and virtually no time can be invested in would-be career changers. In fact, if you lack a track record in the particular field or specialty that interests the agency's client, most agencies will not deal with you.

What a Headhunter Is—and Isn't

As a job hunter, your tendency is to think that the employer holds all the cards. Certainly, he holds the jobs—like some wonderful treasure, which he will dispense only to the person deemed worthy. Ah! To be an employer, it is to be a king!

Now, back to planet earth.

Employers are actually in the same position as job hunters. Job hunters are bewildered by the task of finding an employer, just as employers are overwhelmed by the task of finding employees. For this reason, they often hire so-called headhunters to perform this task for them.

But what, exactly, is this task, and how is it any different from what an employment agency does? Both employment agencies (usually) and headhunters (always) act on behalf of the employer. Agencies serve as candidate clearinghouses, drawing their prospects chiefly through ads they place and from people who call on the phone or walk in the door. Headhunters, as the name implies, are far more aggressive. They are given a specific assignment from the employer company—a set of specs for the desired employee—and they go out and find him or her. Sometimes, headhunting firms will use want ads—especially in professional and trade journals—but, usually, they will aggressively canvass the ranks of firms (other than the one that hired them, of course) in an effort to lure desirable candidates away from their present position and into their client's camp. This done, the headhunter collects a fee.

Because of the differing fee structures involved—headhunters cost the client much more than employment agencies do—headhunters are typically retained only to fill executive or highly skilled creative positions. Middle-management positions and below are usually the province of the employment agency. And, whereas employment agencies invite you to walk on in and take a swim in their candidate pool, headhunters do not. Generally, they come after *you*—though you are free to send them a cover letter and résumé. Chances of anything productive coming of this are slim, but it is just one more option to exploit.

Buzz Word
Headhunters, officially known as "executive search firms," are also called talent scouts—as well as body snatchers and flesh peddlers. (Just kidding.)

Pitfall
As we shall see in a moment, some private employment agencies operate by charging the job hunter rather than the employer. As long as this is made clear to you, there is nothing shady about the deal. However, no legitimate headhunter—executive search firm—operates this way. If you are called by a self-proclaimed "headhunter" and asked for a fee, be assured that your pocket is about to be picked.

State Employment Agencies

Regardless of your politics—left, right, or center—it's hard getting away from the notion that good ol' Uncle Sam (or a state-level equivalent) will at least *try* to provide for you. Maybe—you hope—your local federal or state employment service will have a comprehensive file of available jobs. You may be encouraged in this hope by the fact that the nation's local agencies are tied together in a federal network called the United States Employment Service (USES). I mean, look at this: "United States" *and* "Employment" *and* "Service." With those particular words strung together, how could you possibly go wrong?

In fact, your local USES or Job Services office does have access to the Interstate Job Bank listings, which provide information about opportunities not only locally, but also nationwide. The drawbacks are that the listings are usually two weeks old or older, and, of course, employers are not required to list openings with USES.

Bastion of the Minimum Wage?

State and federal employment services can be significant resources for information, but they have a reasonably well-deserved reputation for primarily listing low-paying and non-professional jobs. Worse, many employers post jobs with these agencies only as a last resort, after they have already tried to fill the vacancies by other means.

The Odds Are...?

USES fails to place a majority of those who seek employment through it. Depending on whose studies you believe, the hit rate varies from just under 14 percent to as much as 30 percent. However, more than half of the people who find jobs through USES quit or are "let go" within 30 days. This reflects the fact that some of the jobs are temporary positions, but also suggests a high turnover rate in positions that are supposed to be permanent.

Private Agencies

Approached and used realistically, private employment agencies can be a useful *adjunct* to (*not* mainstay of) your job hunt. Always consider who pays (and what that means), and, remember that you are in a strong position to pick and choose among agencies. After all, you are presenting them with an opportunity to make money *because of who you are.*

Who Pays?

In most cases, all fees are paid by the employer. Congratulations—but, remember, that means the employer is the client, not you.

Theoretically, there are advantages to seeking out an employment agency that will work for you in return for your paying a fee. Theoretically, such an agency will work harder for you—and spend more time with you—to get you the job you want. Whether theory and practice coincide depends on how well connected the agency is within its specialty or specialties. You can make using such an agency a low-risk proposition by ensuring that the fee you pay is your only cost and that it is 100 percent contingent on your securing and accepting a job obtained through the agency. If the agency fails to get you a job you want, you don't pay. Typical fees are as high as 60 percent of one month's salary—generally payable in weekly installments of 10 percent.

Pitfall
Be careful! Even if an agency collects its fee from the employer, it is possible that you will be held liable for the fee if the employer fails to pay it. Read all application materials carefully before agreeing to any arrangement that may put you at risk financially.

Evaluating an Agency

Check out a prospective employment agency the same way you would check out a doctor, lawyer, or other professional you hire to perform a critically important service. Basic steps include finding out how long the firm has been doing business in your geographical area and in your professional field. Also, make a call to your local Better Business Bureau and ask if any complaints have been filed against the firm. If employment agencies in your area are regulated by a state or local authority, call to inquire if any complaints have been lodged. Beyond this, obtain recommendations. These may come from friends or even from "failed" interviews. When Ms. Smith of Acme Widgets tells you that she has no openings "just now," thank her anyway—then ask her what firm she considers to be the best employment agency specializing in the widget industry.

Winner
This tactic also makes it possible for you to tell the agency's counselor that "Ms. Smith at Acme recommended that I see your firm. Said you were the best in the business." With such a rep to live up to, the agency may just go that extra mile for you.

The final step in evaluation is when you come face to face with the counselor for the first time. Think about this: You are more than halfway through this book. You already know a great deal about job hunting. Ask the counselor what he or she thinks of the usefulness of résumés, or ask for suggestions on negotiating salary. Compare his or her answers with what you've learned here. If this conversation goes nowhere, find another employment agency.

Presenting Yourself

Despite its limitations, a really good employment agency can be a valuable adjunct to your job search. Prepare for your first meeting with the agency's job counselor as you would prepare for an employment interview (see Chapters 18, "Preparing for the Interview: How to Plan for Spontaneity," and 19, "Dressing for the Interview") and conduct the interview accordingly (see Chapters 20, "To Give the Right Answers, Get the Right Questions," and 21, "Asking Questions and Making the Sale"). Be clear about what you want. If you feel that you are being pigeonholed, bullied, or ignored, stop trying to "sell" yourself. Reject this agency and go on to the next. However, don't make the mistake of pigeonholing *yourself*. The trick is to define yourself and your needs broadly enough so that you are not eliminated from consideration for jobs that, as far as the agency is concerned, don't *quite* fit your qualifications, yet not to define yourself so broadly that you waste everyone's time getting called for jobs you'd never even think of taking.

Whatever else your encounter with the employment agency may or may not do, it can be profitably exploited as an opportunity to practice your interview skills. For this reason alone, it is useful to make a visit to at least one employment agency a part of your job hunt.

I SEE...

Case Study

Mary Williams wanted to break into magazine work. She did research, combed the want ads, made inquiries—and she also decided to sign up with three employment agencies specializing in publishing and magazines.

Mary was savvy enough to realize that she could not afford simply to "put herself in the hands of experts." She understood that registering with the agencies was just one of several job-hunting strategies she would use. She also understood something else. Employment agencies may try to define your qualifications either too narrowly or too broadly. By far, the worse of these two alternatives is to be defined too narrowly. It may cut you out of some very good jobs. Therefore, Mary went to the three agencies, emphasizing three variations on what she perceived as her skills and interests: At one agency, she stressed editorial qualifications; at another, publicity qualifications; at the third, she underscored her experience as a college newspaper journalist. She did not lie. She merely provided a different slant on her very real background and interests.

Mary did one other thing. She consciously used her employment agency interviews as practice for actually employer interviews. At the conclusion of each interview, she said to the employment counselor, "Thanks. I really enjoyed talking with you. I know you'll be a big help to me. I suppose it was pretty obvious that I was practicing my interview technique with you. Could I ask you—and please be very frank with me—how did I do? Do you have any advice about how I might put myself across more effectively?"

As it turned out, Mary ended up working for a major consumer audio magazine as an editorial assistant. She got the job because of a letter and résumé she sent on her own—not through any of the three agencies.

Monogamy vs. Polygamy

If your chances of getting "placed" by any one agency are about 1 in 20, it stands to reason that, by registering with more than one, you increase your chances of hitting a job. Don't feel guilty, and don't misplace your loyalty. Unless you have signed an exclusive agreement with an agency, you have every right to register with as many as you want. And, don't worry, few employers will become clients of more than one agency for any single position, so you're not likely to get duplicate job offers.

Headhunters

Most folks feel flattered if they receive a call from a headhunter. Such indulgences in vanity are forgivable; a call from the headhunter is acknowledgment that you are wanted. Headhunters go after the gainfully employed, usually people who are not actively looking for new employment, and they try to lure them from their present berth into a new one.

Pitfall
Read your application form—and anything else you are asked to sign—*very* carefully. Beware of agreeing to give the agency exclusive handling. If you do, you may well have to pay a fee for *any* job you get—whether you obtain it through the agency or on your own.

How to Find Them

Mostly, headhunting is a don't-call-us-we'll-call-you proposition. But there is no law that prevents you from taking steps to make headhunters aware of your presence. You can

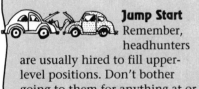

Jump Start
Remember, headhunters are usually hired to fill upper-level positions. Don't bother going to them for anything at or near entry level. Worried that you aren't qualified for an upper-level position? Let the headhunter do the worrying.

locate these firms in the Yellow Pages by looking carefully under "Employment Agencies." Find agencies that describe themselves as "executive search specialists." A more effective way to identify such firms is to look through professional and trade directories relevant to your field or industry and to peruse industry-related periodicals for ads. After you have located some firms, send a cover letter and résumé, making the same appeal that you would make directly to an employer. Emphasize qualifications and abilities rather than mere experience. Stress problem solving. Conclude—do not begin—the cover letter with a statement of the kind of position for which you are looking.

Answering the Call

What if a headhunter calls you? I'm assuming that, since you're reading this book, your present position affords you something less than total bliss. Chances are, then, that you will be interested in what the headhunter has to say. But even if you are fairly content in your present job, it can't hurt to listen.

At the first contact, polite skepticism is the prudent attitude. If the call takes you utterly by surprise, and you have no résumé prepared, tell the headhunter that you are interested in speaking further about the position, but that you won't be available for a meeting before the end of the week (or the middle of next week). Don't explain the reason for the delay. Use the time to prepare a résumé (see Chapter 8, "Looking Good on Paper"), not only for the employer, but also for your own reference and study prior to the interview. Remember to tailor your résumé to the target company. This means using part of the time before your interview to research the company.

Even if you have a résumé ready—and you have been thinking about changing jobs or have been actively job hunting—it is usually advantageous to stall for enough time to research the target company and tailor your existing résumé to its needs.

You Are Not the Client

The headhunter has a very hefty fee riding on you. If you take the job, his or firm may collect the equivalent of as much as one-third of your first year's salary. Breathe easy: They don't collect from you, but from the employer. This means, of course, that the employer, not you, is the client. Do not, therefore, make the mistake of using the head-hunter as an employment counselor. Do not confess to the headhunter current dissatis-faction or anxieties about the future.

Do recognize that the headhunter is pulled even more intensely by the same opposing forces that act upon the employment agency. On the one hand, he or she is highly motivated to send you to the client; only after a hire is made does the headhunter collect a fee. On the other hand, he or she is motivated to demonstrate selectivity. After all, the firm was hired not just to find candidates, but to keep every Tom, Dick, and Harriet from pounding down the client's door. So the headhunter is both a finder and a screener. Getting found is great, but as long as you are dealing with the headhunter rather than directly with the target employer, you are running the risk of being screened. Convey your enthusiasm for your work and your interest in the position. Be cooperative and increasingly forthcoming with the headhunter, but always bid for an interview directly with the client.

What to Say—and Not to Say

Chapters 18, 19, and 20 will help you prepare for and conduct an interview with a headhunter just as they help you with direct employer interviews. The overriding rule is to be positive—positive about your achievements, your abilities, and your qualifications; positive about accepting challenges and solving problems; positive about your love for your work. Do not complain about your present position. Do not express frustration with it. The impression you want to create is that your professional life is just great now and has always been just great; however, you are a person who thrives on fresh challenges and derives tremendous satisfaction from solving problems, increasing profits, and creating innovation.

Odds...?

Don't expect much from a headhunter if *you* make the contact. However, if you are called by the headhunter, and the call leads to a direct interview with an employer, you are in an extremely strong position among a select group of candidates.

One More Breed: The Job-Search Agency

Nestled among the agencies and the headhunters is another kind of "specialist," variously called a career counselor, professional placement specialist, management consultant, or even (confusingly enough) an executive search firm. Whatever such a firm calls itself, it is distinguished from the other services by charging a flat fee *in advance and irrespective of results* for the following services:

➤ Helping to determine your best job field

➤ Preparing your résumé and cover letter

➤ Creating a list of employer prospects

➤ Reproducing a résumé and mailing it

➤ Advising on interview questions and techniques, salary negotiation, and so on

Can such an agency really help you? The answer is *yes*—with a lot of *if*s and other qualifications. The biggest *if* is if you don't have enough time to conduct a job hunt yourself. If the alternative to hiring an agency is not to conduct a necessary job search, then you probably should think about hiring an agency. Here are other considerations:

The fee: We are talking about $900 or more for "processing" 100 résumés. Some outfits want a flat fee up-front and an additional fee contingent on their securing you a job.

Reputation: Get references. Interview the agency carefully and make sure that they can furnish you with the names and contact numbers of at least three individuals they have helped "place." Check out these references. If the agency pleads "client confidentiality" and will not furnish references, walk out the door. Call the local Better Business Bureau and any applicable licensing agencies. Check for any complaints.

Tune into the vibes during your interview. If you get negative feelings, trust those feelings and bid these folks a prompt adieu.

In the end, be aware of this fact: No one can conduct *your* job hunt better than *you* can—provided that you have the time and the inclination and are willing to summon up the imagination to do the work that is necessary, including preparing individual résumés and cover letters tailored to the needs of the target employer (something no agency will do for you).

The Least You Need to Know

➤ Do not turn your job-hunt over to an agency, but use the agency as an adjunct to other strategies. As a rule, it is most useful to register with multiple agencies.

➤ Do not make the mistake of using the employment agency as a vocational counseling service; this is crucial to avoid being screened out.

➤ Make certain that you understand the terms of your agreement with the agency. If you pay the fee, is it contingent on the agency's success in finding you the job you want?

➤ Prepare for an agency interview as you would for an interview with an employer as practice for the "real thing."

Chapter 16

Job Hunting When You're Unemployed

> ## In This Chapter
>
> ➤ Coping with your emotions
>
> ➤ Emergency measures and interim strategies
>
> ➤ The advantages of unemployment
>
> ➤ Using your company's outplacement service
>
> ➤ Explaining being fired or laid off, or resigning

Mark Twain, author of *Adventures of Huckleberry Finn* and many other classics of American literature, knew wealth and knew poverty. He once remarked that banks were institutions very willing to loan you money—just as long as you could prove you didn't need it. Trying to land a job when you're out of work can feel a lot like that. You're most attractive to employers precisely when you don't *need* a job.

It's true, job hunting when you are unemployed presents special challenges, and you can explore them here. But this uncomfortable situation also presents special opportunities for the job hunter. And you can explore these as well.

Aside from That, Mrs. Lincoln, How'd You Like the Play?

If you are out of work, you are not alone. It's not that the economy is bad just now. In fact, as I write this, the economy is healthier than it's been in quite a while. Unemployment is at 5.7 percent as of July 1995, which means that some 6,612,000 people are out of work nationwide. That's a lot of people—I said you're not alone—but it certainly could be worse, and it has been.

More important than percentages and numbers, for you, an out-of-work job hunter, are people and attitudes. They've changed. The world of work has always had its harsh side. Yet, for much of the 20th century, at least, there was a sort of unspoken contract between the majority of employers and employees. If you worked hard and remained loyal, all other things being equal, there was a very good chance that a single company could be your life's work. In recent years, however, two contradictory trends have developed. On the one hand, businesses are investing in personnel as they never have before. Whereas the watchword was once technology and hardware, and corporate bucks were accordingly poured into buildings and machines, funds are now increasingly devoted to developing *people*. Employers are investing in in-house training and development, as well as funding education in the public and private sectors, in the belief that doing so will create the caliber of workforce necessary to compete in a global marketplace. Unfortunately and paradoxically, they are not investing nearly as much in direct employee compensation, with 1995 merit raise averages at only about 3.5 percent.

Jump Start
In the United States, on average, people stay with a job—or the job stays with them—4.2 years.

That's the one hand. Here's the other. Even as corporate America has come to value trained personnel more highly, people have become more expendable. More accurately, as companies place greater emphasis on staffing, they have tended more aggressively to try to put the right person in the right job. That means that if John Jones has worked reasonably well as a widget marketing maven for ten years, but Acme Widgets comes across Mary Maxwell, who appears to have two or three more ideas about widget marketing, Acme will take John out and put Mary in. Employees have come to be seen as extremely valuable *parts* of the organization, but, as valuable as they are, they are also *interchangeable* and *upgradable* parts. It may be that many employers have come to regard permanent employees as expensive overhead that can readily be replaced by cheaper help.

The bottom line: While it has always been true that nobody owes you a job, nowadays nobody even *thinks* that they owe you one. Unless you have a contract or are protected by civil service regulations, your employer may lay you off or fire you whenever he, she, or it wants to.

It gets even worse. In many organizations, company policy prescribes certain warning, reprimand, and probationary procedures as an overture to dismissal. In some states, you are guaranteed either two weeks' notice or two weeks' severance pay. Even where policy guidelines and government regulations do not mandate warning and severance procedures, it is often in the employer's best interest to practice them in order to forestall litigation by disgruntled former employees. Despite all this, however, your employer may fire you or lay you off without any advance warning and without notice. Old Henry Ford was famous for "letting people go" by locking them out of their offices when they left for lunch. The employee returned, couldn't get into his own office, and most definitely got the message.

Such things still happen.

But what about your colleagues, friends, and confidantes? Surely, they will help look after you. Some even promised they would go to the mat for you. When proverbial push comes to proverbial shove, don't count on it. These people are scared, and they have families, mortgages, and car payments. The thought running through everyone's mind: *Better you than I.*

> **Buzz Word**
> *Lay off* is termination through no fault of your own (the company shrinks, technology changes, the economy sours, whatever), whereas getting *fired* is the result of your employer's judgment that you have failed to perform adequately, that you have performed poorly, or that you have committed some serious violation of company rules or the terms of your employment.

Emotional First Aid Kit

Getting laid off or fired feels lousy. There are actually books out there that try to tell you how you'll feel: angry then depressed and, ultimately, beset by feelings of worthlessness and meaninglessness. I suppose that this is true enough. I'd vote for adding *ashamed* and *panic stricken* to the list—especially if you have a family to support. But I won't pretend to tell you how you'll feel, except that I can guarantee you'll feel lousy.

You know what else I'm not going to tell you? I'm not going to remind you that you are a "unique" and "valuable" person. I'm not going to advise you to (in the words of that old song) "pick yourself up, dust yourself off, and start all over again." I'm not even going to tell you that losing a job isn't the end of the world—because, as a matter of fact, it *is* the end of at least one world: Remember when we were talking about "transferable skills" in

Jump Start Do you like acronyms? Here's one. It's my favorite dog: FIDO. *Forget It. Drive On.*

Chapter 1? Most of us don't think about them, but, instead, define ourselves one dimensionally in terms of what we do: "I'm director of sales at Hell-To-Pay." Each weekday morning, for months, years, or even decades, we got in the car, got on the bus, or boarded the train bound for The Shop or The Office—a place, the same place, a world. Suddenly, all that is gone.

You will have feelings, bad feelings, bewildering feelings. They will be made even worse by two things: total uncertainty (about when your joblessness will end) and sleeplessness.

That's the bad news, and I have even more—namely, I can't do much to help you with these feelings. Seek counsel from your friends and love from your family. All *I* can provide are a few pieces of commonsense advice and one unavoidable truth. Let me begin with that: Somehow or other, you will have to *deal with* your negative feelings. And not just because, otherwise, they will drive you deeper into despair, but because they will drive you into the past. Depressed and angry, you will brood yourself into the deadly realm of *woulda, shoulda, coulda.* That is one place where, right now, you do not want to be. Your mind, all your wits should be focused not on the past, but on the future. Forget and forsake *woulda, shoulda,* and *coulda.* Deal with your feelings and move ahead. Ahead is the only way out of unemployment.

Now for the common sense. If you are facing imminent financial collapse, seek the help of relatives and friends and, if necessary, the help of the federal government, the state, and the county. Make certain that you collect the unemployment compensation to which

Pitfall Whatever else you must skimp on, move heaven and earth to pay your mortgage or rent. As long as you can pay your rent, do not tell your landlord that you are out of work. You do not need to add homelessness to joblessness.

you are entitled. You might also cautiously invest in a good book: Charles Long's *How To Survive Without a Salary* (available from Firefly Books at Box 838, Ellicott Station, Buffalo, NY 14205). You might want initially to concentrate your efforts on obtaining freelance work, part-time work, or even "menial" work (flipping burgers, punching a cash register, whatever) just to bridge the gap, reduce your want, and decrease your anxiety.

Do not avoid your creditors during this period. Instead, deal with them proactively. Call your local utility companies; most offer programs to reduce or spread your payments. Do the same with credit card companies and others to whom you owe money. Stress that you want and intend to pay and that your situation is temporary. Ask them to work with you. Do you know why you pay so much interest on your credit card? It's not just because the credit card people want to make a lot of money (of course, they *do* want this), but because they *lose* so much money in bad debts. Credit card companies write off millions in bad debts every year. To avoid adding you to the zero-pay rolls, most are very willing to work out temporary terms with you in an emergency.

Sleep difficulties are common during periods of stress. Pills are usually not a good solution at a time like this because they may deepen depression. Alcohol, although it may make you drowsy, ultimately tends to disturb sleep patterns, resulting in poor-quality sleep that is not very restful. Try instead to keep regular hours, going to bed at the same time every night. It is usually best to go to bed before midnight and to avoid drinking coffee, especially after dinner. Avoid the temptation to work in bed or to pore over want ads and revisions of your résumé. The bed should be associated with sleep, not stress. Finally, sleeplessness is in itself anxiety producing. After about a half-hour of lying awake, you begin to worry about not being able to get to sleep, thereby increasing your anxiety and making it even more difficult to get to sleep. If you lie awake more than a half hour to forty-five minutes, try getting out of bed and reading or watching television until you get drowsy. Do not read anything related to your job-hunting efforts. (If it's past midnight, put this book away right now!)

There are other things you can do during a period of joblessness to keep yourself physically well. If you've had much occasion to watch weekday daytime TV, you have seen that every other commercial is directed at the unemployed: There are ads for training programs, correspondence courses, and debt relief. Clearly, the assumption of the enterprises that are paying for these ads is that, jobless people sit all day on the couch watching television. Prove them wrong. Remain as active as possible during the day. Part of the day, of course, will be devoted to job-hunting efforts, but part of your day should be taken up with walking, jogging, working in the yard—something, anything physical, preferably outdoors.

If you do mope in front of the television set, you're also likely to eat and drink poorly, snacking or grazing all day instead of eating regular meals. Not only will this make you feel unwell, it will contribute to your sense of having lost structure and meaning in your daily life. Eat regular, healthy meals.

> **Jump Start**
>
> The great Yiddish humorist Sholem Aleichem once said, "To be poor is no disgrace. But it's no honor, either." Substitute the word *fired* (or *laid off*) for *poor*, and you pretty much get the picture.

Exploiting the Advantages of Unemployment

Do you think you're out of work? Think again. You may be out of a job, but you have plenty of work to do. You've got to get employed, and that can be very hard work indeed. That's why you've got to stay healthy (you'll need your energy) and focused (you need to keep up your momentum).

Regular sleep, physical activity, and healthy meals are all important to maintaining structure in your daily life. But these things are hardly enough. You need also to set daily goals. Now, at first, this is easy. There is but a single goal: to find a job. But if your unemployment extends beyond 60 days or so, this single-minded focus will not sustain you and will likely begin to frustrate and depress you, ultimately making your job hunt that much more difficult.

We all know the *disadvantages* of unemployment. Why not start exploiting its significant *advantages* by setting a variety of goals for yourself each and every day?

First, in case you haven't figured out what advantages unemployment offers, here are the two most important:

➤ An interruption in your life that compels you to examine who you are and what you do.

➤ Time to examine your life and what you do.

Set your goals accordingly. Your number-one goal is always to find the job you want. If unemployment has dragged on more than six to eight weeks, however, set a secondary goal of learning as much as you can about yourself. Use some of your time to take the kind of self-inventory outlined in Chapter 2, "Where Do You Want to Be (and Should You Really Go There)?" Try to apply what you learn directly to your on-going job hunt. Perhaps what you discover will expand your search. Perhaps it will focus it more sharply.

If joblessness stretches beyond 12 weeks, persevere in your number-one goal, but consider also doing meaningful part-time unpaid volunteer work in your community—working with the disabled, working with the homeless, working with children, working with a local arts organization, and so on. Alternatively, at this point, you may consider embarking on a course of study you've always wanted to pursue. Perhaps the subject—taken at a community college or in a high school adult education program—will be directly relevant to your job hunt. Maybe you need to sharpen your computer skills, for example. Or perhaps it is simply something you always wanted to study: guided reading in the works of William Shakespeare, for example.

The point is that you should not punish yourself by putting your life on hold just because you're out of a job. Doing so will, at worst, drive you crazy and, at the very least, impede your job search. Use the time you have to find a job you want, to examine yourself, to maintain your usefulness within the community, and to expand your knowledge as well as self-knowledge.

Can Outplacement Place You?

Unemployment may offer two additional, more concrete opportunities. One is the chance to use your firm's outplacement service, if it has one, and the other is to write a different kind of cold letter. We'll get to the second opportunity in just a moment, but, first, let's look at outplacement.

Outplacement service is sometimes provided to terminated employees as part of a severance package. Aimed at helping the employee find a new job, the outplacement effort may range from a one-day seminar to an ongoing program, including counseling, the use of an office, want-ad monitoring, and so on.

Many larger firms provide outplacement assistance, either through in-house staff or by compensating you for calling on an independent outplacement service. The aid your firm may offer ranges from zilch, to a one-day job-hunting seminar, to "as long as it takes."

A good outplacement service will provide you with job leads as well as counseling and assistance with preparing résumés and cover letters. Use the outplacement counselor as another set of eyes and ears to help you identify job openings within your field or industry.

Winner

YOU'RE HIRED!

Maybe I should write *The Complete Idiot's Guide to Getting Fired the Way You Want.* You can often negotiate a pretty decent severance package, including one week's severance pay for every year you've been with the firm (this is an accepted standard), outplacement assistance, and maybe even some office space and a phone to help you conduct your job search. Don't sign any severance documents until you are convinced that you've received every severance benefit you can cajole or extort.

Case Study

When Karen Spain was laid off from her position as a customer service representative at a mid-sized regional retail chain, she blamed herself. The fact was that the company's sales had been slumping, revenue was down, and people were laid off. None of this had anything to do with her performance, but she felt like a failure. She was embarrassed and wanted to slink off, away from her fellow employees, alone.

But Karen thought about these feelings. They were highly unpleasant, and, because of that, she thought some more. She thought about how powerful an emotion guilt is. Then she continued to think: "Why should *I* feel guilty? The company—or, at least, somebody in the company—should be feeling this guilt."

Now, Karen didn't expect much more than two weeks' severance from the mid-sized firm she worked for. Certainly, the company had no outplacement program to offer. "What right do I have to expect special treatment?" Karen asked herself. But then she decided to answer herself: "I have every right to special treatment."

So she went to her boss and presented her case: how she had dedicated herself to her job for five years, how her colleagues admiringly called her "iron lady" because she was never out sick, how some of her customers had actually sent her notes and letters thanking her for going the extra mile to help them.

"I know what kind of financial pressures we've been under," she told her boss. "I don't expect my job back. But I do expect something more than two weeks' severance. I've spent a lot of time helping our customers. Now I think I'm entitled to some help."

Karen went on to list what she wanted. She secured five weeks' severance pay—arguing successfully that one week per year of service is standard and fair. She also secured three counseling and aid sessions with a leading outplacement firm, at her former employer's expense.

The point: Getting laid off does not instantly terminate your relationship with your employer. Use that relationship to negotiate the best severance package you can. And don't hesitate to exploit and manipulate your employer's feelings of guilt.

A Different Kind of Cold Letter

Unemployment gives you special license to write a unique kind of cold letter. It is, really, an appeal for help, and it can be quite effective.

Begin by identifying your peers within your industry. If you are an account executive for a widget supplier, identify other account executives for similar firms. Next, go one or two levels above your position: identify sales managers for widget suppliers. Combine these lists and send a cover letter and résumé to each of the names. Begin by making two points:

➤ Do not mention that you were laid off, just that you are job hunting in a "tight market." Don't lie. Do not, for example, refer to your most recent position as your "current" position. If you include a résumé, give the dates of employment in your last position—nothing more or less specific than this.

➤ You are not asking your correspondent for a job, but for a moment's attention.

➤ Add a third point: "In a tight market, all experts recommend getting as much exposure as possible." This not only helps explain what you are about, it unites you and your correspondent in acting not on what *you* want, but on what *experts* recommend. This is a persuasive motive for cooperation.

Continue with the rest of the letter as you would with the kinds of cold letters discussed in Chapter 14, "How to Heat Things Up with a Cold Letter or a Cold Call." Don't focus on *your* needs, but, rather, those of a potential employer. This chapter includes two illustrations of example cold letters. Each requests that the letter's recipient pass along the letter writer's name to other parties who may be in need of the letter writer's expertise.

But Lemme Explain...

If you look at employment advice books from a generation or so ago, you'll detect a universal theme of taboo concerning how to field questions about your having lost a previous job. Today, most employers are savvy enough to realize that lay offs and even firings are part of the *normal* life cycle of any worker. This does not mean that getting fired or laid off can go unexplained, but most employers are now grown-ups who've long ago lost their callow innocence. They understand and accept the facts of life.

You're Fired!

We're starting with the hard one. Remember, a *lay off* is due to circumstances such as corporate downsizing, a workforce reduction, and so on. Getting *fired* is due to what your employer perceives as your failure to perform satisfactorily or to your having committed some transgression. How do you deal with this when you are hunting for a new job?

An appeal to "fellow professionals" for job-search help. This letter is meant to stand on its own, without an accompanying résumé.

BRUCE A. KLARIT
65 FRANLIN ROAD
WORDLY, PA 50045
215-555-2222

August 18, 1995

Ms. Eleanor Glynn
Assistant Director of Human Resources
York Corporation
Highway 45
York, PA 50098

Dear Ms. Glynn:

As a fellow human resources professional, I am requesting your support in my current job search. I am not asking you for a job. I am asking that you take 60 seconds to read this letter.

In a tight job market, all the experts recommend getting as much exposure as possible. So I have been contacting other human resources professionals to ask a simple favor: if you are contacted by a recruiter, a friend, or business acquaintance who is looking for a human resources professional, I would be grateful if you would mention my availability and suggest where to contact me.

Allow me to fill you in on my background. I have operations and administrative experience in manufacturing and service environments and have performed successfully in small and mid-sized, union and non-union companies. My particular strengths are in:

* Employee and Labor Relations
* Compensation
* Benefits
* Safety
* Employment
* Training and Development
* Employee Involvement/TQM
* Administration
* HRIS

I am a generalist with a strong background in compensation and benefits.

I am seeking a generalist position in a small or mid-sized organization or a specialist (compensation and/or benefits) position in a larger organization, which might allow me to move into a generalist role later on. I am also open to a position in compensation, benefits, management, and software consulting.

With the staff reductions that have occurred in many human resources departments, those who remain are often working longer hours just to keep up with the required load. This situation has brought the cost-effective concept of outsourcing such activities as recruiting, compliance reviews, and training to management's attention. While I am conducting my job search, I am also available for temporary assignments.

Thank you for the minute of your time, and for your help. I will appreciate whatever support you can provide should you know, or learn, of an opportunity that you can refer me to. I hope I can return an appropriate favor in the future.

Sincerely,

Bruce A. Klarit

Be honest, but don't strip to your long johns. Never volunteer, let alone advertise, that you were fired. However, if you are asked, give a full and forthright reply that nevertheless puts the event in its best possible light: "I have to say that my termination was my fault. I had personal problems at the time, which are now completely resolved. But, at the time, I was frequently late. My supervisor—with whom I am still very much on speaking terms—was under orders to reduce the workforce in any case, and, quite honestly, my attendance record at the time gave him the reason he needed to let me go."

An appeal letter to accompany a résumé.

Bruce A. Klarit

65 Franklin Road
Wordly, PA 50045
555-555-5555

August 18, 1995

Mr. Thomas Jones
Human Resources Specialist
XYZ Industries
123 Main Street
Mortin's Mill, NJ 09101

Dear Mr. Jones:

During my years in human resources management and consulting, I periodically received calls from recruiters looking for qualified candidates for various search assignments. Given your position, I'd be surprised if you don't get calls like this. And that's why I'm writing.

In a tight job market, all the experts recommend getting as much exposure as possible. So I have been contacting a number of human resources professionals, not to request that they hire me, but just to ask a simple favor: If you're contacted by a recruiter, I'd be grateful if you'd mention my availability and perhaps suggest where to contact me.

Please understand, Mr. Jones, that I'm not asking for a reference. That would be presumptuous. But if you could just get my name in play, I'll carry the ball from there. I'm enclosing a copy of my resume just to give you a feel for my background and experience. I am a generalist who can also stand alone in compensation and or benefits. If you want more information for any reason, I'd be happy to chat with you.

Meanwhile, thanks for your help. I hope I can return an appropriate favor in the future.

Sincerely,

Bruce A. Klarit

Enclosure

Unless you can make a very persuasive case that you were fired unjustly, do not blame other people for what happened to you. Avoid abject wallowing in guilt and orgies of self-blame, but do take responsibility, *and* take the opportunity to demonstrate that you understand how you failed and, more importantly, how to avoid repeating the failure. Convey the impression that getting fired taught you about commitment and responsibility, taught you the "hard way," a way you'll never forget.

Jump Start Why should you be honest? There are two answers to this question. 1. Honesty is right, whereas lying is wrong. 2. Deceptive answers in an interview or on a job application are always grounds for summary dismissal a day later or ten years down the road. If you are caught in your lie, you will be fired. Again.

Finally, to the maximum degree possible, put your firing in context. Try to find out how many others were fired, laid off, or even left voluntarily during the period in which you were fired. After responding forthrightly to the interviewer's question, add: "I am one of twenty-six people who have left so far this year."

However you decide to deal with the issue of having been fired, make certain that you prepare your response in advance of any job interview. You can further prepare by contacting your former employer. This may be emotionally difficult for you, but you should ask that employer what he or she intends to say about you now. "I'm in the process of looking for a new job, and I'd like to see just how I stand with you. If you are asked as part of a pre- or post-employment reference check, how would you describe the circumstances of my leaving the company? Would you say that I was fired? Would you say that I was laid off? Would you say that I resigned? My problem is that, every time I tell a prospective employer about my termination, I blow another shot at a paycheck." In this way, maybe you can persuade your former employer to use less pejorative terminology in describing your parting of the ways.

Laid Off but Not Laid Out

A lay off—provided that it is a genuine lay off and not just a euphemism for firing—is easier to cope with when you are trying to get a new job. As with a firing, however, do not advertise the fact that you were laid off, but if you are asked, respond straightforwardly with a carefully prepared answer: "Sales had fallen 35 percent at Acme Widgets, and management cut back the work force by 20 percent. Our department was particularly hard hit: ten of us, one-third of the staff—were laid off." Of course, this answer assumes that you were not one of the *sales* staff—the department responsible for the decline of Acme.

Jump Start Do what you can to establish or reestablish good relations with your former employer. This is important— but maybe not quite as important as you may think. Only about 10 percent of successful job candidates actually get their references checked.

Your object is to attribute the loss of your job to external circumstances entirely removed from your performance.

You Can't Fire Me. I Quit!

Ideally, job changers secure a new job before quitting their current one. But it doesn't always work out that way. Sometimes an anticipated job falls through, and you are left to twist slowly, slowly in the wind. Or perhaps you quit with the intention of freelancing or pursuing an independent course, and that failed to pan out into a sustainable living. In some cases, you decide that you just cannot stand the job anymore, and you quit, plain and simple.

The problem with any of these scenarios, from the perspective of the target employer, is that they seem to reflect poor planning or the total absence of planning on your part. And if you cannot plan in your own professional life, how will you manage to plan the many activities and operations the prospective job requires?

Without fabrication, put the best possible face on resignation. From the perspective of the target employer, decent reasons to quit a job include:

➤ I had *earned* a hiatus to spend more time with my family.

➤ I wanted time to study in order to broaden and develop my skills.

➤ I felt that I owed it to myself to take time off in order to investigate possible new career directions.

"I'm a Consultant" and Other Lies You Can Use

If you did quit in order to strike out on your own as a freelancer, an independent contractor, or a consultant, and you enjoyed any tangible degree of success in this endeavor, then, by all means, use it as your reason for having left your previous employer and feature it prominently on your résumé and in interviews. (If you've been fired or laid off, and unemployment is shaping up to be a long haul, try to set up on your own, at least for the time being. This will not only help put beans on the table, it will also fill in the ever-widening gap in your résumé.)

If you set up as a consultant—or a freelancer or independent contractor—the best thing that can happen is for your business really to take off: You get good clients, and you make good money. Maybe you go into business for yourself—permanently. The second-best thing, however, is that your enterprise works out just well enough to get you a few clients on whom you can call as references when you approach your target employer. Job hunters habitually tell prospective employers that they are currently "consultants" or "contractors" or "freelancers" or "independents" or something equivalent. Unless you really do have some clients to show for it, however, your target employer is likely to interpret all these terms as synonyms for *long-term unemployment*.

The Least You Need to Know

➤ Prepare for a working world in which losing your job is not a remarkable catastrophe, but a feature of business as usual.

➤ You may be out of a job, but you're not out of work—for no work is more challenging and, ultimately, rewarding than finding a job.

➤ Use your "unemployed" time to take a self-inventory and to formulate a job-hunt strategy accordingly.

➤ Learn to set realistic and appropriately varied goals during your period of unemployment.

➤ Appeal to people in your field or industry for help with job leads.

➤ Don't advertise the fact that you were fired or laid off, but do prepare effective responses to the likely questions of prospective employers.

Chapter 17

In Limbo or Out the Door: How to Profit from Inaction and Rejection

The theme of this chapter is *not* "if you get turned down." That would be silly. There's no *if* about it. You *will* be turned down. Repeatedly.

I'm not saying this just to "harden" you, much less to discourage you, but to assure you that rejection is part of the process of getting the job you want. It's not unusual, and it does not mean you've lost or you've failed. Learn to use rejection, and learn to learn from rejection.

In fact, rejection is not the worst job hunt outcome. Indifference—the total absence of response—is even more disheartening. Even more frustrating, it is more difficult to learn from the lack of a response than it is from a negative response. Still, even indifference is a job-hunting experience, and experience—of *any* kind—is a most effective teacher.

You Will Meet with Indifference, and You Will Get Turned Down

If you are in an all-out job-hunting campaign and are sending out cold letters and résumés in addition to answering ads, you will become more familiar with indifference than with rejection. Most of your letters will go unanswered, while most of those that do elicit an answer, will elicit a negative answer. Depending on your field, you can expect a certain number of rejections following an interview, too. Some companies will even have the insensitivity and plain bad manners to follow up interviews with indifference, leaving you in limbo instead of delivering a yes or no.

I SEE...

Case Study

Statistics on indifference are hard to come by, probably because few employers are eager to admit to bad manners. But here's a bit of anecdotal evidence from a freelance editor I know.

Like most freelancers, even busy ones, Lana Best is always on the lookout for a "real job"—that is, a full-time position with an established employer. During the late 1980s, she sent out a wave of letters and résumés, receiving, she recalls, personal replies to the majority of them, including from those employers who were not interested in taking her inquiry to the interview stage. Much more recently, in the mid 1990s, she reports that no more than 15 percent of the employers she queried even bothered to reply—and the vast majority of those who replied did so in order to arrange an interview.

Lana's experience is corroborated by other war stories I've heard of late. Few employers respond to letters and résumés unless they're serious about you as a candidate.

First, Rescue Yourself

Getting rejected or getting nothing at all does not *necessarily* mean you have done something wrong. (Although maybe there are some things you could do better.) *Certainly*, these responses do not mean there is something wrong with you. Consider the following: If you are sending out cold letters, even cold letters backed with the kind of research we discussed in Chapter 14, "How to Heat Things Up with a Cold Letter or a Cold Call," you need to know that rejection and indifference are the responses to expect. Remember, nobody asked you to send that letter. When Acme Widgets sent you that colorful multipart mailing with a "one-time-only" offer ("exclusive to our special customers") for a deluxe widget at only $49.95, what did you do? The chances are only about 1.5 in a hundred that you wrote out a check and placed an order. It is 98.5 times more likely that you threw the offer in the trash, wholly or partly unread. And yet an entire direct-mail industry thrives on such odds, considering a 1.5 percent success rate to be just fine. Unless you have mass produced your cold letters and have sent them out shotgun fashion, without any research at all, you have reason to expect a better reply rate than 1.5 percent. But you still have to learn to live with a majority of turn-downs and no-replies.

If you were to draw up a list of the reasons why your cold letter or even your response to an ad met with either rejection or indifference, at the very, very bottom would be the employer's perception that you were somehow inadequate—didn't measure up to the job. Far higher on the list would be the following reasons:

➤ In the case of a cold letter, the employer has absolutely no openings remotely related to what you do.

➤ In the case of a response to an ad, the employer hired his son-in-law and placed the ad just to placate his investors.

➤ The position was filled from inside the company, but the job was posted in order to comply with company policy or equal opportunity employment regulations.

➤ The position was filled before you even read the ad.

➤ The position was advertised but never funded.

➤ The position was planned, advertised, but then the home office decided not to expand that division after all.

➤ The ad was a fake (see Chapter 11, "Trekking the Want Ad Jungle").

➤ The employer never read your cold letter, because it was intercepted by her secretary, who sent it to Human Resources.

➤ The sight or smell of an unsolicited résumé induced an uncontrollable reflex action in the employer's arm, forcing him spasmodically to throw your inquiry into the trash.

Even supposing that your cold letter or ad response is given genuine and careful consideration, the target employer has at least two good reasons to reject you:

➤ He or she is an idiot who doesn't know a good thing when he or she sees one; has a closet full of 8-track tape cartridges; turned down an opportunity to buy stock in a leading photocopier manufacturer back in 1967, remarking, "Who'll buy a machine like that, when they've got carbon paper?"

➤ You can't be all things to all people.

The point is, don't assume that rejection or indifference means you've failed to make the grade. Only if consistent patterns of rejection emerge, should you reconsider your strategy. Otherwise, do what the direct-mail marketers do: Keep on plugging.

Responding to No Response

In an ideal world, you'd get a response to your answer to an employer's ad within two weeks of mailing your résumé. In the case of cold letters, you should head your target off at the pass by closing the letter with an announcement of your intention to make a follow-up call: "I'll call next week to learn if a meeting can be arranged" or "May I call you on Monday?" So let's begin by talking about how to deal with an employer's failure to respond to your answer to his or her ad.

Why Should I Bother?

This is not a rhetorical question. You need to decide whether it is worth your while to follow up on indifference. If the ad was of great interest to you, then the employer's attention is worth fighting for. If, however, what it offered was of marginal appeal, take the demonstration of indifference as an omen and move on to other, more promising things. Then again, if you are one of those folks who is made sleepless by the thought of having let opportunity pass by, you should make the effort to follow up. When you're in the middle of a job hunt, just about nothing is worth losing sleep over.

Step 1: The Helpful Follow-Up Letter

If you are going to do something, begin with a follow-up letter, which you should send within two weeks of *mailing* your response to the want ad. If you sent the original response via expedited mail or overnight courier service, then mail your follow-up after 7 to 10 days.

Jump Start Reread the ad. Some employers are thoughtful enough to announce, "We will respond only to those résumés we are considering." If you receive no response from the firm that posted such an ad, assume a rejection—and a rejection that is probably not worth following up.

In writing the letter, you have a choice of taking a high-pressure indignant tone or a helpful one. The former may make you feel good, but the only action it is likely to elicit is a rejection letter. If you want the job, it is far more effective to help the employer act positively.

The single most helpful thing you can do is to put another copy of your résumé before him or her. Assume that the target employer is buried under an avalanche of paper. Sarah Abramowitz—hey, I'm talking to you—don't expect that the target has carefully filed your application under "A" and, once reminded, will sprint over to the filing cabinet, pull out your neatly prepared "jacket," and refresh his or her memory. The more likely scenario is that your letter and résumé are in a heap with the rest of them. Therefore, include a résumé with your follow-up.

Keep the letter simple and helpful:

> Dear Mr. Vogel:
>
> On May 12, I responded to your ad for an assistant book buyer.
>
> Because the position seems tailor-made to the qualifications I offer, and because I have not heard from you, I thought you would find it helpful to have another copy of my résumé for ready reference.
>
> I look forward to your response.
>
> Sincerely,
>
> Sarah Abramowitz

The keynote should be an offer of help rather than a reminder of the employer's *failure* to respond. This is not an occasion to play on the target's guilt or to arouse any negative emotions, which are likely to produce nothing more than additional avoidance behavior. An example follow-up letter is illustrated in this chapter.

> **Jump Start**
> Whatever you do, don't imply that you think the employer is incompetent, inconsiderate, or has too much to handle.

Step 2: The Gentle Wake-Up Call

If your follow-up offer of help produces no response within ten days of mailing it, you can either choose to assume that your application is a dead letter (or at least a dormant one) or you can make a follow-up call.

The first step is identifying the person to call, if that person's name is not given in the ad. If you are dealing with a large organization, call the main number and ask for the director of the department relevant to the target position. If the target organization is small, call and ask for the owner or president.

> **Pitfall**
> In the course of this book, I've advised breaking some "rules": avoid going through Human Resources, evade requests for your "salary requirements," and so on. But if an ad specifies "No calls, please," do not call—even as a follow up.

Here is a follow-up letter that offers help rather than a guilt-inducing plea for attention.

Alvin Darkwood

1632 Penrod Street
Monckton, MA 02233
555-555-5555
Fax: 555-444-4444

August 21, 1995

Mr. Dean Foxhall
Marketing Director
Holbrook Press
79 Garden Drive
Westminster, MA 02134

Dear Mr. Foxhall:

Could you use some help?

My five years of success in selling printing for a major East Coast book manufacturer thoroughly convinced me that I offer precisely the combination of skills and qualifications you need. That's why I responded so quickly to your ad in the August 9 *Times*.

I believe you will find it useful to have another copy of my resume to review, and I look forward to hearing from you.

Sincerely,

Alvin Darkwood

Do not begin by reminding the callee that he or she has replied neither to your original response to the ad nor to your follow-up letter. Instead, launch into the kind of attention-getting pitch discussed in Chapter 14—that is, begin by appealing to the target employer's self-interest:

"Hello, Mr. Perkins. This is John Burton. When I saw your ad in the *Times* earlier in the month, I thought, *This is an organization that can really use what I have to offer.* I just completed a major marketing campaign to roll out Acme's new line of executive widgets, and sales have already exceeded projections. This was no accident, and I learned a great deal from the experience, which, I believe, would interest you."

Only now do you allude to your original response. You need not refer to your subsequent follow-up. After all, your object is to get an interview, not to admonish the callee, let alone remind him that he has *twice* failed to respond to you. (To do so will get him thinking, *If he wrote me twice, and I did nothing, I must really not be interested.*)

> "That's why I rushed out to you a response to the September 2nd ad. If you've had the opportunity to review my résumé, I was hoping to learn if we could set up a meeting."

The language is important here. Nothing is said about the employer's failure to respond. Nor is the employer directly asked if he has read the résumé. Instead, use the call to bid for an interview. Just because the employer has not taken the next step doesn't mean *you* cannot take it. Note further that it is a good idea to avoid the word "interview"—which suggests a pro-forma employment procedure—and substitute the word "meeting" instead, which conveys a peer-to-peer relationship. If you are particularly bold, you can also substitute the phrase "learn *when* we might set up a meeting" for "learn *if* we could set up a meeting."

The callee may respond in several ways to the follow-up. He or she may:

Pitfall
Avoid offering an *excuse* for making a follow-up call. It will make you sound feckless and lame. The lamest of all excuses is—"I was just calling to see if my response to your ad had arrived—the mail service being what is, you know." If you cannot keep the follow-up call absolutely positive, do not make it at all.

➤ Set up a meeting.

➤ Retrieve your résumé and discuss it with you over the phone.

➤ Explain that he or she has been swamped and will get back to you in two weeks. (You will discover that this is the basic unit of time for purposes of blowing you off.)

➤ Retrieve your résumé, fall silent while he or she skims it, and then tell you that you're not what the company's looking for.

➤ Tell you that the position has been filled.

➤ Simply put you off indefinitely.

Rejection we will deal with shortly. If, however, you are "simply put off indefinitely," try—gently—to set a finite time limit: "I see. I'm going to have to make some decisions within the next ten days. Do you think you'll be ready to proceed to the next step by that time, and may I call you back, say, on the 15th?"

The techniques that work with following up want-ad responses should also be helpful in following up cold letters. If a cold letter does not result in a response after two weeks, consider making a call. The most likely reply you will get is that "no position is available at this time." If you are significantly interested in the target company, you can reply, "I understand. Yet I am very interested in Acme, and I believe what I have to offer will interest you for the future. Would it be possible to set up a strictly informational meeting? I promise I won't hit you up for a job you don't have to offer."

Of course, all of this assumes that your phone call gets through to someone with the power to hire you. And that, unfortunately, is no slight assumption. Even in smaller organizations, the gates are often guarded by assistants who pride themselves on insulating the boss from all intrusions—no matter how "helpful." In Chapter 14, we've already explored some tactics for getting by these guardians. You can also try disarming the guard with informality. Instead of announcing, "Hello. My name is Samuel Sherwood. I would like to speak to Ms. Hopkins," try, "Hi. This is Sam. Is she in?"

If the secretary is particularly efficient, he or she may also be the bearer of the bad tidings: "Oh, Mr. Sherwood. Ms. Hopkins asked me to tell you that she is sorry, but we have no openings at the present time."

You need not fold your tent, if you don't want to. Reply without disappointment: "I understand. Nevertheless, I'd still like to speak with her—get her advice on current trends in the industry. It would be very helpful to me. May I speak with her for just a moment?" If this gets you through, do make a sincere attempt to set up an informational interview.

Greeting Rejection

Pollyanna was the heroine of a popular early 20th-century American novel. Her name became a part of the language as a byword for someone afflicted (or blessed) with blind, blithe optimism. Should you follow the example of Pollyanna and greet rejection blindly and blithely?

No.

But it helps to view it optimistically. First of all, rejection is preferable to indifference—especially if the rejection reflects any thought given to your ad response or cold letter. Rejection also means that you have at least succeeded in commanding attention, however briefly. Even more valuable than this is the fact of contact. Every contact with a potential employer—even if that contact fails to produce a job—is valuable. You can parlay rejection into an informational interview—which may eventually lead to a position with this or another employer, and which, at the very least, will yield practice and exposure. You may even get a referral: "Is there anyone you would suggest that I contact?"

Step 1: Is It Worth Another Step?

As with following up on employer indifference, there is no hard and fast rule that obligates you to butt your head up against every brick wall you meet. Do follow every rejection with a thank-you letter, but pick and choose which rejections to follow up with a thank you *and* something more. Pursue those employers who really interest you, especially those in which you are willing to invest time laying groundwork for future employment.

Step 2: Thanks—No, Really: Thanks

To everyone who bothers to reject you—as opposed to simply ignoring you—send a thank-you note. To those in whom you are still particularly interested, send a thank you with a little extra (a "business" card, as illustrated next in this chapter):

Dear Ms. Kline:

Thanks for taking the time to review my résumé so carefully. Of course, I'm disappointed that there are no positions available at Acme just now. But needs and circumstances do change, and I hope that you will continue to keep me in mind, should you find yourself in need of a thoroughly seasoned marketing professional with a proven track record in special sales and premium promotions.

I know *I* shall keep Acme in mind.

Sincerely,

Thomas Morton

Bruce A. Klarit **Human Resources Professional** · EMPLOYEE RELATIONS · LABOR RELATIONS · COMEPNSATION · BENEFITS · SAFETY · EMPLOYEMNT · TRAINING AND DEVELOPMENT · EMPLOYEE INVOLVEMENT · ADMINISTRATION · HRIS **65 Franklin Road • Wordly, PA 50045 •** **215-555-2222**

A creative way to get extra mileage from all your communications is to include a personal business card with your note or letter. This one incorporates a mini-résumé along with the usual name, address, and phone information.

An interview that does not result in a job may result in two thank-you notes. The first is written immediately after the interview, before you receive the bad news. The second comes in response to the turndown. Express your gratitude and your continued interest in the company. Assume that you performed well at the interview; do not engage in apology or self-analysis:

> Dear Mr. Johnson:
>
> I'd be lying if I said I wasn't disappointed by the news. However, I greatly appreciate the time we spent in conversation, an experience that was very valuable to me.
>
> Needs and circumstances do change, and if Johnson Chemical should again find itself in need of a seasoned and innovative plastics engineer, I ask that you keep me in mind.
>
> Sincerely yours,
>
> Frances Borth

Step 3: Self-Review (Not Self-Torture)

Failure need never be final—not if you appreciate it for the great teacher that it is. If you are turned down for a job—especially after getting as far as the interview—recognize that you will be disappointed, go ahead and feel the disappointment, then move on to a self review. See "Woodshedding: Self-Review and Self-Revision" in Chapter 23, "Think You're DOA? Here's CPR for a "Dead" Job Search," for a discussion of the self-review process.

The Least You Need to Know

➤ Rejection is a normal and inevitable part of the job-hunt process, and you cannot avoid it.

➤ The overwhelming majority of reasons for rejection have little or nothing to do with you, your qualifications, or your personality.

➤ Selectively follow up in cases where you initially meet with indifference; use a letter, a phone call, or a combination of the two.

➤ All contact with a potential employer is valuable, even if initial contact results in rejection.

➤ Use rejection as an occasion for self-review, but not futile self-doubt and self-flagellation.

Chapter 18

Preparing for the Interview: How to Plan for Spontaneity

In This Chapter

➤ Dealing with fear

➤ Researching before the interview

➤ Preparing yourself for a winning interview

So you ride up the elevator with men in blue neckties and medium-starched white shirts, women in tastefully tailored jackets accented with a single stick pin over the heart. An aggressively jaunty version of "The Girl from Ipanema" churns from an unseen loud-speaker as the doors slide open, revealing the blond wood of a reception desk partially camouflaged by some leafy potted plants. A corporate logo stands in relief against the wall behind the receptionist, to whom you announce yourself, then take a seat on a chrome-frame chair upholstered in an irritatingly nubby material. Basically, the same people who were in the elevator are now deployed on other chairs in the room. Like you, they wait. The fluorescent lights hum faintly. There are magazines to look at, but no pattern in the dove-gray carpeting.

The decor is more than a trifle bland. It's meant to be reassuringly routine, a typical business environment, the product of a civilized society. The truth? It is the holding pen of an Arena of Mortal Combat. You are about to be interviewed for a job.

Jump Start Most supervisors and executives see interviewing job candidates as an unwelcome intrusion into their routine. Most are downright uncomfortable with the whole process. Want to score interview points? Prepare yourself with questions, comments, and issues *you* can raise during the interview, so that the interviewer doesn't have to do all the work. The easier you make it on him or her, the better the impression you'll create.

Friends, family, the colleagues to whom you have confided, they've all told you, "You've got nothing to worry about. You'll ace it. Why should you be nervous?" But an annoying voice from that movie you saw a few years ago—What was it? Oh yes, *The Fly*—keeps tugging at you from inside.

"Be afraid," it says. "Be very afraid."

And sitting in your suit, on the nubby upholstery, amid the hum of fluorescent lighting, you feel much the same sensations our ancestors felt hunkering down in a lightless cave, beyond which lay a world populated by saber-fanged beasts and driven by continual hunger. Your tongue is practically glued to the roof of your mouth. Your heart is beating in your throat, and your stomach's not far behind it.

"He's ready for you now," the receptionist says.

Be Afraid. Be Very Afraid.

Let's not try to gloss over the fear. True enough, you're not *really* a Neanderthal faced with wrestling a woolly mammoth (and I'm not paleontologist, either). I mean, nobody will walk away bloody. It's not really life-and-death here, right?

Right. You're not fighting for your life. But you *are* fighting for your livelihood.

The fact is, a lot does ride on a job interview. Maybe it's the difference between paying your rent and not. Maybe it's the difference between paying rent and owning a house. Maybe it's the difference between a job and a career, putting in time and drawing a check or turning time into self-fulfillment and satisfaction. Whatever this particular interview means, it's always about getting something you need or something you want. It's about making a difference in your life and the lives of those who depend on you.

No wonder you're scared. It's perfectly normal, and you don't have much of a choice. After all, why should you expect to be any different from, say, our greatest athletes, musicians, race-car drivers, and actors? Read the life stories of folks like these, and the common theme you'll find is fear. In fact, the great ones don't try to ignore that fear or "conquer" it. Instead, they learn to use it, to savor it, to harness it, so that it energizes them and sharpens their reflexes, senses, and sensibilities. How do they do this? By learning their craft. By careful, thorough preparation. If you know just how to take the hurdles, how to hit C above high C with the clarity of crystal, how to speed through to the groove at Indianapolis, how to find the heart and soul of Prince Hamlet, then fear becomes the very fuel that supercharges your performance.

Jump Start
Forty-seven out of every one hundred job interviews lead to a job.

Doing Your Homework

Now you've got this job-hunt adviser wagging a finger at you: "You can't just walk into a job hunt unprepared!" You take it to heart, dutifully sit yourself down, and start to think. Before long, the process of thought transforms itself into more worry and anxiety.

But preparing for the interview does *not* mean devoting yourself to unfocused worry about the interview. Instead, concentrate on performing eight actions:

➤ Learn about the organization to which you are applying.

➤ Learn about the role of your target position within the organization.

➤ Anticipate the organization's special needs, goals, and problems; then figure out how you can fulfill the needs, help achieve the goals, and solve the problems.

➤ Prepare a concise list of your *relevant* and *specific* accomplishments.

➤ Formulate your salary needs.

➤ Read Chapter 20, "To Give the Right Answers, Get the Right Questions." The chapter will help you prepare answers for the Ten Interview Questions You Should Always Expect and to prepare the Ten Interview Questions You Should Always Ask. Use the tear-out card at the front of the book for review.

➤ Prepare your Interview Kit, a professional scrapbook designed to help you and the interviewer create a productive interview.

In addition, give careful thought to grooming—check out the next chapter, "Dressing for the Interview"—and be sure that you've got the vital practical details straight. This means:

➤ Make certain that you know the exact time and place of the interview.

➤ Get clear directions to the interview, if you are at all unsure how to get there.

➤ Make certain that you know how long it will take to travel to the interview. Count on the traffic being a disaster and a taxi strike being in full swing. Allow extra time.

➤ Take along names and contact numbers. You should have the names and numbers of everyone you may have spoken to on the telephone in connection with the interview.

➤ If your interview invitation came by letter, be certain to bring that letter along.

Getting on the Inside from the Outside

Doubtless the Oracle at Delphi was a smart guy. He (she? it?) advised, "Know thyself." However, what will cut even more ice with the folks who are thinking about hiring you is how well you know *them*. The fact that you have taken the time to learn about their organization conveys the intensity of your interest and the high level of your initiative. It also suggests that yours will be a very smooth learning curve, that you will hit the ground running and be an immediate asset to the operation. Ideally, you should acquire information on a company before you answer an ad, write an application letter, or make a cold call. It will make any of these more effective. Then, in preparing for the interview, try to acquire information in greater depth.

Reliable Sources

If you're a fan of spy novels, you know all about moles. They're the secret agents you've got on the inside of an organization, burrowing into it and feeding you information. Do you need a trench-coated mole to break you into the job you want? Well, it couldn't hurt, but it is not likely that you will have access to such a source. Take heart. Even the CIA gets the bulk of its information from public sources. Does a federal spook want to find out about a foreign government? He or she starts out by reading its constitution, its laws, its newspapers, and its travel brochures. You can do much the same to learn about your target company. When Acme Widgets calls you for an interview, check out the following:

➤ Acme's annual report.

➤ Acme's catalogs, brochures, ads, and other published material.

➤ Material supplied by Acme's Public Relations and/or Customer Service departments.

Jump Start
Chapter 13, "Cruising the Infobahn," tells you how to use the Internet and other on-line resources to obtain company-specific information.

➤ Journals and newsletter articles devoted to Acme.

➤ Books (available in the public library) that mention Acme.

➤ On-line sources: Check out the Internet and commercial on-line providers. Does Acme maintain its own on-line BBS?

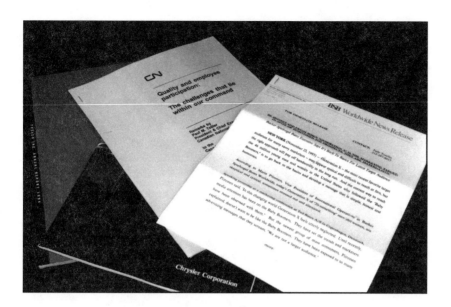

Some examples of the corporate "insider" information available for the asking. Annual reports, press releases, and CEO speeches are rich sources.

What Do I Need to Know?

It is true that a job interview should be a two-way street. The interviewer wants to find out about you, and you want to find out about the company. However, the more you know (and *show* you know) going in, the more successful the interview is likely to be. At minimum, walk into the interview knowing something about:

➤ The business of the company: What does it do or make?

➤ The scope of the company: How large? Where does it do business?

➤ The competition: Who are they, and what is the target company's standing among them?

This is the minimum. To go the extra mile, read "Scoping Out What the Organization Needs" later in this chapter.

Hey, Get a Job Description

Obtaining a job description would seem to be almost too elementary a research step even to mention. Surprisingly, however, many applicants neglect to ask for such a description. The solution to this is simple: Always ask for a full job description when a company calls to schedule an interview.

A tougher problem is the yet more surprising fact that many organizations fail to prepare this very basic document. In this case, you'll have to do your best to assemble a description for yourself.

A revealing document about a software firm downloaded from an electronic bulletin board system (BBS).

```
--------------------------------------------------------------
STACKER NOTE                          STACKER NOTE
STAC ACQUIRES NOVELL NETWORK BACKUP AND DISASTER RECOVERY
PRODUCT
     Purchase of Rememory and Crossware Backup Business Adds Data
     Protection to Stac Family of Software Products for Managing and
                         Accessing Information

STAC FAX  1135 (03-27-1995)
--------------------------------------------------------------
```

NETWORLD + INTEROP, Las Vegas, Nev., March 27, 1995 - Stac
Electronics (NASDAQ:STAC), today announced the acquisition of
REMSERVE, the popular Novell network backup, archiving and data
recovery software, developed by Crossware Development and
marketed by Rememory Corporation.

As part of the purchase, Michael W. Harris, president of Costa
Mesa, Calif.-based Rememory, will serve as director of Stac's new
Backup Product Group, and John Matze, founder of San Diego-based
Crossware will serve as principal architect for the new Stac
product group. Harris, Matze and their combined team have
relocated to Stac's San Diego corporate headquarters from which
the new operation will be based. The amount and terms of the
acquisition were not disclosed.

Gary Clow, Stac chairman and chief executive officer, said
acquiring the assets of the two companies' backup software
business adds crucial data protection software to Stac's plan for
building a diversified family of products for managing, accessing
and protecting information assets. Stac is best known for its
award-winning ReachOut remote access program, and its line of
Stacker data compression products that can significantly increase
the storage capacity of Windows, DOS, Macintosh and OS/2
computers.

"Stac's new REMSERVE product was one of the first backup NLM's to
be NetWare 4.1 certified and is now ideally positioned to service
the growing number of companies and departmental groups that are
utilizing the power of our newly released version of NetWare,"
said Toby Corey, vice president of marketing for Novell's NetWare
Products Division.

REMSERVE is a Novell-certified backup and data recovery NetWare
Loadable Module (NLM). Fully compliant with Novell Storage

Tactfully pump the employer for information. You are called for an interview. You prudently ask for a job description. "We don't have one," comes the reply. You say, "Well, I certainly understand what a widget wonker does in most corporate environments, but is there anything special and specific I should know about the position at Acme Widgets? The information will help me prepare some specific answers for the interview and give you a better idea of just who I am and how I can meet your needs."

Tap the sources mentioned in "Reliable Sources" to construct a generic description of the position.

Contact people who do the job in question—but *not* anyone who works for the target company. If you are applying for the position of widget wonker, call friends and friends of friends who already are widget wonkers. If you don't know any, call a widget company and ask to speak to a widget wonker. Introduce yourself, explain your situation, and ask for help. Does this sound difficult? The fact is that most people welcome the opportunity to be helpful.

So much for what to do in the absence of a formal job description. If you are more fortunate, and an official job description is available, seize it and devour it, not just to make a mental list of the duties and responsibilities involved, but to determine just how the position fits into the operation of the organization.

I SEE...

Case Study

You are about to be interviewed for the position of Production Coordinator for a book publisher. According to the job description, one of the responsibilities of the position is to "traffic work flow." Another function is to "track production schedules." Sounds harmless enough. But train yourself to consider the real-life *organizational* implications of such functions. You may not be the party responsible for assigning workload or setting schedules, but, as one who "traffics" and "tracks," you will be in an ideal position to monitor the progress of projects and to facilitate the movement of the work. To your co-workers—even your supervisors—you will be the living embodiment of The Schedule, a combination of departmental ramrod and collective conscience. Be prepared, therefore, to highlight to the interviewer your skills as a manager, a diplomat, and an all-around "people person": "I'm not only well organized, I take a proactive approach. I work to help people stay on schedule and deliver on time, making certain that Editorial can deliver what Design needs when Design is ready for it."

Scoping Out What the Organization Needs

Wouldn't it be wonderful if you could walk into the interview with an insider's knowledge of the needs, goals, and problems *specific to* the organization? Obviously, if you have a reliable source of information within the company, use it. Ask him or her to identify for you just what the organization requires. Trouble is, you can't count on having a friend on the inside, let alone somebody in a position to give you truly useful information. Where else can you turn? Consult the same sources you used for finding general information about the organization, but filter these for the specifics concerning needs, goals, and problems. Here are the key sources to tap:

➤ Obtain the organization's annual report, brochures, and other published material.

➤ Talk to people in the industry. It's a good bet that the needs, goals, and problems of one company in a given industry will be shared by others in the same industry.

➤ Scan the most recent three months' worth of journals and newsletters devoted to the industry.

➤ Go to the public library and look for books about the industry.

Your objective is to identify the following:

➤ Company issues: Do your sources emphasize certain themes or issues as critical to the firm?

➤ Industry issues: Do your sources emphasize certain themes or issues as critical to the industry as a whole?

➤ Relevant current events: What's going on in the world, nation, community, or neighborhood that affects the company or the industry?

Winner

Everybody's got an opinion. Read widely, not only in publications directly relevant to your industry, but also in general-interest newspapers and magazines. Work on focusing your opinions into well-informed statements about trends, issues, problems, and opportunities.

There is another, even more direct approach. In his best-selling book, *What Color Is Your Parachute?*, career advisor Richard Nelson Bolles suggests obtaining an informational interview with someone in an organization that appeals to you. This isn't a job interview, but only an information-gathering exercise. You set up the interview by identifying a supervisor or manager in an area relevant to your interests, you contact that person, and you ask to speak to him about general career prospects in the industry.

This is a useful approach to information gathering—*if* you have the time to invest in it and *if* you can find a supervisor or manager with the time and inclination to speak with you (in fact, many *are* happy to help). Here's a more direct alternative:

You have sent your résumé to Acme Widgets. Two weeks later, you get a phone call. "Ms. Prynne would like to see you," says the secretary.

You could reply with, "That's great! I'll be there!" Or, more productively, you could ask to speak with Ms. Prynne, on the telephone, now. If she is available, tell her how much you look forward to speaking with her on Thursday, then continue, "Before we talk, are there any specific company goals or needs or problems you would like me to address at the interview?"

Straightforward? Absolutely. And if Ms. Prynne is not available at the moment, obtain her phone number and call her back later.

Keeping Score

Chances are, you've succeeded in preparing an effective résumé. (That's why you've been called for an interview!) As we hammered at in Part 3, "A Résumé Handbook," an effective résumé includes listings of your *specific* accomplishments. Review these accomplishments before the interview, and mentally highlight the ones most relevant to the position in question and, even more importantly, to whatever goals, needs, and problems you have managed to identify as being of concern to the organization.

If—by some wild chance—you have secured an interview without having inventoried your achievements on a résumé, prepare a list now. If you're stuck, here is an exercise that should help:

Think of a job-related problem you had to face within the past two or three years. Jot it down.

Next, describe, in step-by-step fashion, your solution to the problem.

Finally, assess the results of your solution, stating those results in terms of money earned or saved for the company.

Now, just to keep things interesting, let's interject a disturbing thought. What if the accomplishments you think are so great don't mean a thing to the interviewer? It could happen, but, fortunately, there is a way to insure against it. The real danger is not so much failing to be an impressive candidate, it's failing to be *heard*. Customer service authority Michael Ramundo advises people who want to be *heard* by business to *speak the language of business*. That language is nothing more than dollars. So, don't get ready to tell an interviewer that one of your great accomplishments was redesigning your present firm's shipping labels. Instead, be prepared to say, "My redesign of our shipping labels reduced shipping errors by 12 percent last year, which meant a savings of $23,000." Or, "Last quarter, I sold 10 percent over my target. That meant another $12,500 added to our gross."

> **Jump Start**
>
> It's 9:30 on Tuesday morning. You are called for an interview at 11:30. What do you do? Arrive as early as possible. Survey the lobby for annual reports, monthly newsletters, product catalogs, and so on. If you don't see anything on the end tables and brochure racks, ask the receptionist. Tell him or her that you are early and say, "Please don't announce me yet." Start reading.

These items—CEO speeches and an annual report—were available in corporate lobbies. They're useful for emergency interview cramming.

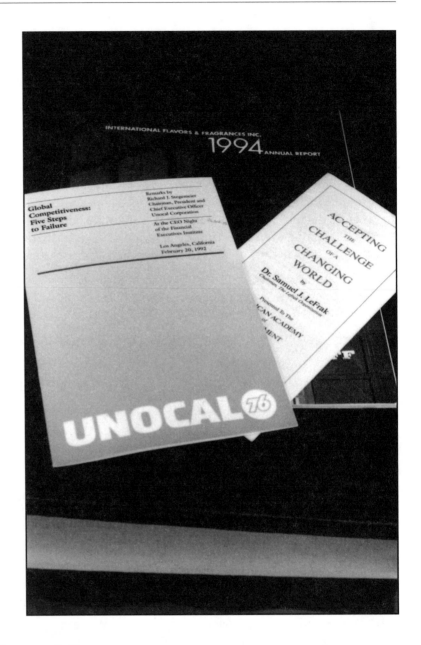

How Much Is Enough?

As we will see in Chapter 22, "Negotiating Salary and Other Matters," you should try never to be the first one to mention a salary figure in an interview. (If asked, "What kind of salary are you looking for?" reply, "It's a position you created. You must have some figure in mind.") The fact is, he who mentions a figure first, loses at the last. Nevertheless, you must go into the interview knowing the minimum you need. You might also want to know how much you would, ideally, like to make. You can review the guidelines for determining these figures at the end of Chapter 2, "Where Do You Want to Be (and Should You Really Go There)?"

Boilerplate Questions

The world of work offers dazzling variety, but, to paraphrase the old French saying, the more interviews change, the more they remain the same. You can pretty much count on always being asked certain stand-by questions. You will find these—and suggestions for answering them—in Chapter 20, "To Give the Right Answers, Get the Right Questions." By the same token, there are certain questions *you* should always *ask* at an interview, regardless of the target job. These, too, are covered in Chapter 20. The tear-out card at the front of this book provides a handy review of the boilerplate Q&A.

Your Old Kit Bag

Now that we're about at the end of the chapter, let me point you back to something I said near the beginning: *Employers hate interviews*. Not only are they usually interruptions in a busy day, but, more importantly, they put the interviewer on the spot. *You* might have prepared carefully for the interview, but rarely has the interviewer done *his* homework, and now he must come up with something to talk about with you. It is a pain, and it is a strain. Remember, it is your prime objective to appear to your prospective employer as part of the solution rather than just another part of the problem. Right off the bat, you can supply a solution to a problem.

Problem: The interviewer wants to get through the interview.

Solution: You.

Prepare for a proactive interview not only by coming armed with questions and comments (don't make the poor interviewer do all the work), but also by furnishing a handy prop—the Interview Kit.

> **Jump Start**
> Somewhere in the back of every prospective employer's head is a cliché that just won't stop buzzing around as she or he looks into your eyes: *You're either part of the solution or you're part of the problem.* To the degree that you unmistakably appear as part of the solution, you maximize your odds of landing the job.

Winner

If what you do—or want to do—for a living involves creating ads, artwork, and so on, you will need more than an Interview Kit. Prepare a full-scale portfolio of your work. These days, such a portfolio might even be put on diskette and presented using a color laptop computer you bring to the interview.

This is a kind of scrapbook, which may contain such items as an additional three copies of your résumé, letters of commendation, awards, copies of (nonproprietary and nonclassified) business presentations you have made, photos of equipment you have worked with, and so on.

You control the Interview Kit. Although you may give the interviewer one of the copies of your résumé, the Interview Kit itself stays in your hands. You do not give it over to the interviewer, but merely let him or her look. The idea to convey is that the work it contains is yours, it is of value, and it most definitely is not up for grabs. The Interview Kit functions quite literally as a conversation piece—something to look at and something to spark comment. It is a visual aid for selling yourself and for underscoring how your accomplishments can be applied to your prospective employer's needs, goals, and problems.

The Least You Need to Know

➤ Research the prospective employer and position, concentrating on how to show that you are the solution to the employer's problems.

➤ Inventory your skills and achievements, with special emphasis on specific accomplishments, problems solved, profits made, and money saved (speak the language of business: dollars).

➤ Establish your salary needs (especially a salary floor) *before* you go into the interview. Avoid being the first to mention a figure.

➤ Use the tear-out card in this book to help you anticipate interview questions.

➤ Prepare an effective Interview Kit to help you as well as the interviewer have a more productive interview.

Chapter 19

Dressing for the Interview

In This Chapter

➤ Dressing "appropriately"

➤ Savvy grooming strategies: learning the code

➤ Self expression versus conformity to the "mainstream"

➤ Wardrobe guide for men and women

"Dress for success" has been a concept both celebrated and reviled since it was first introduced during the 1970s by John Molloy in his series of books on the subject. Most of us are simultaneously fascinated and repelled by the notion that what we wear has such a powerful influence on how people respond to us. Henry David Thoreau warned us to "beware of all enterprises requiring new clothes," and while Thoreau was a great natural-ist, a wonderful writer, and a stimulating philosopher, it is well to remember that he held only one steady job (running his father's pencil factory for a year) and that he lived much of his life on money borrowed from his friend Ralph Waldo Emerson (who, judging from 19th-century photographs, was always well dressed).

Dressing "right" is no magical open sesame to the job you want. However, poor, indiffer-ent, or inappropriate grooming will often get you screened out of the job you want. Even if you resist the notion of "dressing for success," you can't afford to make mistakes that will sabotage you before you've even had your shot at letting the employer know who you are and what you can do.

Dress Code

The single fact that fashions change is enough to make it impossible to prescribe a foolproof interview outfit. But there's more than a single fact involved. Winning interview dress is a combination of what makes you comfortable, what expresses how you feel about yourself, and what is appropriate to the field or industry in which you are seeking employment.

Buzz Word

Comfortable. Of course, we all know what that word means. Or do we? A T-shirt and jeans may make you very comfortable at home, but not when you are trying to sell yourself as a candidate for a job in investment banking. Comfort is compounded of physical, psychological, social, and situation-specific factors. Looked at this way, *comfortable* dress is winning dress for any interview situation.

I suppose that just about all of us feel we should be judged for "who we are," not for what we wear. Certainly, this is what we expect from our spouses, our friends, and our family. But they have *years* to get to know us for ourselves. The person interviewing you has a matter of minutes. It's not that you've got to wow 'em with your clothes—in fact, that's a risky strategy—but that you must convey the message that you've been able to get yourself together in a professional manner. The impact of succeeding in this is subtle, quietly suggesting efficiency, self-control, and an appropriate pride in yourself. The impact of failing in this, however, is dramatic, triggering the following thought in the mind of the interviewer: "If she can't put herself together professionally, what will she be able to put together on the job?"

There are certain rudimentary and general rules for "putting yourself together," which I'll discuss in a moment. But a savvy grooming strategy can provide a remarkably specific advantage at an interview. Many career fields and professions have more-or-less unspoken dress codes. To the degree that you can demonstrate your understanding of the code, you are likely to advance in the estimation of the interviewer—before you even utter a word. In a logical world, you would be hired strictly on the perception that you can do the job. In the real world—which is governed as much by impulse and emotion as it is by logic—your being hired is based, in no small part, on the employer's perception that you will "fit in." The business, after all, is not only a business, but also an organization, a kind of club. You're either in or out. Approach the club looking like you are already a member, and you begin the interview with a significant head start.

There are any number of dress-for-success books on the market, including N. J. Golden's *Dress Right for Business,* Anne Fenner and Sandi Bruns's *Dress Smart,* and Pamela R. Satron's *Dressing Smart.* The problem is that few of these explore the dress codes of specific industries, let alone how those dress codes may be influenced by regional preferences and individual corporate cultures. So how can you crack the code? It's not a well-kept secret. In fact, the "code" is on exhibit everyday, for everyone to see. Pay a visit to the target company, and observe. If the firm publishes a newsletter or other literature illustrated with photographs, look at these. Plan your interview wardrobe accordingly.

Pitfall
Don't visit on Friday. In many firms, Friday is "jeans day" or "casual day," and does not reflect the prevailing dress code.

This Above All: Be Sharp and Clean

Above and beyond getting in sync with "the code," make certain that whatever you wear is sharp and clean. Suits—for men and women—should be dry-cleaned immediately prior to the interview. Shirts and blouses should be freshly laundered. The clothes you wear need not be brand-new, but they must be in impeccable repair.

Look to your personal hygiene as well. Shower or bathe, of course, and be certain to use deodorant. However, avoid the excessive use of perfume, cologne, or after-shave. This actually makes some people ill by provoking a mild to severe allergic reaction. More important, using too much perfume, cologne, or after-shave conveys the subtle psychological message that you are trying to "cover up" something. The olfactory senses are emotionally charged and work at a primal level. Those who emanate an excessive scent may be perceived as annoying, intrusive, or at least insensitive and inconsiderate. On the other hand, the sparing use of your favorite perfume, cologne, or after-shave can create a pleasant and inviting aura. Just make certain that the scent is *barely* perceptible.

Bad breath is a turnoff in any situation. It's usually best not to eat just before an interview, and, certainly, you should avoid garlic, onions, liquor, and the like. Brush your teeth or use mouthwash before the interview, if possible. A breath mint is okay—just make sure that you're not sucking or chomping it during the interview!

Hair length, especially for men, was a highly charged issue during the 1960s and 1970s. It is less so now, but it is still a factor. Very long hair on men is still perceived in many quarters as a token of rebellion or, at least, a hang-loose kind of sloppiness. Nowadays, however, excessively *short* hair may connote a different, more sinister kind of rebellion. If you cut your hair very short, you risk being identified with ultra-conservative values or, worse, with the "skinhead" philosophy of intolerance.

Jump Start
What about self-expression? Personally, I'm all for it. But if your hair shouts for attention, it's going to be that much harder for the interviewer to hear *you*.

Women enjoy greater "political" latitude so far as hair length is concerned, but it is also true that even a relatively worldly and sophisticated interviewer (male or female) may be put off by hairstyles that appear "mannish."

Certain "creative" industries—fashion, the arts, magazine work, and so on—invite a liberal array of hair fashions for men as well as women. It pays to get in tune with the codes that prevail in the industry.

By law, no employer may discriminate in hiring on the basis of age, gender, or race. However, no law can regulate the emotions, including humanity's uglier sentiments. Despite a wider acceptance—indeed, in some companies, the positive embrace—of ethnic and cultural diversity in the workplace, you may want to reconsider "ethnic" hairstyles that represent significant departures from what is generally perceived as the cultural mainstream.

Just as it is illegal to discriminate on the basis of race or ethnicity, it is also unlawful to do so on the basis of age. Yet employers continue to place a premium on youth or, at least, the appearance of youthful vigor. Veteran TV game show host Bob Barker created a mild sensation in the early 1990s when he stopped dyeing his silver-gray hair. You will have to decide for yourself whether gray hair is an advantage—conveying your well-deserved reputation for wisdom—or a disadvantage, suggesting that you are older than your years.

If you have a mustache or beard, be sure that they are neatly trimmed.

Where Safety Ends and Panache Begins

Please note that the observations in the preceding section—particularly the last two paragraphs—are not meant as prescriptions for your appearance at an interview and even less as judgments of value. They are, however, offered as a barometer reflecting the climate currently found in most corporate cultures. The observations are intended to set a *safe*, even conservative, course for your appearance at an interview. Because the fact is, if you do want a single-sentence prescription for interview grooming, the safest look, for men and women, is conservative and traditional.

Accept this as the base on which you can build a more individual look. But heed this important exception to the conservative concept. Dress appropriately for the position you seek, not the position you currently have. If you are an office assistant accustomed to wearing a sport jacket, shirt and tie, and jeans, invest in the best conservative-cut suit you can afford when you interview for the position of assistant account executive. If you are a secretary now, strive not to look like one at an interview for an entry-level executive position. Depending on your personality, dressing "above your station" may require a deep breath and a plunge into the credit card account. But, then, nobody ever said a job interview should be comfortable or that earning a living should be a walk in the park.

In the balance of this chapter, I'm going to run down the items of interview attire for men and for women. These are guidelines and points of reference intended simultaneously to spark your creativity and to curb any tendency to excess.

> **Jump Start**
> Fashion is communication. Set clear goals for what you want to communicate to the interviewer. Let those communication goals guide your fashion choices.

Gentlemen, Suit Up!

Dress to convey an impression of reliability and attention to detail. You do not want any single article of your attire to become the subject of undue attention or discussion. (*You*, not your outfit, should be the subject of attention and discussion.) Two general rules:

Dark colors convey authority. Dark blue conveys the greatest degree of authority—which explains the color of a police officer's uniform. Avoid black, however, unless you are applying at a funeral home.

Wear natural fabrics. Synthetics tend to have a sheen and texture that makes them look cheap. Generally, they don't "drape" as attractively as natural fibers. They also tend to retain body odors stubbornly. On a more subtle level, it is a mistake to associate yourself with anything "synthetic," which implies phoniness or a lack of depth.

Suit Yourself

Remember, dark colors convey authority—though the most extreme dark color, black, is more appropriate to an undertaker than a job hunter. Solids and subtle patterns are fine; muted, narrow pin stripes, for better or worse, always smack of conservative finance and politics. The style is often called "banker stripes," and some interviewers will be impressed, while others mildly intimidated. Avoid checked patterns, which (in the minds of many) conjure up images of a more or less disreputable used-car salesperson.

Your choice of fabric is simple: 100 percent wool. If you are interviewing in the summer, select a

> **Jump Start**
> New York City maintains a small army of "traffic agents," men and women whose principal and entirely unenviable duty is to write parking tickets in the jam-packed streets of that town. Originally, they were uniformed entirely in brown. As comic Rodney Dangerfield might have put it, they didn't get no respect. The city soon started dressing them in blue.

summer-weight wool suit rather than a light-colored linen or linen-blend suit, which tends to wrinkle quickly.

Monitor prevailing fashions. A decade or two ago, three-piece suits were *the* business uniform. For the past several years, two-piece suits have predominated, and you will probably be perceived as pretentious or even over-the-hill if you wear a three-piece suit to an interview. This, of course, could change.

Smart European cuts are fine *if* you are interviewing in a "young" industry and *if* you have the slender build such a cut flatters. Generally, you are safest with a more generous—and conservative—American cut.

The Shirt on Your Back

The shirt *must* be long-sleeved. French cuffs, with *simple* cuff links, convey an extra measure of attention to detail. The shirt should be white or very pale blue—not patterned and not striped. Monograms can work for you or against you. Some interviewers may interpret the presence of a monogram as a mark of individualism, prosperity, and pride in appearance, while others will see in it nothing more than ostentation, even a faint hint of vulgarity. The safest course is to avoid monogrammed shirts.

As with the suit, natural fabrics are most desirable for the shirt. Wear a closely stitched, all-cotton shirt, *professionally* laundered and medium (crisply) starched. Polyester blends may wrinkle less readily than 100 percent cotton, but, ultimately, they just don't look as good, and they don't absorb perspiration as effectively.

Fit to Be Tied

Some experts say that the necktie is the first article of clothing noticed when you shake hands with the interviewer. Others say that the shoes make the first visual impression. Whether in first or second place, the tie is important. It can make an expensive suit look cheap, or it can significantly upgrade the impression made by otherwise modest attire.

Choice of fabric is a no-brainer here: pure, 100 percent silk. Avoid linen, which wrinkles instantly, and avoid wool, which is too casual. Synthetics look cheap and never knot beautifully.

If you are wearing a white or very pale blue shirt, coordinating your tie with your shirt presents no challenge. The tie should complement the suit, but not match it. If your suit is patterned, be careful not to select a tie that does mortal combat with the suit pattern. Tie widths vary with changing fashion, but, in relation to the suit, a safe rule of thumb is that the width of the tie should approximate the width of the lapels.

Any of the traditional patterns are acceptable, including solids, foulards, stripes, and muted paisley prints. Executives have long favored broad, solid stripes—the so-called "power stripes." However, always shun polka dots, pictures (animals, the heads of hunting dogs, naked ladies, and so forth), sporting images (golf clubs, polo mallets), and designer logos. Many interviewers find the latter particularly offensive, feeling that they suggest insecurity—as if you need a designer's imprimatur to certify your good taste.

Tie the tie carefully. For some years now, fashion has favored a small, tight knot. The tied necktie should not extend below your trouser belt.

Pitfall
It's just as well that few of us anymore know how to tie a bow tie, because you should never wear one to an interview. Clip-on ties? Don't even *think* of wearing them.

Well Shod

As I just noted, it's a toss-up as to whether neckties or shoes make the first impression when you first meet the interviewer. Wear black or brown leather. Avoid other colors and materials. Make certain that your shoes are well polished. A British chemical engineer I know once remarked to me about what he called the American businessman's obsession with highly polished shoes. "American executives always wear these *bright, blank* shoes," was the way he put it. An American *obsession*? All the more reason to ensure that your shoes are polished. Also, look to your heels. These should be even and relatively unworn. The expression "he's well-heeled" entered into the language long ago as a synonym for prosperity.

Err well toward conservatism in choosing shoe style. Managers tend toward lace-up wing tips, while accountant types seem to favor tasseled slip-on dress shoes. Those in "creative" positions—such as advertising art directors—often wear expensive Italian loafer styles. If you feel wing tips are too heavy, go with a conservative slip-on dress shoe. Do not wear casual shoes to an interview.

Sock It to 'Em

These are especially important if you choose a slip-on shoe with a low vamp, but in all cases, the color of the socks should complement the suit. Usually, this means a choice of blue, black, dark gray, or dark brown. Make certain that your socks are long enough to permit you to cross your legs without showing hairy bare skin, and be sure that they've got enough elasticity to keep them from sliding down your leg or bunching up.

A Brief on the Briefcase

A simple and slim attaché is the best choice. If it is appropriate to your profession, carry a neat portfolio. Avoid anything that suggests a salesperson's clunky sample case. Also ensure that the clasps work correctly—holding the briefcase closed when they're supposed to, and opening at your will and without a struggle.

Complete with the Accessories

Carry a plain white cotton or linen handkerchief. Wipe your hands on it before your interview in order to avoid a clammy handshake. A decorative pocket square tucked (not folded) into your suit pocket can be a nice accent, but avoid the matching tie-and-pocket-square look, which went out with the polyester look, exposed stitching, the OPEC oil embargo, and other unpleasant fixtures of the 1970s.

Your leather belt should match or complement your shoes, and the buckle should be simple, small, and entirely unobtrusive. Avoid the cavalry look (Union *or* Confederate) in buckles, and steer clear of biker styles as well.

Suspenders (or "braces") became very popular as tokens of corporate power in the late 1980s and early 1990s. They are seen far less frequently nowadays, and many reviewers may find them pretentious.

Beware of Jewelry

Simple cuff links and a wedding band (if you're married) are always safe jewelry choices for men. Neck chains, stick pins, bracelets, and pinky rings are 100 percent taboo. In most industries, earrings are a medicine that's too strong for interviewers. If you are passionate about your class or fraternity ring, wear it; however, if you feel comfortable without it, it is safest to leave it at home.

Topcoat—Only If You're Really Cold

If weather permits, avoid wearing a topcoat. It is likely to get in the way. (What if there's no place to hang it?) But there's no reason for you to freeze to death, either. Wear beige, black, gray, or blue. Wool—in camel hair or cashmere—is most attractive and most impressive.

For the Women: More Choices (and Higher Prices)

Even in the conservative realm of interview attire, women have a greater range of choices than men. They are also under greater economic pressure to invest in current fashions. A man can easily get away with a two- or three-year-old suit (provided that it is in impeccable repair) at an interview. A woman cannot. Sexism? Without doubt. But that's the way it is.

Suit du Jour

In most interview situations, a suit is appropriate. However, the suit need not be an imitation of a man's wardrobe, drab and gray. (Nevertheless, a charcoal gray suit with a white blouse remains the safest, solidest interview combination.) Solids, pinstripes, and muted plaids in a variety of colors are all acceptable. Whereas men are cautioned to favor all-natural fabrics, women's wool or linen suits tend to wrinkle readily. Consider natural-synthetic blends to combat wrinkling. In warm weather, a cotton-polyester combination works well. If you are committed to an all-natural fabric, go with wool.

Skirt length varies from season to season. You and the interviewer will be most comfortable if you opt for a rather more conservative length than you might wear on a social occasion or even in an *everyday* business situation. A rule of thumb here is actually a rule of fingers: If your skirt is above your fingertips when you hang your arms comfortably at your sides, the skirt is too short for business interview purposes.

About the Blouse

Long-sleeve blouses are most desirable. Showing a quarter to a half inch of cuff beyond your jacket sleeve suggests professionalism and authority. Short-sleeve blouses are not a good idea, and sleeveless blouses are absolutely to be avoided.

For blouses, stay with natural fabrics, preferably cotton or silk. Unlike men, women need not restrict themselves to white or pale blue; however, be aware that, even for women, these are the most universally accepted colors in the business world. Pearl gray and the deeper shades of blue are also good color choices.

Keep it simple. A front-tie bow is always appropriate. You might consider a blouse that buttons up to the collar rather too severe, but it works great in more conservative companies or industries.

The Neckwear Accent

A beautiful scarf can add a dramatic accent to the interview wardrobe. Avoid the matching scarf-and-blouse look, however, which many regard as mechanical and even a bit tacky. Pure silk in a color and pattern that complement your suit is most desirable. Avoid large polka dots (though small ones are fine).

Pitfall
While women may wear shoes and belts made in a wider variety of materials than such articles for men, exercise caution here. Snake skin, alligator, and lizard shoes and belts may be attractive, but an interviewer who happens to be sensitive to environmental issues will be offended if you wear the skin of endangered or near-endangered animal species.

Jump Start
Whenever I stay at a hotel, I take the little sewing kit (you'll find it with the miniature soap bars and shampoo bottles) and toss it in my suitcase. I have a collection of them. Women as well as men should consider packing one of these emergency repair kits in their briefcase for an interview.

Jump Start
Whether you carry a purse or stow a clutch bag in your briefcase, don't forget to include a handkerchief. It's as practical an accessory for women as it is for men. Male or female, you'll miss it, if you need it.

Well-Heeled

Conservative is best here, and a closed-toe pump with a 1 1/2 heel is a safe choice. Avoid very high heels, which may make your walk less self-assured. Choose colors to complement your suit and accessories, choosing from navy, burgundy, black, and brown. In some "creative" environments, red shoes will make a positive impression, but they should be avoided in the majority of business situations.

Boots are an iffy proposition. To some interviewers, they convey a degree of confrontational "attitude." Avoid risk by not wearing boots to an interview.

If your suit doesn't incorporate a belt, it is best not to wear one. They are not an essential feature of interview attire for women.

Hosiery in a Low Key

Unobtrusive is the keyword here. Wear neutral or skin tones, and since Murphy's Law mandates a run at the most inopportune time, keep an extra pair of pantyhose or stockings in your briefcase or purse.

The Briefcase vs. The Purse

Take one or the other with you, not both. In most interview situations, carrying a briefcase projects more authority than carrying a purse; you can put the essential contents of your purse in a small clutch bag, which you store in the briefcase.

Jewelry: Where Less Is More

Take a minimal approach to jewelry. Wedding bands or engagement rings are always fine, but avoid the Gypsy look of rings on multiple fingers. Thumb rings are out. Earrings should be small and discreet. For the sake of your own comfort and concentration, avoid long, dangling earrings that jangle or make noise, tickle your neck, or even catch on clothing. Pierce your ears, not your nose.

A simple necklace is fine, but avoid fake pearls or gaudy costume jewelry. While an attractive bracelet is quite acceptable, charm bracelets should be avoided, as should any jewelry with your initials on it. Never wear an anklet to an interview.

Make-up

The rule here is very simple: less is more. Strive for a natural look. If you are comfortable without lipstick, avoid it, but if you do use it, apply a subdued shade sparingly.

Go very easy on your favorite cologne or perfume. In our polluted world, there are plenty of people walking around with allergies, which perfumes and colognes (no matter how expensive) irritate. The main thing an allergy sufferer wants is to get away from sources of irritation. You don't want to be such a source.

The Least You Need to Know

➤ Dressing "comfortably" for a job interview means, in large part, dressing appropriately for the field or industry.

➤ Part of interview preparation is learning the "dress code" of the target employer.

➤ How we dress involves intensely personal choices; dressing effectively for a job interview may involve compromising some of these choices.

➤ When in doubt, err on the side of a conservative appearance.

➤ Dress appropriately for the position you seek, not the position you currently have.

Chapter 20

To Give the Right Answers, Get the Right Questions

In This Chapter

➤ Helping the interviewer to create a great interview

➤ Questions interviewers almost always ask—and how to answer them

➤ Responding to inappropriate questions

If a great job is the Holy Grail, then the interview is the path leading to it. It is a passage both coveted and feared. And what inspires the most terror is the prospect of being asked hard questions.

"I'm no good at thinking on my feet," nervous job seekers have confessed to me.

My answer to them: "You'll be sitting down."

In this chapter, I'll suggest some strategies that are aimed not at getting you *through* the interview, but that will let you take charge of the interview and direct it to your areas of greatest strength. Let's fact it, the interview situation can make you feel like some sort of insect in a collection, pinned and wiggling against the wall. In truth, you can usually take much of the initiative and seize much of the control.

Why an Interview Is Easier Than a Midterm Exam

The first mistake is to face an interview thinking that the interviewer holds all the cards, that he or she has a carefully prepared stack of cleverly crafted questions designed to probe you and expose your every flaw. The fact is, almost nobody enjoys interviewing job candidates. Most managers regard interviewing as an intrusion—albeit a necessary one—into their routine, an unwelcome distraction from daily deadlines and other pressing matters. Moreover, most managers are uncomfortable in an interview. They feel that the candidate is judging *them* and judging the company through them. They feel *they* are on the spot.

Jump Start
Most inter-viewers don't *mean* to ask you hard questions, but they end up ask-ing vague questions open to so many possibilities that you may be overwhelmed if you do not prepare for them in advance.

What makes it even worse for most interviewers is that they are usually ill-prepared, often having rushed through your résumé and often at a loss for meaningful questions.

Few interviewers want to make an inherently uncomfort-able situation worse by contriving trick questions to trip you up. Indeed, few even want to inflict particularly demanding questions on you. Basically, they just want to get the interview over with.

So, you're saying, this isn't such a bad deal, after all. The interviewer is uncomfortable, is fresh out of really hard questions, and just wants to get this thing over with. Sounds easy enough.

The trouble is that all of this leads to a disappointing interview. Sure, it won't be your fault, but that doesn't matter. The interviewer will recall the *event* as unimpressive, and you, of course, are very much part of the event.

Here's the drill, then. Like so many other business situations, the interview that results from the typically inept and unprepared interviewer is not your fault, but it *is* your problem. You address the problem in three related ways:

➤ Learn as much as possible beforehand about the company and the job. Come to the interview armed with topics of conversation related to hot-button issues, leading trends, major challenges faced by the company or the industry, and so on.

➤ Anticipate questions and prepare answers that will play to your strengths—that will guide the interviewer to subjects you know well and that will give you an opportu-nity to demonstrate your abilities, talents, accomplishments, and qualifications.

➤ Prepare specific questions about the job and about the industry that demonstrate your having given the job and the industry careful and creative thought.

In other words, address the interviewer's inadequacies by taking responsibility for the interview. Not only will this result in a more intellectually stimulating and valuable exchange, it will create gratitude on the part of the interviewer. You will have lifted from him or her an onerous burden. The interviewer has a problem: *How will I conduct this interview?* Talking about how you're a problem solver is important, but coming into the interview and actually solving a problem—namely, the interview—is far more persuasive.

Ten Interview Questions You Should Always Expect

What follows are hardly the only questions you might expect. For example, you must prepare for industry-specific questions ("How would you handle outsourcing in the widget business?"). But you can pretty well count on being asked at least five of the following questions, in one form or another, during any interview.

1. What can you tell me about yourself?

This is a favorite. On the face of it, it is a generous, inviting question. In reality, if you're not prepared for it, it's a question that will denude your mind of quick responses as mercilessly as fire sweeps through a droughty forest. You could pull yourself together and ramble on with a full-scale autobiography. But where do you start, and where do you stop? (When the interviewer's eyelids begin to quiver and descend?) It is better to *help* the interviewer by focusing on the question: "What about me would be most relevant to you and what this company needs?" Then answer accordingly, focusing on one or more of the relevant terms listed in Chapter 23, "Think You're DOA? Here's CPR for a 'Dead' Job Search." "I find nothing more rewarding than *troubleshooting* a problem—*analyzing* a situation and working as a team to solve the problem."

2. Why do you want to leave your present company?

If you have a good, *positive* reason for wanting to leave, use it. Make sure that you think about this question beforehand and prepare an answer. Avoid negative reasons: "I don't get along very well with my boss," or "My supervisor is uncreative and won't let me try out new ideas," and so on. Avoid what may be interpreted as frivolous reasons: "I want an office with a window."

Instead of letting the question focus your answer on why you want to *leave* your present company, redirect your response to explain why you want to *move to* the target company. For example, instead of answering, "I don't get enough challenges at XYZ Industries," respond: "I am eager to take on more challenges, and I believe I will find them at ABC Industries." Framing your response in this way does not evade the question, it simply ensures that the response will express a positive motive rather than a gripe.

3. What do you know about us?

Learn all you can about the target company, using the approaches outlined in Chapter 18, "Preparing for the Interview: How to Plan for Spontaneity." For there is no formulaic answer to this question. If you have done no research and can't come up with an answer, don't expect to get the job. If, however, you've done your homework, the question is your chance to shine.

4. How much experience do you have?

This is another opportunity for a great interview moment. If your pre-interview research has revealed areas in which the company is concentrating its efforts, and these areas coincide with your field or with the specific job you're applying for, marshal your relevant experience. For example, if you know that ABC Industries is revamping its customer service operation, and you are interviewing for a customer service representative position, you might summon up your experience in leading-edge customer service issues: "I've been concentrating on cost-effective strategies for automating customer service." Or you might give a distinctive spin to routine matters: "I have particular expertise in the information side of customer service, and, as we both know, 90 percent of customer service is clearly and effectively conveying information."

Winner
Having trouble putting your reasons into words? Employment counselors, who have a fondness for acronyms, offer the CLAMPS formula. Express your reasons in terms of Challenge, Location, Advancement, Money, Pride (or Prestige), or Security. Singly or in combination, positive responses embodying any of these motivating factors should persuade the interviewer that you have a sound, intelligent, thoughtful reason for wanting to leave your current position.

If your research has failed to reveal any clear-cut areas of concern to the target company, you must answer the question with a question in order to get the interviewer to define the areas of most concern to him or her. Try, "Are you looking for overall experience or experience in some specific area of special interest to you?" This will not be perceived as an evasion, but as a demonstration of your thoughtfulness, perceptiveness, and analytical skills. The interviewer's response should allow you to frame your answer in a way that will directly address the target company's needs.

5. What do you most like and most dislike about your current job?

Try to minimize the negative part of this question—something that may not be easy to do because it is human nature to complain, especially when you are so graciously invited to do so.

How to answer, then? Consider replying, "I like everything about my current position." Next, go on to list some vital skills, abilities, and qualifications that position has given you or allowed you to hone. Conclude with, "I'm now ready for a new set of challenges and an opportunity for greater advancement and greater responsibility."

> **Pitfall**
> Avoid negativity. Even if you are very specific in talking about what you don't like about your present job, the interviewer will tend to forget the specifics, but vividly remember the negativity.

As to the positive part of the question—What do you like?—emphasize the opportunities to acquire and develop vital skills, abilities, and qualifications. These, after all, are the very items you bring to the target employer's table. In essence, you want to tell the interviewer that what you most like about your *present* job is the opportunity it has given you to develop assets for the *target* employer.

6. How many hours a week do you need to get your job done?

If you are of a somewhat uncharitable nature, you might call this a trick question. The "trick" is that if you reply with something like 40 hours, you risk labeling yourself as a clock watcher, yet if you say 60, you might be implying that you're slow, inefficient, and easily overwhelmed.

Here's a sound piece of advice for answering just about any trick question. When you are invited to mount the horns of a dilemma, simply decline the invitation. Instead of pinning down to a specific number ("I work 46.4 hours each week."), reply, "I make an effort to plan my time efficiently. Usually, this works well. However, as you know, this business has crunch periods, and when that happens, I put in as many hours as necessary to get the job done." Usually, that's all the interviewer needs—or wants—to hear. However, it is remotely possible that he or she will persist, asking you to furnish a number. Try to turn this around: "That really does depend on the project and the priorities. What's typical in your business/department?"

7. How much are you making now and how much do you want?

You'll find an entire chapter—Chapter 22, "Negotiating Salary and Other Matters"—devoted to the subject of salary. But it is important to note here and now that you should frame your response to the first part of the question very carefully in order to *divorce* it from the second part. And, as to the second part, you should do everything you reasonably can to avoid responding with a specific figure. Ask for either too much—or too little—and you can be eliminated as a candidate for the job. Saddle yourself with a low figure, get hired, and you'll start the job already feeling bitter and disappointed.

Pitfall

"Honestly report..." Should you just lie about your current salary? Although it is *fairly* unlikely that the target employer will verify your salary, he or she might ask for your W2. This request might come after the handshake and, worse, after you have given notice to your current employer.

You cannot avoid answering the first part of the question, of course, but you can frame the reply effectively: "I'm earning $35,000, but I'm not certain that helps you evaluate my 'worth' because the two jobs differ significantly in their responsibilities."

And let's think about that figure. Of course, you know what your salary is, but what happens when you figure in benefits—insurance, profit-sharing, bonuses, commissions, and the like? Make certain that the figure you furnish is the absolute maximum you can honestly report.

As to the second part of the question, avoid stating a figure. Instead, itemize the skills, talents, abilities, and responsibilities the target position entails: "If I understand the full scope of the position, my responsibilities would include..." Then, for good measure: "Have I missed anything?" Finally: "Given all of this, what figure did you have in mind for someone with my qualifications in a position as important as this?"

An alternative is to reply, "I expect a salary appropriate to my qualifications and demonstrated abilities. What figure did you have in mind?" Or: "What salary range has been authorized for this position?"

8. What's the most difficult situation you ever faced on the job?

A favorite question among interviewers—and not a bad one at that. The problem is, if you search your soul, you might respond with a situation so difficult that it resulted in personal failure or general disaster. ("Our department was terribly late with a rush widget shipment. I led a team effort to crash those widgets through. We worked hard, but we were still late—and the client canceled the order, a move that cost my company a gazillion dollars, resulting in massive layoffs that, in turn, eroded the tax base of our community, resulting in a reduction in the police force and a horrible crime wave that wiped out half the town.")

Prepare yourself in advance by thinking of a story with a happy ending—happy for your company. Avoid discussing personal or family difficulties. Avoid discussing problems you've had with supervisors, peers, or subordinates. However, you might discuss a difficult situation with a subordinate, provided that the issues were resolved inventively and to everyone's satisfaction.

9. What are you looking for in this job?

Stand this one on its head. You may be looking for money, self-fulfillment, an easy commute… whatever. But don't tell the interviewer any of this. Put words like *contribute*, *enhance*, *improve* in your response. "At ABC Industries, I discovered just how much one person could contribute to a company. As production supervisor, I increased efficiency an average of 14 percent, which meant a quarterly bottom-line increase of $27,000 in net revenue for our department. I'm looking to do even more for XYZ Industries. That's what will give me satisfaction in this job."

10. Why should I hire you?

"Because I need the work."

WRONG!

> **Jump Start**
>
> An interview is not a game show—no 60-second clock is running. Take the time you need to formulate a response. A brief silence between question and answer is better than hemming and hawing. If you need to buy more time for thinking, repeat the question back to the interviewer in a thoughtful tone: "The most difficult situation I ever faced on the job…."

This is really a request for an "executive summary" of what you bring to the company table. Keep the response brief. Foolproof your response by recapping and repeating, in laundry-list fashion, any job requirements the interviewer may have enumerated earlier in the interview. Point by point, match your skills, abilities, and qualifications to those items.

Inappropriate Questions—and How to Answer Them

Employers are forbidden by law to ask any questions bearing on your marital status, your sexual orientation, your age, and your ethnic or national origins. So what are you going to do if one of these taboo questions is asked? Take offense? Invoke the law? You are within your rights to do either. Trouble is, you probably won't get the job.

Are you married?

Usually, this question reflects a concern that your family duties may interfere with your job. "Yes, I am. My wife/husband and I are both professionals, who have spent *X* years very happily keeping our professional lives separate from our family lives."

Do you plan to have children?

This is almost exclusively directed at women. You might answer, "Could you explain what bearing this has on the position? I'm not sure I understand the relevance of the question." You would be perfectly justified in making such a response. However, you risk putting off the interviewer. You might simply reply, no. But if you want children, and you feel strongly inclined to answer frankly, why not turn the question to your advantage? "Yes, eventually. But those plans are directly dependent on the success of my career."

What is your sexual orientation?

This one's strictly out of bounds, and there's no graceful way to respond. Avoid indignation, but ask the interviewer to "explain the relevance of the issue to the position." Or you may simply reply, calmly, evenly, and neutrally: "I don't think that question is appropriate."

How old are you?

An inappropriate as well as stupid question. Inappropriate, because age discrimination is prohibited by law. Stupid, because, if you are turned down for the job, the very fact that the question was asked lays the interviewer's company open to a lawsuit. (But do you really want to spend your time litigating, or do you want to find a job?)

The best way to respond is to translate the question into terms of experience. "Now that I'm in my forties, I've had more than a quarter-century of experience in the widget industry."

Do you believe in God? / What is your religious background?

If you *want* to answer, keep it general: "I worship regularly, but I make it a practice not to involve any of my personal beliefs in my work." (If you are active in charitable work, this is a good time to bring that up.) If you have no religious beliefs, it is usually better not to make an issue of the fact. "My personal spiritual beliefs are very important to me, but I don't let them get involved with my professional life, and I make it a practice not to discuss them."

Were you born in the United States?

If you were born here, just say so. If not, but you are a citizen, reply: "No, but I became a citizen by very proud choice in 19XX." If you are not a citizen, you might want to reply, "No. I'm currently working toward becoming naturalized as a citizen."

Case Study

Is being asked to take a drug test an inappropriate question? You may find it an offensive question, but, alas, it is not inappropriate. As many as half of the *Fortune* 500 companies include some form of drug testing either during or after the hiring process.

Stan Williams (that's what we'll call him) was not a drug user. But he had read enough about false positives to know that agreeing to a drug test is not a matter to be taken lightly. He also knew that if he indicated that he would not be willing to take a drug test, would almost certainly be found guilty without a trial—and would not be hired.

Stan had been called for an interview and had just received in the mail—a few days prior to the scheduled meeting—a form for him to sign, granting the employer permission to administer a drug test. He asked me what he should do.

I told him that, first of all, if he answered that he had "no problem" taking a drug test, the chances were only about fifty-fifty that he would actually be given one. But I suggested that he call the contact number given on the release form and ask whether the testing company will fully explain the test and provide a complete list of food, nondrug, over-the-counter medications, or prescription drug items that may cause *false positive* results. At least 5 percent of drug tests yield false positives due to the presence of innocuous substances. (One authoritative source places the figure at 14 percent!)

I told Stan that if he became the victim of a false positive, that he should insist on being given a backup test of a different type. Document your request in writing.

As it turned out, the drug test was never administered.

The Eleventh Question

And the inevitable question number eleven is, "Do you have any questions?"

You'd better. And that is how we begin the next chapter.

The Least You Need to Know

> ➤ Most employers are unprepared to conduct an effective interview, and it is up to you to help them.

> ➤ Prepare—in advance—answers to the ten questions discussed in this chapter, but also try to anticipate industry-specific questions and prepare answers for them, too.

> ➤ Express yourself in positive terms, even when you are invited to respond negatively.

> ➤ If necessary, refocus questions to address how you will satisfy the target employer's needs.

Chapter 21

Asking Questions and Making the Sale

In This Chapter

➤ Why you need to ask questions

➤ Questions you should ask

➤ Questions to get the "inside" story on the target employer

➤ The five-step formula for making the sale

➤ Responding to "buy signals"

Aside from falling victim to an ultra-rare case of SHC ("spontaneous human combustion"), the worst that can happen at an interview is your failure to ask questions. If you don't ask questions, the interviewer will assume that you are neither very bright nor very interested in his or her company. Worse, you will miss an opportunity to find out some of the things you need to know in order to make an intelligent decision, should you be offered the job. But, even more important than either of these very important points is something every sales professional knows. Questions are vital to making a sale. Making a sale depends on persuading your target to respond to you positively. A crucial step in eliciting that response is to get the target to verbalize his or her needs and desires, as well as reservations. And this is accomplished by asking questions.

In this chapter, I will suggest what questions you should ask to reveal yourself in the best light. I will also show you how you can use time-tested sales techniques to put yourself across to an interviewer.

Ten Interview Questions You Should Always Ask

Don't limit yourself to the following questions, but they are designed to help you gather the information you need in order to make an informed decision about the job while simultaneously helping you drive the sale home. Use as many of the following questions as possible on your first interview with an employer. If there is a follow-up interview, get to the questions you didn't ask the first time around.

1. Have you had a chance to review my résumé?

Do not fail to open with this one, and take care to phrase it just this way. A staggering number of interviewers do not read your résumé beforehand. A staggering number of interviewers will not admit this fact. It is, therefore, unlikely that you will get a simple "no, I haven't" in response to this question. More likely, it will elicit something like, "I haven't had the chance to review it as thoroughly as I'd like to." (Translation: "No, I haven't read a word of it.")

Do not be chagrined by such a response. It's the rule rather than the exception. Your task, then, is to continue: "Well, then, perhaps you'll find it helpful for me to hit the highlights of my qualifications." And then do just that, using the strategy outlined in "Making the Sale: A Five-Step Formula" later in this chapter.

Jump Start Watch your tone. Keep it bright and conversational. Never let your manner become inquisitorial. The interview should be a polite and pleasurable conversation.

2. Is there anything else I can tell you about my qualifications?

Buzz Word Wherever possible, use the word *qualifications* instead of *experience*. "Qualifications" conveys active achievement, while "experience" is more neutral and passive.

Should the interviewer answer yes, he or she *has* read your résumé, or after you finish reciting your verbal review of it, invite further questions. This is not putting yourself in harm's way, but giving you an additional opportunity to present yourself in the best possible light. Also, the more *time* you can get the target employer to invest in you, the more valuable you will become in the target's eyes. This is a good question for a first interview as well as for any follow-up interviews.

3. How would you describe the duties of this job?

If you did your homework, you may think this question superfluous. You've read the job description. You know what the duties are.

But that is not the question. It specifically asks the *interviewer* to describe the duties. His or her take, you may discover, may be a far cry from what's in the official job description. At the very least, by asking the interviewer to describe the duties, you may get a handle on which functions are perceived as most important and, therefore, really *are* the most important. Not only will this information aid you in your own deliberations, but it should provide a springboard to launch a description of your particular skills and qualifications. ("Oh, I'm very happy to hear that you consider client contact a major part of the position. I place a high premium on creating customer satisfaction. It's building a business, each and every day, one client at a time.") If you are exposed to new interviewers at a follow-up interview, don't hesitate to try this question on them: "I've already spoken to Mr. Jones about the duties and responsibilities involved in this job, and I know what the official job description says. What's *your* take on the most important aspects of the position?"

4. What are the principal problems facing your staff right now?

A dual-purpose question. First, understanding the target employer's problems gives you an opportunity to present yourself as a solution to those problems. Anyone can say, "I'm a problem solver," but if you know what the problems are, you can address the issues specifically and head-on.

The second purpose of the question is to help uncover any truly terrible situations that might make you think twice about taking the job. ("The biggest problem is that people just don't seem to be buying buggy whips right now.") Feel free to repeat this in a follow-up interview, if you are exposed to new interviewers.

5. What results would you like to see me produce?

Just by asking the question, you demonstrate your intention to *do* a job rather than *take* a job. For you, a job means more than earning a living. It means serving the company, creating profit, saving money, solving problems, and increasing productivity.

Attempt to respond point by point to whatever list this question elicits: *This is what* you *want; this is what* I'll *do.* If new interviewers are present at a follow-up interview, ask this question again.

6. What do you consider ideal experience for this position?

If the interviewer's response is light-years away from anything you expected, reconsider the job. However, the main purpose of the question is to get the interviewer to describe a profile into which you, verbally, can step. Once again, try to respond to the interviewer's laundry list point by point.

7. How would you describe the 'weather' in this company? Stormy? Hot? Cool? Breezy? Calm? Brisk? Or what?

This is a creative question about the work environment. Its primary purpose is to catch the interviewer slightly off-guard and to discover if you are about to walk into a snakepit. There is a secondary benefit to the question, too. It gives you a chance to say that you thrive in the target company's environment. "I like intensity, and I'm energized by pressure situations. To me, nothing's more stimulating than stormy weather."

8. Was the person who held this job before me promoted?

The bad way to put this would be, "What happened to the last marshal of Dodge City?" So don't put it that way. The question aims to find out why the job is vacant. It is also an opportunity to assess the chances for advancement at this particular company and from this particular position.

9. May I talk with the person who held this job before me?

Don't overlook this opportunity. It is an intelligent and prudent request, which will suggest that you are likewise intelligent and prudent. Your conversation with this person should provide valuable insight into the position.

But what do you do if the answer is no? If the previous incumbent is still with the company, you have to be suspicious of such a response. Ask what the objections are. If the person has moved on, you might ask the interviewer if he or she knows where you can get in touch with the former employee.

10. Based on what I've told you, don't you think I could give you all that you need in this position?

This is the kind of question an experienced salesperson would use to close a sale. It invites a positive response. More accurately, it invites the kind of thought that is likely to generate a positive response—and this is a valuable distinction. You want the positive response to come from the interviewer's conviction, to be, in effect, the interviewer's idea, as if to say, *You've judged for yourself.*

Of course, as phrased, the question is a loaded one. It would be difficult—but certainly not impossible!—for an interviewer to answer negatively. The question helps force the issue, but it also coaxes it toward a *yes*.

Aren't We Forgetting Something? (Like, What Do I Get Paid?)

For many—perhaps most—of us, the most important question is, *How much would I get paid?* But as I've observed elsewhere, and as we'll explore in depth in Chapter 22, "Negotiating Salary and Other Matters," you should do all that you can to avoid being the first one to bring up the question of salary. Popping the question first is not impolite or uncool, but it does put you in a weaker negotiating position. The more time you have to sell yourself, the more committed to you the interviewer will be. If you raise the salary issue prematurely—before the interviewer is thinking *We gotta have this person*—chances are, you will be pegged to a lower salary than you might otherwise have commanded. Even worse, you might come up with a figure that seems too high at this point in the interview, but which might have seemed reasonable had you waited until you'd reached the *gotta have* stage.

Leaving the Garden Path

We all hope for a pathway to a rewarding career, and we would love that path to lead to a pot of gold. But sometimes interviewers lead us down the garden path, and, after a few twists and turns, we sense that, at the other end, lies not a pot of gold but a pile of—well, it's not a pot of gold.

Two unpleasant things can happen. Sometimes, despite your best efforts to guide him or her, the interviewer will respond vaguely or reluctantly or even misleadingly. Other times, you may discover that the job you thought you were interviewing for (parts department manager at $45,000) is something very different (parts department assistant at $19,500).

Let's start with the vague interviewer. Your natural impulse will be to pretend that you understand. This is a laudable and decent impulse—if the person you are talking to happens to be your aged grandmother, who has a "tendency to wander just a little bit." But pretending you understand will only dig a pit for you in an interview. Look, this is an important occasion. The chances are very good that you are paying careful attention. That means, if you don't understand the interviewer, he or she probably isn't making much sense. Your next move? Ask for clarification. If need be, probe. "I'm not following you. What do you mean by 'realignment of secondary priorities?'"

259

If you become convinced in the course of the interview that your questions are being evaded, insist—as politely as possible—on an answer. "Ms. Reston, what I'm still unclear about is the full range of my responsibilities. Does the position include supervising three territories or only two?

If evasion persists, and you are convinced that this is not due to the nervousness or ineptitude of the interviewer, you are perfectly justified in suspecting a deliberate attempt to mislead you. Seriously rethink the prospective job.

The second disturbing mid-interview crisis is the realization that the job the interviewer is talking about is not really the job you thought you were applying for. To begin with, this revelation, shocking and disappointing though it may be, is not a bad thing. After all, it's better to discover problems now than after you've accepted the position—and turned down others. If you begin to sense that your understanding of the position differs significantly from what you are being told at the interview, explore the differences with the interviewer: "Your ad specifically mentioned extensive customer contact, but what you are describing is essentially back-office work. Just how much customer contact is involved in the job?"

If you discover that the position is not at all what you want, terminate the interview—politely, even if you are angry and upset: "I am very happy that I had the opportunity to talk with you. You see, the position, as you describe it, is not at all what I was led to believe it was. I appreciate the time you've given me. Perhaps another position—one that really is focused primarily on customer contact—will develop at a later date. I'd certainly be grateful if you could keep in touch.

Making the Sale: A Five-Step Formula

But how do you get *them* so they "gotta have" *you*? I mean, you're either right for the job or not. Correct?

By now, dear reader, you can probably smell one of my rhetorical questions a mile downwind. But this one isn't totally rhetorical. I'd be lying to you if I said that qualifications, background, and accomplishments counted for little in getting the job you want. They mean a lot. However, *you* can manage the interview to make the most of whatever qualifications, background, and accomplishments you have.

Unless you are contemplating a career change well down the road, there isn't much you can do, immediately prior to the interview, to alter or add to your inventory of qualifications, background, and accomplishments. What you can do, however, is shift the focus from yourself to the target employer (review Chapter 18, "Preparing for the Interview: How to Plan for Spontaneity"). Then spend some prep time thinking about how you can match your inventory of assets to what the target is looking for. Your goal is not to change yourself or to concoct a picture of yourself distorted to fit what you perceive as the target's mold. Rather, it is to position yourself as the person most qualified to meet the target's needs.

Step 1: Persuade with Your Ears

Ideally, then, you arrive at the interview primed with research that has revealed something substantial about what the employer needs. But bear in mind that this is a dynamic situation. It is not possible to prepare for the interview the way an actor prepares for a play—that is, by memorizing a script. Unfortunately, the other "actor's" part is not written out. Therefore, even if you are well prepared, go into the interview aware that your most important tools for persuasion are your ears. Listen.

Really listen.

Listen to what the interviewer says about his or her company, its needs, its goals, its problems. Listen to what the interviewer says he or she needs. Then respond to what you hear. In this way, you quickly transform yourself from a stranger looking for a job to a potential partner with a commitment to pitching in and solving problems.

"We don't always move as quickly as we would like in evaluating new projects," says the interviewer. You respond: "What you could really use is a facilitator—someone who brings out the best performance in all your people." Or: "Sales is where it's at. That's where the money starts." You respond: "That's what I like about selling. I know that designers believe everything starts with them, and production folks look at themselves as the center of the universe. But, I've always thought that sales is the genesis of it all. We produce money—and that's the fuel that makes the whole thing move."

Jump Start
An effective way to listen—and to demonstrate that you are listening—is to underscore the interviewer's most important points by repeating and rephrasing them: "What I hear you saying is…" or "If I'm understanding you correctly…."

Step 2: Spark Attention

It is quite possible that you've gotten the interviewer's attention through Step 1. In large part, this depends on how forthcoming the interviewer is in expressing what he or she or the company needs and wants from you. Be prepared, however, to take the initiative yourself with a statement that reminds the interviewer of why you're sitting in his or her office.

I don't mean that you should begin by saying something like, "Hey, you remember, I'm here about the administrative assistant job." No, you command attention by reminding the interviewer of why *he* or *she* called *you* in for an interview.

But how should *you* know why?

It's easy, really, because there's only one answer—at least, only one answer that matters. You were chosen because the interviewer believes that you're probably the right person for the job. Get his or her attention, then, with a reminder of that fact: "Good morning. Mr. Perkins. I'm really delighted to be here, since it seemed to me that my qualifications so closely coincided with what you need." Or: "I'm very excited about being here. What I have to offer seems to me a perfect match for this company."

Step 3: Develop Interest

There is no mystery to this step. You develop the interviewer's interest in you as a potential employee much as you develop any new acquaintance's interest in you. Unless you have lived the life of a hermit, you are already accustomed to developing interest in what you have to offer. That's how strangers become acquaintances and how acquaintances become friends. The only difference is that, in the case of a job interview, you must develop interest in a specific direction, by demonstrating your potential value as a member of the employer's team. This is done by making an effort to turn everything you say into an expression of accomplishment, achievement, or qualification. Be specific. "I'm a super executive assistant" will not get you very far, but "I specialize in handling the details and anticipating needs, so that you can be more efficient" addresses what the target employer wants.

Step 4: Transform Interest into Involvement

Persuasion is, of course, a two-way street. You don't just define and describe your qualifications, then recite your accomplishments. You constantly gauge the interviewer's responses to what you are saying. You listen for "buy signals." These may be quite obvious. "That interests me," the interviewer says, or "I like that," or "Great!" More frequently, the buy signals are expressed more neutrally: "Tell me more about…" or "Can you be more specific about…." Either way, the buy signal indicates that you've pressed the right button. Once you elicit a buy signal, it's time to zero in on the point that triggered the positive response. You've just said, "I specialize in handling the details and anticipating needs, so that you can be more efficient," and the interviewer responds, "Can you tell me more about that?" What an opportunity! You respond:

> "Well, for example, I'm a great believer in maintaining 'hot files.' I track the issues of most immediate importance and keep the relevant documents instantly accessible. I would like to work with you to develop a list of hot contacts—people who must be given immediate access to 'the boss,' as opposed to those I can safely put on a call-back list. In some ways, I see the most important aspect of my position as a contact manager. The most important benefit I provide is more *useful* time for you."

At this stage in the interview, be specific—not specific about yourself, but about what you can do for the target employer. In the preceding instance, the candidate has addressed the unspoken—but always-present—question, "What will you do for me?" with a specific and powerful answer: "I will give you time." And, in most businesses, nothing is more valuable than that.

I have deliberately chosen an example of someone interviewing for an entry-level or near entry-level position: an executive assistant. The reason I've done this is to show how even an entry-level position can be defined—and defined quite specifically—in terms of its most valuable function. If you are moving from one position up to another, concentrate on presenting your track record. But even if you are just starting out—and your track record is brief or nil—define what you do (or what you *will* do) in the best possible light and in the most vividly specific terms possible. Involve the interviewer by offering something he or she *must* have. In the example, that "must-have" is *time*, whereas for a widget sales representative the "must-have" offered is sales. If you were a candidate for such a job, you would do best if you demonstrated that, in a department generating $2.3 million in sales last year, you were personally responsible for $640,000. Moreover, if you know that widgets are subject to a 30-day return period, you might further note that *your* sales generated a lower rate of returns than anybody else's.

> **Jump Start**
> Nothing develops the interviewer's involvement more strongly than money: money you will bring into the company and money you will save for the company. Money is the language of business. Whenever possible, speak this language.

Step 5: Prompt Action

The final phase of the interview offers the opportunity to prompt action. Assuming that, as the interview winds down, *you* remain interested in the job, you should try to end with a provocative question. Don't ask, "Well, do I get the job?" but try question number 10,

Winner

I've compared the interview to a sales situation. However, there is one important difference between the two. In sales, your only goal is to sell the product. In an interview, you are also asking yourself, *Do I really want this job?* It is best to observe all that you can *during* the interview, but to reserve your evaluation for *after* the interview.

stated previously: "Based on what I've told you, don't you think I could give you all that you need in this position?"

If your sense is that you haven't quite connected with the interviewer, try this alternative: "Mr. Perkins, I've enjoyed talking with you, and I believe I've got a great deal to give to this company. Tell me, please, is there anything I haven't addressed to your satisfaction? What could I tell you that would prompt you to make an offer?"

No matter how the interview has gone, the object is to push toward some form of closure, a specific action. If you are told that the whole matter must now be reviewed by "The Committee," be certain to thank the interviewer, then ask when you should expect a decision: "Well, thank you very much. It's been a pleasure. When should I expect to hear from you concerning The Committee's decision?"

A push toward action—or, at the very least, closure—conveys a certain urgency. It does not make you look over-anxious or desperate, but it does reinforce the impression that you are important and valuable and, further, that you are well aware of your importance and value.

The Least You Need to Know

➤ Ask questions that reveal information that will help you make a decision about the job and exhibit your skills and qualifications in their best light.

➤ Formulate questions to discover the target employer's needs and problems, as well as the work environment and your prospects for advancement and growth.

➤ Treat the interview as a sales negotiation. Listen to the "customer," get his/her attention, develop his/her interest, transform that interest into involvement, and then move the interviewer to action.

➤ Your "sales" effort should prompt the interviewer to ask questions and make "buy signals," which you can develop to *close* the "sale."

➤ Tie up loose ends with follow-up questions.

Chapter 22

Negotiating Salary and Other Matters

In This Chapter

➤ Why salary negotiation makes you uncomfortable

➤ Putting yourself in the strongest possible negotiating position

➤ Calculating a target salary range

➤ Responding to a salary offer

➤ What you can—and cannot—negotiate

➤ The common employer objections—and how to overcome them

Like the fabled Sword of Damocles, the question of compensation hangs over each and every interview. You and the interviewer both know that the issue must be raised and resolved, and you in particular are anxious to know what you'll be getting. You're also anxious because you are afraid to ask for too little or too much, either of which can take you out of the running. Add to this mix the fact that most of us are naturally uncomfortable setting a price on our own heads, and your palms start to sweat. And if you don't have sufficient cause for anxiety, remember what we've said repeatedly in the course of this book: You want to be careful to avoid being the first one to pin down a salary figure.

Salary negotiation is a landscape obscured by confusing and contradictory emotional features. It is best, therefore, to go into it with a clear and rational road map.

Homework Review

If you've gotten as far as the interview, I'd guess that you've already done a good deal of homework on the target employer. As far as salary negotiation is specifically concerned, your preparation should involve two steps:

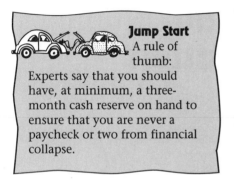

Jump Start A rule of thumb: Experts say that you should have, at minimum, a three-month cash reserve on hand to ensure that you are never a paycheck or two from financial collapse.

1. Work out your own minimum cash requirements. (The Minimum Monthly Cash Needs Worksheet in this chapter can help.) By minimum I do not mean the least you need just to keep yourself and your family alive, but the least you need to feel reasonably secure and comfortable. This is a very personal matter, of course, but a good starting point is to figure what you need to meet all of your monthly obligations *and* be able to save at least 3 percent of your monthly income *and* have another 10 percent (on average) that you can count on to meet emergencies.

2. Determine the going price of your qualifications and skills on the current market.

This may have emerged clearly as a result of homework you've already done. If not, try the following:

➤ Contact the local office of the U.S. Department of Labor to obtain a copy of the latest report of the Bureau of Labor Statistics.

➤ Use the Internet to access the BLS at **http://www.bls.gov** or at **umslvma.umsl.edu** (for *The Occupational Outlook Handbook*).

➤ Consult Les Krantz's *Jobs Rated Almanac*.

➤ Contact a headhunter for an informational interview (see Chapter 15).

➤ Consult professional and trade journals in your field or industry; these often publish annual salary surveys.

➤ Pick up the *National Business Employment Weekly*, which runs salary surveys. Back issues are available through the publisher, or you can check your local library.

Minimum Monthly Cash Needs Worksheet

Housing

Rent or mortgage payments	$_____
Electricity/gas	$_____
Water	$_____
Telephone	$_____
Garbage removal	$_____
Cleaning, maintenance, repairs	$_____

Food

Groceries	$_____
Eating out	$_____

Clothing

Purchase	$_____
Cleaning, dry-cleaning, laundry	$_____

Automobile/transportation

Car payments	$_____
Gas	$_____
Repairs	$_____
Public transportation (bus, train, plane)	$_____

Insurance

Auto	$_____
Medical	$_____
House and personal possessions	$_____
Life	$_____

Medical Expenses

Doctors' visits	$_____
Prescriptions	$_____
Fitness costs	$_____

Support for Other Family Members

Child care costs	$_____
Child-support	$_____
Support for your parents	$_____

Try taking two passes through this list. First, supply the minimum figures, then fill in the amounts you would ideally like to earn.

continues

267

Charity	$_____
Education	$_____
Pet Care	$_____

Bills and Debts (Monthly Payments)

Credit cards	$_____
Local stores	$_____
Other	$_____

Taxes

Federal	$_____
State	$_____
Local/property	$_____

Amusement

Movies, video rentals, and so on	$_____
Other entertainment	$_____
Newspapers, magazines, books	$_____

Gifts	$_____
Savings/Investments	$_____
Contingency Fund	$_____
TOTAL MONTHLY AMOUNT NEEDED	$_____

Your homework should produce two figures: the minimum salary you need and a midpoint salary associated with your target position. Using these two figures, formulate a third: what we might call your (reasonable) dream salary. This is what you would really like to earn.

Timing Is Critical

You enter the interview armed with a clear idea of what salary you absolutely need, what salary you can expect, and what (reasonable) dream salary you might shoot for. Now you must add one more task to your interview list. In addition to doing all that is necessary to sell yourself—that is, to demonstrate how you are the answer to everything the employer needs—you must ensure that you are alert to the signals that tell you just when to get into a salary discussion with the target employer.

Never Be the First to Mention a Figure

And try to ensure that the salary discussion does not come until the end of the interview. Despite your own anxiety, it is relatively easy to avoid being the first to raise the salary issue. If, however, you are preemptively asked what kind of salary you are looking for, use some of the delaying responses offered as answers to Question #7 ("How much are you making now and how much do you want?") in Chapter 20, "To Give the Right Answers, Get the Right Questions." Chances are, one or more of these answers will do the trick. But, if the employer is insistent on getting a figure from you, respond with a broad salary range. Calculate it this way: Let's say that you've decided that you need a minimum of $36,000. Your research suggests that the salary range for the target position is $33,000 to $41,000. Bracket the range you tell the prospective employer so that it interlocks with the upper range of what you can expect as an industry standard and exceeds your own minimum requirement. In this case, a good range would be $38,000 to $43,000.

> I SEE...
>
> ## Case Study
>
> My friend Susan Ford calls it the "salary dance." "Actually," I said to her, "it's more like a contest." "Yeah," she replied. "The trouble is that you get so into winning that you forget what your real purpose is—*not* to keep from being the first to mention a salary figure, but to get a job offer!"
>
> "I was in an interview once," she said, "dancing around the salary issue. Finally, the guy says to me, 'Come on, let's not play games. I need to have a firm figure from you.'
>
> "I was tempted to give nothing more than my name, rank, and serial number—like on a war movie. But then I remembered, 'Hey. I really want this job.' So I came up with a range. I wanted at least $35,000—absolute, drop-dead minimum—so I said that I was looking for something in the range of $38,000 to $43,000. I figured that would get me $41,000 or so.
>
> "We ended up settling on $40,000."

Recognizing the Phases of an Interview

The issue of timing sounds more complicated—or, at least, more mystical—than it really is. Look at it in terms of a checklist. You should avoid the subject of salary until:

➤ You're in the final interview (if there is more than one).

➤ You're convinced the interviewer has gotten to know you.

➤ You're confident that you fully understand what the job entails.

➤ You're sure you want the job.

➤ You're confident that the interviewer has reached the *gotta have you* stage.

If an interview goes really well, it progresses from a starting point at which the target employer "sort of" knows you (if he or she has read your résumé carefully) or doesn't know you at all (if—as is often the case—he or she has hardly glanced at your résumé), through a process of increasing involvement with and commitment to you, and to a point at which the interviewer decides *we gotta have you*. It is at this point that salary negotiation should take place.

Now!

Well, not *quite* now. Remember, *you* should not be the first one to bring up the subject of salary. But the beauty of delaying the issue until the interviewer has reached the *gotta have* stage is that he or she will usually raise the issue at this point. The "buy signal" will be something like this: "I think we see eye to eye about the duties and responsibilities of the position. Now, what about salary?" Or, "I believe you can do the job we want. What salary were you looking for?"

Winner
Watch your body language! Practice your best poker face. Avoid looking disappointed or enthusiastic in response to the figure or range that emerges. Don't grimace. Don't smile. Don't look down. Don't squint or shut your eyes. Don't look up at the ceiling or roll your eyes. Don't cross your arms (it indicates defiance). Don't bring your hand to your face or mouth (it indicates insecurity). Just maintain neutral eye contact.

Respond with, "This is the first time we've really broached the subject. Could you tell me what the authorized range is for someone with my qualifications?"

Once a salary range is on the table, you have four options for responding:

➤ You can accept the range, remarking that, "the upper end of this range is certainly what I had in mind and would be acceptable to me."

➤ You can negotiate further by responding with your own range, which overlaps the top end of the target employer's.

➤ You can thank the interviewer for the information and ask for additional time to consider the figure.

➤ You can tell the interviewer that the range is out of the ballpark.

There is nothing wrong with the first alternative, if you really are pleased with the figures offered; however, be aware that most employers tend to leave some negotiating room beyond the top end of the range. If the employer is well within your ballpark, it is usually worth the extra effort to respond with the second option, which may define a new, somewhat higher range.

Let's say that the employer proposes a range of $38,000 to $40,000. You know from your research that this fits industry-standard patterns, and it is at or above your own minimum requirements. Respond, "Yes. This is quite near what I was expecting. I'm thinking in terms of $40,000 to $45,000." This will position you to negotiate for a final figure greater than the employer's stated low-range figure, probably settling at—or even slightly above—$40,000.

Of course, you can't expect the employer to give you what you want just because you topped his or her top range. Reemphasize your qualifications—why you are worth top dollar. Demonstrate your knowledge of the industry:

Winner

Will the interviewer think you're a greedy pain in the old gluteus M if you bargain for more money? Not if you do it in a professional manner. Most employers *expect* you to haggle. Indeed, the ability to negotiate intelligently is a highly valued qualification. Bargaining with the employer is itself a positive demonstration of your potential value to the company.

> "As you can imagine, I've been doing a good deal of poking around in industry salary surveys. They are very much in sync with the range I just stated. Now, because we're agreed that I have the qualifications that will more than satisfy your needs, I can say with confidence that I'll be up, running, and producing for you within 30 days. This is why I feel that compensation somewhat beyond your upper range is appropriate and fair—fair for me and, certainly, a fair value for you."

Hardball

The final option, telling the interviewer that his or her offer is not even in the ballpark, may be seen as a way of ending the negotiation, the interview, and your candidacy for this particular job, or it may be seen as a hardball technique: *Come up with the money or you don't get me. Period.*

271

Unless you've got something very specific and very special to offer, playing hardball will probably get you kicked out of the game. There is a very small chance that such a response will get you what you want. It is far more likely that the interview will end—with both you and the interviewer in a position from which there is no recovery. A better alternative, if the employer's figure is substantially below your range, is to ask for time to think the offer over. Set a specific time when you will call with your response—usually 24 to 48 hours hence—and use that time to evaluate in tranquility the pros and cons of the job. The delay may also get the employer thinking, because it is a signal that he or she really has come in too low and is in danger of losing you. After 24 to 48 hours, "absolute" caps and ceilings and limits sometimes have a strange way of melting, at least a bit.

At the time appointed for the call, assuming the employer has not raised the offer, and assuming that you are resolved to ask for money, reply straightforwardly and politely: "I appreciate that you've given the matter consideration; however, the level of compensation is, as I indicated, below the minimum I need and, I believe, below what is appropriate for the position." Briefly run down the list of the qualifications and responsibilities called for and how you meet or exceed the requirements. State—or restate—your counteroffer, not as an ultimatum, but as a simple fact: "$38,000 is the minimum I need, and the minimum figure I think appropriate to this position." Now it's time for you to make an offer: "I am actively pursuing other positions, but I don't expect I'll have to make any decisions for at least three days. Unless you are absolutely convinced at this point that you *cannot* meet my minimum figure, I'd be happy to check in with you again on the 23rd." Chances are that the employer will hold firm, and the negotiation will end. However, if the employer indicates a willingness to discuss the matter further, then the odds are very much in your favor. Just remember that hardball is a high-risk strategy and should be used only if *you* feel that you have no room left for compromise, and you are willing to pass up this particular opportunity, if necessary.

Everything Is Negotiable?

Somebody once said, *Every silver lining has its cloud*. Alas, that's the fact, Jack. Ask any number of negotiation mavens, and they'll tell you: Anything is negotiable. Well, *I'm* here to tell you that this is not true.

Let's look at reality. At the lower levels, salaries tend to be most firmly fixed and least negotiable. As you go up in compensation, salary ranges tend to increase in flexibility. At the very highest ranges—above $60,000—there is often great room for negotiation.

If you are applying for entry-level positions that pay less than $20,000 a year, you can expect little or no flexibility in salary. These positions are often assigned very specific salaries, and, because the pool of available candidates is usually substantial, it makes more sense for the employer to find a person who will accept his or her offer rather than negotiate with someone who won't.

In the vast middle range between $20,000 and $60,000, there is usually more room for maneuver—albeit within limits. Characteristically, employers hiring in this range can and will negotiate as much as 15 percent above the stated salary figure. But that is about the limit.

Beyond $60,000, candidate pools shrink dramatically, and employers tend to be willing to spend whatever it takes to get the person they want.

The point is that if you're interviewing for an entry-level position with a posted salary of $19,500, and the employer protests that his hands are tied as far as salary is concerned, well, he's probably telling the truth. If you are negotiating in the $35,000 to $40,000 range, and you insist that your qualifications deserve a salary of $50,000, you may very well be right. But you won't get the job at anywhere near that salary.

Overcoming Objections

Objections to your salary requirements are almost always variations on one of four themes:

➤ Your figure exceeds the range authorized for the position.

➤ Your figure is outside of our budget. The employer can't afford it.

➤ Others similarly qualified within the company don't make that kind of money.

➤ Your salary history doesn't warrant what you are asking for.

As we have just observed, depending on the salary range associated with the position, the first objection might be quite valid: a statement of fact. If that is the case, there really is nothing you *can* do to overcome the objection. However, the other three objections are usually less absolute and, therefore, capable of being overcome. Notice that none of the objections bear on your value or performance. Keep this in mind, so that you can communicate to the target employer that the company will get exceptional value and a very high return from your performance. The objections all focus on *cost*. It is your task to refocus the employer on cost versus *benefit*. Your special qualifications, talents, and abilities are an investment in greater profitability. Your "cost" may be greater than what the employer anticipated paying, but the benefits you offer likewise exceed what the employer anticipated. Therefore, the net value you will produce is higher.

> "I understand that you budgeted less than $38,000 for this position, but I know other employers who are willing to pay more. However, more importantly, I think we're both agreed that I bring to the table special qualifications and skills, as well as a deep commitment to performance. Those things justify the $40,000 figure I'm asking for."

If you're told that others presently employed don't make the salary you're asking for, redirect the issue to your own performance. After all, what the employer pays others is a matter between the employer and the others. What he pays you concerns only the employer and you.

> "I understand your concern. However, based on our conversation thus far, I understood that my salary would be based on my performance and my qualifications, and that it was not capped by what others in the organization earn. In fact, this brings up another issue that I'd like clarification on. How will I be rewarded for performance? Are raises based primarily on a cost-of-living formula, or are they tied to performance?"

Just as you need to divorce the issue of compensation for your performance and qualifications from the salaries others are earning, so you must separate the record of what you earned in the past from what you are asking for now.

Winner
The most effective strategy is to try to avoid the issue of salary history entirely and in the first place by not volunteering information concerning your current compensation level.

"I'm not certain I understand what bearing my past salary has on the work I will do for you. What I *do* see as very relevant to salary is performance—performance and my qualifications. We've discussed these, and I think we're both agreed that I offer great value to the company. I've very carefully looked into how this job is compensated in other organizations, and I believe that the figure I'm suggesting is quite fair. Wouldn't you agree that a combination of the qualifications I offer and industry standards is a very fair way of arriving at an appropriate salary figure?"

Alternatives to Cash

In the army, they call it S.O.S.: *Same Old—uh—Stuff.* When the cold, hard cash isn't there, the employer tries to impress you with a benefits package. Most such packages are, in fact, pretty standard and, therefore, a poor substitute for cash.

At least, that's the way it has always seemed in the past. These days, the cost of medical care is nothing less than terrifying, and good, solid employer-provided medical insurance is indeed a great benefit, which should figure prominently in your evaluation of a compensation package. You can use the Compensation Evaluation Worksheet in this chapter to compare the dollar and benefits compensation offered by different employers.

Compensation Evaluation Worksheet

Position

_____

Company

_____

Projected Start Date

_____

Base Salary

_____

Bonus/Incentives

_____

FirstReview Date

_____

Normal Review Cycle

_____

Benefits

        Health _____

        Pension_____

        Other _____

Relocation

_____

Total Compensation Package =

_____

Use this worksheet to help you evaluate and compare employer compensation offers.

If you have reached an impasse in salary negotiation, consider negotiating for valuable benefits that may not be part of the standard package. These items include:

➤ Performance-based bonuses.

➤ An early salary review date (one year is standard, so you may ask for a review at six months).

➤ Longer paid vacation.

➤ Flex time.

➤ Profit sharing.

➤ Day care services.

➤ Professional membership dues.

➤ Relocation expenses (including such items as moving, temporary housing, and guaranteed purchase of your former residence).

In addition, you can negotiate some sort of "golden parachute" severance agreement (a cash payment in the event you are "let go") and you can also negotiate perks that are important to you: an office of a certain size and description, a leased car, a private parking space, special equipment, and so on.

What to Do When You're Just Too Far Apart

The most obvious action is to conclude the interview with thanks and to continue your job search elsewhere. But if you really want—or really need—the job, try to renegotiate the future. Accept the employer's best offer now, with the explicit proviso that your salary will be reviewed in six months in light of your performance. It is a last resort, but it is a viable alternative to locking yourself into a low salary for the long term.

The Least You Need to Know

➤ *Before* you go to the interview, calculate your minimum salary requirements.

➤ Do research to determine the industry-standard salary range for your target position.

➤ Avoid being the first to mention a salary figure, and try always to speak in salary *ranges* rather than a specific figure.

➤ If the salary offer is well below your minimum, buy time to "think the offer over" instead of rejecting it (and the job) outright.

➤ Learn to recognize the critical stages of the interview, and try to delay salary negotiation until the interviewer has reached the "gotta have" stage.

➤ Give the prospective employer a salary range so that your target range overlaps the upper range of what you can expect as an industry standard and also exceeds your own minimum requirements.

➤ The negotiable range of salaries is usually proportional to the level of the position: Entry-level salaries tend to be narrowly fixed, while upper-level compensation is far more flexible (and negotiable).

➤ Overcome objections by shifting the employer's focus from *cost* issues to issues of *cost* versus *benefit*.

GET ME A NEW RÉSUMÉ, A BETTER SUIT, AND THE CLASSIFIEDS, **STAT!**

Chapter 23

Think You're DOA? Here's CPR for a "Dead" Job Search

In This Chapter

➤ How to tell when your job hunt is stalled

➤ Stop gaps to put beans on your table

➤ How to "smokestack" and "woodshed"

➤ Transforming stop-gap jobs into careers

➤ Going it on your own

How do you know when your job search is stalled? There is no hard-and-fast gauge, because so much depends on conditions specific to your field or industry and your specialty within your field or industry. In some industries and geographical locations, you might have reason to become concerned if no job offers were forthcoming after a month of looking. In others, you might reasonably expect several months to pass without producing an offer.

When should you consider your job search stalled, then? When you're running low on energy, ideas, hope, and alternatives.

In this chapter, I propose to combat despair not with pep talks and reminders of your self-worth, but by proposing strategies to jump start a stalled job search and additional strategies to keep your financial boat afloat while you continue your search.

The hard part about protracted unemployment is your very real sense of being boxed in, your options collapsing one by one, your choices being whittled to nothing. This chapter aims to introduce and activate as many options and alternatives as possible.

Taking Your Time

Black Monday. On October 19, 1987, the Dow Jones Industrial Average plunged 508 points, triggering waves of panic and disbelief. Fortunes were wiped out, of course, but that's hardly remarkable. The truly amazing thing is how many fortunes were *not* lost. The reason? When the stock market plunges, you lose money only if you sell at the low point. Those who managed to hold on to their stocks did just fine.

Jump Start
Employment counselors agree—one out of every three job hunters gives up on the job hunt too soon.

The same holds true for those who endure a seemingly endless string of "Black Mondays," workdays without work, and Black Fridays, too: paydays without pay. Despite the hard times, you're defeated only when you give up. If you can hang in—take your time—the odds are overwhelmingly in your favor: You will get a job.

As a matter of course, plan on your job hunt taking longer than you think it will. Keep hunting until you find what you want. There is no substitute for persistence, and there is no viable alternative to it.

Stop Gaps: Temp Work and Freelance Work

In the meantime, you've got to live. Take stock of what you have. Determine realistically how long you can last without an income, and then determine how much of a stop-gap income you need. Sources of such stop-gap income include the following:

➤ Temp work

➤ Freelance work

➤ Part-time work

➤ Job sharing

As you wrestle with depression and frustration over being unable to land the job you want, you may find it hard to believe just how booming the temporary employment industry is. Many employers find it more economical to cut permanent staff and then fill temporary—or even quite extended—gaps with "temps." Even though the employer pays a hefty premium to the temp agency, substantial funds are saved by not having to pay for the benefits usually given to regular employees.

Nor does temporary work necessarily mean a clerical or secretarial job. These days, temp agencies furnish temporary workers in virtually all fields and for just about every industry. Chances are that you can take your skills and qualifications, go to a temp agency, and find assignments in your field. Usually, you can work out schedules that will allow you enough free time to continue your job hunt on a systematic basis, too.

Jump Start
The U.S. Bureau of Labor Statistics says that temporary workers represent almost 30 percent of the work force. They number over 35 million.

Another alternative—and it is one that may be used separately from or in conjunction with temp work—is freelancing. Often, 9-to-5 types make the transition to freelancing after they are laid off. The former employer taps the services of the former employee on a freelance basis. From this, your reputation is spread by word of mouth to other companies. Alternatively, of course, you can set up a full-scale freelance business, either from your home or from an office you rent. I'll discuss this briefly in the next chapter, but, for now, consider freelance work as a stop-gap during your hunt for more permanent employment.

Freelancing can be structured loosely enough to give you plenty of time to carry on your job hunt. However, it does have a significant drawback. Unless your former company keeps you steadily supplied with freelance assignments, you will have to devote a good deal of your "free" time to beating the bushes for more assignments. This, of course, will eat into your job-hunting time—although it is also true that a freelance relationship with a company may well lead to full-time employment there, so that the very act of freelancing can sometimes double as a highly effective job-hunting strategy.

Don't overlook the potential of part-time work. You may be willing to take on part-time work to make ends meet, even if the job isn't right up your alley. Moreover, its part-time nature leaves you with time to conduct your job hunt. Naturally, you cannot expect a part-time job to support you the way your full-time job did, and there is no magical way around this fact. However, you can approach the situation strategically and with a protracted job hunt in mind. Use the part-time position to stretch your cash reserves. If you have three months' worth of reserves in your savings account, part-time work may extend this to six or nine months, which may be ample time to get the job you want.

And one final alternative is the concept of job sharing. Let's say that you locate a full-time job that will put beans on your table, but it is by no means *the* job you really want. It's a rock-and-a-hard-place situation: You hate to pass up the money, but you don't want to get stuck in this full-time job, unable to devote time and energy to continuing your quest for more rewarding employment.

Perhaps there is an alternative. Find a friend, relative, or acquaintance who is willing to *share* the job with you. Call on the employer and propose that your partner work from eight to twelve while you work from one to five.

Downside? Sure—and plenty of it. For one thing, many employers want no part of job-sharing arrangements. Then, of course, sharing a job requires a partner—somebody who happens to be looking for part-time work, who happens to be highly competent, and who happens to be willing to take on this somewhat unconventional arrangement. Yet, despite all the *ifs* involved, job sharing can make a viable alternative, on the one hand, to taking on a full-time job you don't like and that puts a major crimp in your job hunt, and, on the other hand, simply turning down an income.

Smokestack: Making the Job Hunt Part of Your Daily Routine

You won't find this definition of "smokestack" in any dictionary I know of: "*Verb*. To monitor routinely job possibilities in one's field or industry." The word comes from a practice of itinerant job hunters during the Great Depression of the 1930s. They would wander into a town and look for industrial smokestacks that were actively *smoking*. Here, they assumed, was a still-productive industry offering the potential for a job. Today's job hunters don't look for literal smokestacks, but figurative ones. They keep alert to what's going on in their field or industry, as well as in related fields and industries: who's doing what, who's ordering what goods, who's coming out with what new products, who's offering new services, who's gearing up for new projects and products, and what new opportunities will arise because of the introduction of new products and services. Identify where the activity is, and, chances are, you've identified where the jobs are.

Whether you are currently employed or not, keep your feelers out for new opportunities by making it a habit to smokestack. Learn what's hot in your industry or field—not just from the employer's or producer's point of view, but from that of the consumer. Make yourself an active and alert citizen of your industry. You become an "insider" not because somebody lets you in, but through your own alert and responsive curiosity.

Woodshedding: Self-Review and Self-Revision

Divide your time between *smokestacking* and *woodshedding*. Now that's a term jazz musicians use as synonym for going off alone in order to practice and review and improve. (Old-time rural musicians used to work on their licks in the privacy of the woodshed, where they wouldn't be disturbed and where they would disturb no one.) A stalled job search presents a perfect opportunity for such self-review. However, this does not mean engaging in a self-destructive and utterly fruitless round of *woulda, shoulda, coulda*, but in answering the following:

➤ What skills, abilities, and qualifications do I have that I so far failed to communicate to potential employers?

➤ Do I need to *acquire* certain skills, abilities, and qualifications that are desirable to potential employers?

A productive shortcut in the self-review process is to ask yourself how many (or how few) of the following terms you have applied to yourself in the course of creating cover letters, résumés, and in conducting interviews:

➤ Accomplished	➤ Improved	➤ Promoted
➤ Achieved	➤ Initiated	➤ Published
➤ Activated	➤ Innovated	➤ Qualified
➤ Administered	➤ Installed	➤ Reconstructed
➤ Advised	➤ Interpreted	➤ Reduced expenses
➤ Analyzed	➤ Invented	➤ Reengineered
➤ Changed	➤ Judged	➤ Reorganized
➤ Communicated	➤ Launched	➤ Restored
➤ Composed	➤ Led	➤ Reviewed
➤ Conceived	➤ Learned	➤ Saved time
➤ Contributed	➤ Managed	➤ Sold
➤ Controlled costs	➤ Marketed	➤ Set goals
➤ Converted	➤ Mentored	➤ Streamlined the process
➤ Coordinated	➤ Motivated	
➤ Created	➤ Organized	➤ Succeeded
➤ Delegate	➤ Performed	➤ Supervised
➤ Designed	➤ Persuaded	➤ Taught
➤ Developed	➤ Planned	➤ Trained
➤ Evaluated	➤ Presented	➤ Troubleshoot
➤ Facilitated	➤ Problem-solved	➤ Understand
➤ Forecasted	➤ Produced	➤ Updated
➤ Implemented	➤ Progressed	➤ Wrote

283

The more of these and related terms and phrases you can apply to—and convey about—yourself, the better. Begin your self-review process by setting as a goal the incorporation of more of these terms into your résumés, your cover letters, your telephone conversations, and your interviews. Take whatever steps are necessary to be able to use this vocabulary to describe yourself.

Turning a Stop Gap into a Career

If you work at the stop gap long enough, it may become a way of life—or even lead to a new, and better, way of life. It is possible to make a career out of full-time temp work, and many temporary positions have led to regular, full-time careers. Also, you don't have to work from your home very long before you begin to like it. Stop-gap freelancing may evolve into your own full-time business.

The Temp Work Smorgasbord

Some people find working with a temporary agency unsettling. After all, you move from office to office, and you move into one new situation after another. Rarely do you get the satisfaction of seeing an entire project through to completion, and there is also the feeling that you are the perpetual stranger—treated politely enough by the others in the office, but never quite accepted as one of them. Yet many people see temp work as a great opportunity to experience the smorgasbord of jobs and companies within your field or industry and, in some cases, beyond your field or industry. Finally, a significant percentage of temps use their assignments to get a foot in the door and are eventually hired by the temp agency's client company on a full-time basis.

Pitfall

Traditionally, temp work was strictly entry-level work. It is still generally true that, the more advanced you are in your career, the less satisfaction you are likely to find in temp work. However, temp agencies continue to offer increasingly specialized and advanced positions these days. Even if you are a seasoned pro, it pays to investigate temporary employment.

To find out more about effectively integrating temp agencies into your career, consult Peggy O'Connell Justice, *The Temp Track: Make One of the Hottest Job Trends of the '90s Work for You* and Karen Mendenhall, *Making the Most of the Temporary Employment Market* (Betterway Books, 1993; 1507 Dana Avenue, Cincinnati, OH 45207).

Forget the Office—Forever

For many of us, the hardest part of the work day is getting to and from work. The dreaded commute! Perhaps you spend an hour or more staring down your hood at a faded bumper sticker ("Have you hugged your pillow today?") or strap-hanging in a subway car, jockeying for your cubic half-foot of fetid oxygen. By the time you get to work, you're disheveled and dispirited, you put in your eight hours, then repeat the commuting process in reverse.

Few of us have *not* thought about setting up on our own. We decide to commute not from suburb to city, but from bedroom to spare room, setting our own schedule, keeping our own time. You think, you calculate, you dream about this—and then you get up, get in the car, or get on the train, and go to work.

Now you're out of a job, and your job hunt hasn't gotten you very far. You're doing freelance work to make ends meet. It suddenly dawns on you: *Maybe the time is now.*

Let's get the wet blanket stuff out of the way first— because, great as it can be, working at home is not always the working person's nirvana. To begin with, you can expect to earn 30 percent less than what your office-bound colleagues earn. Next come the pressures of working in a home rather than at a place of business. Can you balance your business time against your family time? And, just as important, can your family accept this balancing act? Do you have the physical—as well as emotional—room to set up the home business? Do you have the discipline to work at home, to set your own schedules, to avoid going into the kitchen every five minutes for a cookie or going out into the yard to water the begonias? How do you feel about working alone for most of the day—no water cooler conversation, no cafeteria, no break room, no across-the-desk interchanges? These are serious issues, and you need to resolve them or you will surely falter.

> **Jump Start**
> Thinking about working from home? You are most definitely not alone. Approximately one-third of the American workforce—39 million people—do at least some part of their work at home. Of these, 23.8 million run their own businesses, while another 8.6 million take home work from their regular employers, and 6.6 million are officially "telecommuters," working at home, for their employers, during regular business hours.

But the most formidable problem that self-employed solo operators face is the continual need to get new business. If you hate job hunting now, be aware that running your own home business is, in many ways, committing yourself to a never-ending job hunt. You are always beating the bushes for more work, and you can rarely afford to "take it easy" on the work you have.

What Kind of Home Business?

Once you have reconciled yourself to the challenges of setting up on your own at home, you need to decide what you're going to do there. The possibilities go far beyond the scope of this book but, fortunately, are the sole subject of dozens of others. Check out Paul and Sarah Edwards's *The Best Home-based Businesses for the 90s: The Inside Information You Need to Select a Home-based Business That's Right for You.* For you, the most obvious home business is the one that exploits what you already know, perhaps using freelance work assigned by your former employer as a foundation on which to build.

Out of the House and Into a Franchise

If you are not committed to working at home, but you've decided that you want to work for yourself, consider a franchise. Again, the obvious direction to take is to build on what you have learned working for somebody else. But remember that, whatever job you held, you developed job-specific as well as transferable skills, so you need not limit your consideration to a franchise directly related to the business you presumably know best.

Overall, the track record for franchise businesses is a good one. Overall, fewer than 4 percent fail—far better odds than you can expect setting up entirely on your own. However, buying a franchise represents a serious commitment, usually a commitment binding yourself to a very large and often very powerful corporation. Research prospective franchise opportunities thoroughly. Perhaps the single most important direction that research can take is frank conversations with other people who have bought the franchise you are contemplating. You should talk to at least three owners of the franchise you have your eye on, and you should also talk to a number of owners of related franchises. Take your time to study the franchise company, the product, the industry, the public demand, the trends, and the community in which you'll be setting up shop. Be sure to check with the Better Business Bureau in your community as well as in the community in which the franchise company is headquartered. Inquire about any complaints.

Books on franchises abound. I suggest that you *begin* with *Franchise Opportunities Handbook*, a reprint of a U.S. government publication available from Sterling Publishing Co., Inc., 387 Park Avenue South, New York, NY 10016.

It's Almost the Last Chapter, But It's Not the Last Resort

There's a risk to ending a book on getting the job you want with suggestions for pursuing such alternatives as temp work, part-time work, starting a home business, or buying a franchise. The risk is that you'll think I'm telling you that these are the final ditch and the last resort.

Hardly.

They are nothing more or less than additional options, and options are what this book has been all about. The world of work is full of slings and arrows, one-way streets, and dead ends.

But it is also a field of dreams.

You may have begun reading this book thinking that you were limited by one "lack" or another: a lack of insider pull or insider information, a lack of experience, a lack of confidence, a lack of an academic degree. Make no mistake, there *are* limits and obstacles and brick walls out there, and they are real. But by far the most formidable and confining limits are the ones you impose on yourself. I hope this book has let you see that such limits are just another set of options. You can take them. Or you can leave them.

The chapter that follows introduces you to the special-edition *JobHunt* software bundled with this book. It bulges with 5,000 potential employers (including names and addresses!), and each of those employers may offer who knows how many opportunities, possibilities, ideas, and options.

Good luck and good hunting!

The Least You Need to Know

➤ Use temp work, freelance, and part-time assignments to maintain an income while you continue your job search.

➤ Ideally, whatever stop-gap employment you find will be related to your area of greatest interest and competence; the temporary work may even lead to a permanent job.

➤ Use part-time work strategically to extend your on-hand funds while you look for permanent employment.

➤ Make it a habit to "smokestack," keeping alert to industry trends that may produce job opportunities.

➤ Use your downtime for productive self-review ("woodshedding"), with an eye toward making yourself more attractive to employers.

➤ Consider transforming stop-gap measures into a full-time career.

Part 5
More Strings to Your Bow

The following chapter not only provides an array of techniques for jump starting a stalled job search, it suggests some stop-gap measures to keep beans on the table in case that search stretches from weeks, to months, and beyond. And there is more. The chapter suggests strategies for turning those stop gaps into alternative means of full-time employment.

Many of us look back wistfully at the days of our fathers, mothers, grandfathers, and grandmothers. Those were the days when you got an education, joined a "Good Firm," remained loyal to it, and it rewarded you with a career—that is, a working lifetime of steady advancement and secure employment. Of course, it didn't always happen that way—but it is true that this scenario was at least perceived *as the ideal norm and well within rational expectation. It was not just a dream.*

But it could *be a nightmare.*

I've spilled a lot of ink in this book talking about how to make yourself and keep yourself employable *in a working world with jobs that don't extend over a lifetime, but, on average, a bit more than four years. That sounds like a hard world, and it is. But it is also a world of opportunity and mobility. The nightmarish aspect of your parents' and grandparents' American dream was that workers tended trade choice, mobility, and genuine growth for security. In the 1950s, the "man in the gray flannel suit" became a symbol of the strict conformity expected in the American workplace. Jobs were more secure back then? Well, prison sentences were secure, too.*

Chapter 24

Using the Software That Comes with This Book

In This Chapter

➤ What the *JobHunt* software program is

➤ Installing the software

➤ Using the software

➤ Getting more help

The Complete Idiot's Guide to Getting the Job You Want includes *JobHunt*™ *6-in-1* software, from Scope International, designed to accelerate your job search.

JobHunt 6-in-1 includes:

➤ A national database of 5,000 employers, which you may search by name, region, and/or industry.

➤ A word-processing program, including automatic mail-merge for mass mailings.

➤ A program to print labels, envelopes, and mailing lists.

➤ A phone dialer to make follow-up calls easier.

➤ Résumé and cover letter samples and fill-in forms.

➤ Tips on interviewing, dressing, and other important job-hunting topics.

Requirements

Requires an IBM-compatible personal computer running Windows 3.1 or higher, including Windows 95, and at least 4 megabytes of RAM. Two 3.5-inch, high-density disks supplied with this book contain the program installation files.

Getting Started

Before installing *JobHunt*, start Windows and close all applications that may be running, including terminate-and-stay-resident (TSR) programs such as virus checkers, screen savers and faxing software. **It is very important that you close—not just minimize—all the applications.**

Windows 3.1/3.11 and Windows for Workgroups 3.11

Insert *JobHunt* "Disk 1" in your A drive (or B drive). Ensure that all applications are closed. In the Windows Program Manager, click on **File**, then select **Run** from the drop-down menu. When prompted, type **A:SETUP** (or **B:SETUP**, if the *JobHunt* disk is in Drive B). Press Enter.

Follow the on-screen instructions to complete installation.

Windows 95

Insert *JobHunt* "Disk 1" in your A drive (or B drive). Ensure that all applications are closed, not just minimized. Click the **Start** button, point to **Settings** on the menu, and then click **Control Panel**. Double-click **Add/Remove Programs**. Complete the installation by following the instructions on your screen. (Click the **Install** button.)

If you prefer, you may install this program using the **Run** command, as explained previously in the installation instructions for Windows 3.1/3.11 and Windows for Workgroups 3.11.

Getting Help

JobHunt is very easy to use and requires no printed manual. If you need help, just access the full on-line help system by pointing to **Help** on the menu bar and clicking the left mouse button. You will be able to read (and, if you want, print) tips on the topic of your choice. The Help Index is a handy reference to all Help topics.

Using the Employer Database

When you start *JobHunt* you will be taken to the Main Menu. You will see two lists, "States" and "Standard Industrial Classifications" (SICs). To generate a list from a database of the 5,000 employers in a particular industry in your state, just click on the appropriate criteria—for example, "Building Construction—Gen Contractors" and "Georgia." To broaden your search geographically, click on additional states. To broaden it by profession or field, click on additional SIC categories. Then click on the **View Data** button.

The records generated by the search may be displayed or printed in alphabetical sequence (by name of company) or by a serial number assigned by the software.

Serial sequence is useful when you have added your own records to the Additional List (for example, from the want ads in today's newspaper) and you want to write only to those companies that you added today. Because new records will be automatically appended in alphabetical order as you type them in, it may be difficult to identify exclusively today's records if you display them alphabetically. However, each time you add a new record to the database's Additional List, the program automatically increments the serial number by one; therefore, if you display them serially and know the serial number where you started typing in records today, then you can easily limit your display or selection to today's records.

You can also search for specific companies using the database. In the Begin and End fields in the Range section, type from one to four characters, indicating where you want to start and end searching company names. For example, if you want to search beginning with "General Motors" and ending at "Xerox," enter **GENE** in the Begin field and **XERO** in the End field. If you are sorting serially instead of alphabetically, then you must type numbers instead of letters.

If you want to search for a single company, then Begin and End at that company. For example, type **XERO** in both the Begin and End fields to generate information for Xerox only.

Using the *JobHunt* database is a great way to survey the available major employers in your region and in your field or industry. By helping you to define the scope of your search, it can save you a lot of time and legwork.

Winner

JobHunt lists 5,000 employers in the United States. Use *JobHunt* to identify major employers. For a more extensive database, order the full-blown JobHunt program with 12,000 companies or Scope's HitList CD-ROM with 100,000 records. See the ad at the back of the book for more information.

Using the Phone Dialer

With *JobHunt* you don't have to wear out your index finger punching a telephone keypad. While you are viewing the Employer Database, highlight the employer you want to call, then click the **Dial** button at the bottom of the screen. Pick up the phone when you are instructed to do so.

Well, actually, it's not *quite* that simple. To begin with, you need to have a modem installed in your computer, and then you need to make sure that the Dialer is set to the communications port ("com port") your modem is using. *Usually*—but not always—this is COM 1 or COM 2.

Adding Employers to the Database

JobHunt is a good place to keep track of additional employers your research—or your reading of the want ads—may turn up. To add an employer to the database, view the Additional List by clicking on the **Additional List** option in the Main Menu. Next, click the **View Data** button. The Add option will display an empty screen where you may enter company information. Click on the **Save New Record** button to save the record afer you have entered your data. The fields will be cleared so that you may enter another new record. When you are finished adding new records, click on **Cancel** after saving the last new record.

Exporting Data

In the Main Menu, you can click the **Export Data** button in order to use your *JobHunt* employer data with Microsoft Word®, WordPerfect®, and other word-processors as well as with most popular database programs. This option greatly extends the flexibility of *JobHunt*.

Jump Start The WordPerfect merge file that *JobHunt* creates is in WordPerfect 5.1 format. WordPerfect 6.0 (DOS or Windows version) and 6.1 will automatically convert the file to 6.0 format when you perform the mail-merge. Just answer yes when WordPerfect 6.0/6.1 asks you whether or not you want to convert the file to 6.0/6.1 format.

Export the data to a comma-delimited ASCII file if you want to use it with Microsoft Word®. *JobHunt* also can directly export a WordPerfect 5.1-compatible merge file (also known as a "secondary file"), so that, if you want, you can use WordPerfect rather than *JobHunt* to perform a merge. If you use WordPerfect, create a "primary file"—such as a cover letter or cold letter—in WordPerfect and merge it with the secondary file exported from *JobHunt*.

Consult *JobHunt's* Help index for the names, lengths, and sequence of the exported fields. Refer to your word processor manual for complete information and instructions concerning mail-merges.

For a full explanation of how to export comma-delimited ASCII files from *JobHunt* in order to use the files with third-party database software programs, click on **Export** in *JobHunt's* main **Help** Menu.

Word-Processing Program

You don't have to own a third-party word-processing program to write cover letters using the data generated by *JobHunt*. *JobHunt's* own built-in word processor is all that you need.

Once you have selected the company or companies you want to write to, just click on the **Create and Merge** button at the top of the screen. This will open the word processor. You may automatically place the *Name* of the person (to whom the letter is addressed), *Salutation*, *Title*, *Company*, *Address Line 1*, *Address Line 2*, and *Date* anywhere in the letter by choosing **Form**, **Insert Fields**. This is especially helpful when you want to print a large number of personalized letters for targeted mass mailings.

Once you have inserted the desired fields into your letter and entered the appropriate text, you are now ready to perform the mail-merge. Prepare your printer for printing and click on **File**, then click on **Print Sample**. This will merge sample data into your letter and print out one copy. Examine the printout to be sure of field placement. Once you are satisfied, click on **File**, and then click on **Print All Letters**. This will start the mail-merge process. The data from each record you selected at the Main Menu will be merged into your letter and printed. Select **File**, **Open** then select SAMPLE1.LET or one of the other samples for help with field placement and other important advice.

Jump Start
Please consult Chapter 9, "Judged by Its Cover: How to Write Great Cover Letters" and Chapter 14, "How to Heat Things Up with a Cold Letter or a Cold Call" for advice on creating effective job-hunting letters.

Making Address Labels

In the Main Menu, click on the **Print Labels** button. Select the desired style of label or envelope to be printed. If you select one of the label options, select the Label Type, depending on what kind of printer you have. The One-up Dot Matrix Labels and the Two-up Dot Matrix Labels choices are only for dot matrix printers and are 3 1/2" by 15/16" labels. The Three-up Laser Printer Labels choices are designed to print on Avery® 5160 Laser Printer Labels, which are 1" by 2 5/8" in size. If you select Envelopes or a label option that includes return-address labels, be sure to enter your address in the Return Address fields. This data will be saved automatically for future printing. You may also select the printer, font, font style, size, and color.

Jump Start
Printing employer lists is a handy way to keep track of your job hunt progress and prevent sending duplicate applications. The [N], [E], and [I] boxes in the Detailed List stand for "No Opening," "Evaluating" and "Interview." Check these off to chart your current status, respectively. Use the blank lines for your notes.

Generating Employer Lists

If you want, you may print out—on plain paper instead of mailing labels—lists of target employers. Click on **Print Lists** in the Main Menu and choose either the **Condensed List** or the **Detailed List**. The Condensed List option prints one company per line, showing the company name, phone number, city, state, and zip. The Detailed List option prints all company information.

Creating Résumés

In the Main Menu, click the **Create Résumé** button. You will find a simple form to fill out with the requisite elements of a basic résumé. For help with creating the résumé, click on **Help** while your résumé is on-screen. Use the **Preview Résumé** button to see how your résumé will look before you print it.

With *JobHunt*, you can create a no-frills basic résumé. If the range of *JobHunt* résumé options suits you, great! But you might find it more useful to use the *JobHunt* résumé as a draft to help you prepare a more fully customized résumé you create using your own word processor. Make certain that you read Part 3, "A Résumé Handbook" in this book for advice on how to tailor your résumé to the needs of each target employer you go after.

Tips

For a quick—and I *do* mean quick—last-minute refresher on job hunting dos and don'ts, click the **Power Tips** button in the Main Menu.

Troubleshooting

If you run into any problems, call Scope International at 704-535-0614, ext. 57. The number is available 24 hours a day, 7 days a week. You may also contact Scope International by fax at 704-535-0617, or you may log onto its BBS at 704-535-0610 and download a file named HELPFILE.TXT.

The Least You Need to Know

➤ *JobHunt* can take some of the drudgery out of looking for a job by providing a lot of the preliminary research information for you.

➤ Use *JobHunt* to identify the employers in your field or industry and in your geographical area.

➤ Use the *JobHunt* employer database to help focus your job search. This will save you time and trips to the library.

➤ You may use *JobHunt* to create your résumés and cover letters from start to finish, or you may use the program just to help you plan them.

Buzz Words Glossary

BBS   See **Bulletin Board System.**

Benefits package   Sometimes called "fringe benefits," these are items of compensation you may receive in addition to salary. Benefits are usually fairly standard from employer to employer (health insurance, paid vacation time, and so on), but you may negotiate for genuine extras such as day care for children, more vacation time, education grants, and so on.

Blind ad   A want ad that specifies a post-office or newpaper box number for reply rather than the name of a company.

Body language   The nonverbal cues, usually unconscious, including gestures, postures, and facial expressions, by which we often communicate our "real" feelings.

Bulletin Board System   Often abbreviated BBS, this is the electronic equivalent of an old-fashioned bulletin board, where organizations, companies, and individuals "post" news, notices, documents, software, and other items, making them accessible to anyone who dials in with a computer and **modem.** Some BBSs contain information relevant to employment and potential employers.

Buy signals   Verbal cues from an interviewer indicating interest in you. These range from a simple "Tell me more about…" to "That's just what we're looking for."

Cold call   See **cold letter.**

Cold letter   *Cold letters* and *cold calls* are unsolicited applications. Your target employer doesn't know you and hasn't asked for you. Cold letters and cold calls are the employment equivalent of junk mail, but research beforehand makes the cold letter or cold call less of a shot in the dark.

Comfortable   As applied to interview attire, comfortable dress consists of clothing in which you feel physically and emotionally at ease, but which is appropriate to the business environment.

Cover letter   A letter accompanying a **résumé,** designed to introduce the résumé and to emphasize its highlights and chief selling points.

Destaffing   A neutralized, impersonalized, and sanitized synonym for a systematic **lay-off** program.

Downsizing   A deliberate reduction in a company's staff in order to reduce overhead and achieve a "leaner, meaner" operation. Downsizing inevitably requires layoffs. See also **Lay off.**

Downward move   Any job move involving a decrease in salary.

EDI   See **Electronic Data Interchange (EDI).**

E-mail   Short for "electronic mail," e-mail consists of messages sent electronically, via telecommunication links (usually the phone lines), from one computer to one or more others. Sending and receiving e-mail requires a computer, **modem,** telephone line, **on-line service** provider, and an e-mail address.

Electronic Data Interchange (EDI)   An umbrella term for the technology that allows a wide range of the transmission of data (textual as well as graphic) over a computer network. Job hunters can transmit résumés as well as graphical materials (for example, a photograph of oneself) to companies equipped for EDI. Such material can readily be shared with various departments within the company.

Employment agency   A business that finds jobs for people seeking them and finds people to fill particular job vacancies. Usually, the employer is the agency's client and pays a fee; however, some agencies regard the job seeker as the client and charge him or her a fee. See also **headhunters.**

Executive search firm   See **headhunters.**

Fired   Dismissed from a position because of failure to perform or failure to perform satisfactorily. See also **fired for cause.**

Fired for cause   Dismissed from a position because of wrongdoing (such as theft, sexual harassment, drug use, and so on). This is the most pejorative form of termination.

Flak-catcher   A person hired to make life easier for the boss by deflecting criticism, handling niggling little problems, and fending off would-be job- and favor-seekers.

Flex time   A working arrangement in which employees are given a degree of choice as to when they begin and end the workday. It is an alternative to the strict 9-to-5 routine.

Franchise A privately owned small business authorized to sell or distribute a (usually) nationally advertised company's goods or services. The franchisee gets the benefits of advertising, brand recognition, and other services provided by the grantor of the franchise. In return, the franchisee purchases all of its merchandise from the parent company and may have to adhere to various rules, regulations, and policies prescribed by the company.

Freelancer A self-employed individual who sells his or her services to individuals or companies.

Fringe benefits See **benefits package.**

Golden parachute A **severance package** that provides a substantial cash settlement (and usually other benefits) in the event of termination.

Hardball negotiation Negotiation—usually over salary—of a take-it-or-leave-it variety. Except in very special circumstances, hardball negotiation rarely gets either side what it wants.

Headhunters Officially known as "executive search firms," headhunters are also called talent scouts, body snatchers, and flesh peddlers. A headhunter is hired by one company to recruit usually high-level executive talent from some other company. A headhunter's client is always the prospective employer, not the prospective employee.

Home page An **Internet** site, created by an individual or organization, which contains "hypertext links" to data relevant to the individual or organization. It is roughly equivalent to an electronic table of contents, providing orderly access to whatever information the individual or organization has to offer.

Human being For the purpose of getting the job you want, a human being is an upright biped with **transferable skills.**

Internet The name for a group of worldwide information resources linked together in an electronic network of electronic networks and accessible by anyone with a computer, **modem**, telephone line, and an account with an Internet service provider. A large number of employment-related services, as well as information relevant to all aspects of business and to many professions, is available on the Internet.

Job sharing An innovative work arrangement whereby two individuals obtain part-time employment by sharing a single full-time job, one individual working part of the day and the other working the rest of the day.

Lateral move Leaving one position to move to another offering the same salary or, at most, a compensation increase of three percent or less.

Lay off To dismiss an employee for reasons unrelated to his or her performance or behavior. Layoffs are usually the result of economic reversals, mergers (in which certain departments or individuals become "superfluous"), and so on. This is the least pejorative type of termination and implies no prejudice against the employee.

Minimum salary requirement The salary you need to make ends meet. As used in this book, the phrase suggests more than the least you need just to keep yourself and your family alive, but is the least you need to feel reasonably secure and comfortable.

Modem A computer "peripheral device" that enables the computer to communicate over telephone lines. The term stands for MOdulator/DEModulator; on the transmitting end, a modem modulates (converts) digital electrical impulses generated by a computer into sounds that can be transmitted as analog signals over a phone line and, on the receiving end, demodulates those analog signals into digital electrical impulses the computer can use.

Networking For the job hunter, *networking* is the systematic acquisition of contacts for the purpose of learning about job opportunities.

On-line service A company that provides access for computer users to an array of electronic information services via **modem** and telephone lines. Some of these companies also provide access to the **Internet**. The user pays a monthly and/or hourly subscription fee for the service.

Outplacement service Sometimes provided to **terminated** employees as part of a **severance package**, this is a service aimed at helping the employee find a new job. The outplacement effort may range from a one-day seminar to an ongoing program, including counseling, the use of an office, want-ad monitoring, and so on.

Paperless office A modern myth. Supposedly, the electronic revolution has freed us from paper documents, but American business uses 775 billion sheets of paper per year, enough to make a stack 48,900 miles high.

Positioning A term borrowed from the field of marketing, *positioning* is how a product or service (or an entire company) is perceived by the best potential customer for that product, service, or company. The successful job hunter works to position him- or herself in order to be perceived by the **target employer** as the answer to its corporate prayers.

Proactive Acting in advance to deal with an anticipated problem or issue rather than waiting for the problem or issue to happen, forcing you simply *to react* to it. To be proactive is to *anticipate* problems as well as opportunities rather than to react to them *after* they emerge. Also see **Reactive**.

Qualifications Qualities, abilities, or accomplishments that suit you, the job candidate, to a particular position or task. It is always preferable to refer to your qualifications rather than to your *experience,* which (according to the *American Heritage Dictionary,* Third Edition) is merely "an event or series of events participated in or lived through." *Qualifications* suggest active creativity, whereas *experience* is passive and (at most) reactive.

Reactive   Acting in response to problems, cirumstances, or issues as they arise rather than in anticipation of them. Also see **Proactive.**

Résumé   Also spelled *resume.* As traditionally defined, this is a document designed to summarize a job candidate's experience. As defined in this book, the résumé demonstrates how the candidate's qualifications suit him or her to the needs of the **target employer.**

Reverse ad   Often called a "situation wanted" ad, this is placed by a job applicant, who advertises his or her qualifications in the misguided hope that an employer, desperately scouring the classifieds, will jump at what he or she has to offer.

Rightsizing   Staffing in order to achieve maximum cost-effectiveness—that is, minimal overhead. Almost always, this is synonymous with **downsizing** and therefore entails lay- offs. See **Lay off.**

Screening   The practice, especially among larger employers, of eliminating job applicants considered unqualified in order to avoid "wasting time" through interviewing. Screening is usually carried out by human resources personnel rather than by supervisors—the people with the power to hire.

Severance package   The settlement offered to a **terminated** employee. This may include a cash amount in addition to other benefits (such as the temporary use of an office, access to an **outplacement service,** and so on).

Smokestack   For the job hunter, the term functions as a verb, meaning to monitor job possibilities in one's field or industry. The word comes from a practice of itinerant job hunters during the Great Depression of the 1930s. They would wander into a town and look for industrial smokestacks that were actively *smoking.* Here, they assumed, was a still-productive industry offering the potential for a job. Today, the "smokestacks" are figurative: signs of increased activity and innovation, which suggest that a company may be interested in hiring new or additional staff.

Specific skills   In contrast to **transferable skills**—general skills you can take from one job (or life experience) to another—specific skills are more or less associated with a particular job. Carpentry is a specific skill, whereas an ability to work with materials is a transferable skill.

Staff redesign   A euphemism for a program of layoffs. See **Lay off.**

Target employer   The employer with whom you are trying to get a job.

Telecommuting   A work arrangement in which the employee works, during regular business hours, at home rather than in the office. He or she is linked to the office (or to other employees, some of whom may also be telecommuters) via telephone, fax, and computer/**modem**. Telecommuting is a growing trend.

Temporary agency   A business that specializes in supplying other businesses with temporary employees to fill staffing gaps or to work on special projects.

Terminated   Usually a synonym for **fired**, although not quite as pejorative. See also **lay off**.

Transferable skills   These are the building blocks of any career you choose. They are specific to *you* rather than to a particular *job*. They always describe a function—that is, how you *work* with people, data, or things. See also **specific skills**.

Vertical integration   An exciting new way of thinking about and structuring complex businesses. Vertical integration unites productively related industries, making them work together, so that the sum of their combined operations is truly greater than the parts. Thus a book publishing operation, television production company, and movie studio might be vertically integrated as a "communication company," and any single product (that is, copyright) exploited as a book, a TV show, and a movie. Vertical integration will not only continue to change the way we think about corporate organization, it will also change the way we define our careers.

Woodshed   A term borrowed from jazz musicians, which they use as a synonym for going off alone in order to practice and review and improve. (Old-time rural musicians used to work on their licks in the privacy of the woodshed, where they wouldn't be disturbed and where they would disturb no one.) Job hunters who experience repeated rejection over a protracted period are advised to "woodshed," that is, to undertake a quiet and contemplative self-review, with an eye toward revising résumés, cover letters, and the like.

Index

JobHunt™
6-in-1 Software
(National edition)

12,000 Companies Nationwide

NEW Software! *Find a job FAST, promote your business and make money doing targeted mailings for others.*

• •

"JobHunt 6-in-1" includes a database of 12,000 employers nationwide with full contact information (Name, Address, Phone, Fax-*if available*, size, etc.). Search by Region or Industry. Built-in word processor automatically prints personalized cover letters, follow-up letters, labels and envelopes for targeted mass-mailings. Just attach your resumés and mail by the thousands. **Save months of typing and research effort.** Resumé creator for creating stunning resumés in COLOR. Powerful advice on interviewing and dressing. Phone dialer for making follow-up calls after you have mailed your letters! Ideally suited for administrative, entry-level and upper-management job-hunting.

Product Name: **JobHunt (National)**
Product Code: JHWN
Ships On: 3.5" Diskettes
Price: Reg. $59.95, Now $49.95

only **$49.95**

Who Buys JobHunt™ & HitList™?

Job-seekers, someone who is already employed but either wants to move up or keep their options open, Marketers & Salespeople, Employment Agencies, Career-related businesses, College Placement Offices, Libraries, Counselors, Computer Labs, Investors, Fund-raisers, Consultants, Retiring/Separating Military personnel entering the civilian workforce, Vocational and Rehabilitation Centers and Parents & Friends (as a Graduation or going-away present).

<u>System Requirements</u>: Both programs require Windows® 3.1 and 4 Meg RAM. 100% compatible with Windows® 95.

MICROSOFT® WINDOWS™ COMPATIBLE

JobHunt and HitList are trademarks of Scope International. Product features, prices and specifications subject to change without notice. Copyright © 1995, Scope International.

100,000 Employers'
HitList™
CD-ROM

New! Awesome Power. Check This Out!!

The ultimate in job-searching and sales-prospecting tools. HitList works quite similarly to JobHunt (see detailed description of JobHunt National edition) but contains a database of a whopping 100,000 records nationwide. Just this data is worth over $10,000 if you were to buy it from a mailing-list company—not to mention what you can accomplish with it.

HitList is not to be confused with phone CDs that give only phone numbers, incomplete mailing addresses and do not do mail-merge.

Instead, HitList is an extremely powerful program that provides a full mailing address and phone number, searches by Region and/or Industry and prints personalized cover letters, sales prospecting letters or any other letter that you type into its built-in word processor. It prints labels and envelopes too. Includes Resumé-creator, Interview Tips and a Phone-dialer for making telemarketing or follow-up calls. A goldmine of opportunity—Order HitList today!

Product Name: **HitList**
Product Code: HLNL
Ships On: CD-ROM
Price: Reg. $99.95, Now $69.95

only **$69.95**

 • Order Today •

1. **By Phone: 1-800-448-5478**
   (Visa/MasterCard, 24 hrs) or 704-535-0614

2. **By Fax:** Fax orders to: (704) 535-0617 (FAX)

3. **By Mail:** Please make your Check or Money Order payable to Scope International. NC residents, add applicable NC Sales Tax. Add $5.95 Shipping and Handling (per order, not per product). Mail to: SCOPE INTERNATIONAL (DEPT. ABK-95), P.O. BOX 25252, CHARLOTTE, NC 28229-5252, U.S.A. [CHECK]

Note: College and Government Purchase Orders accepted *ONLY* for orders totalling $100 or more. For orders of less than $100, please *PREPAY* by check or credit card.

About the Author

Marc Dorio, of Dorio Associates, Inc., is an organizational development and training professional with over 15 years of corporate and consulting experience gained with organizations in a wide variety of industries. His clients have included Fortune 100 and 500 corporations, and his professional experience ranges from training, organizational development, and management development to team building and family business advisement.

Prior to forming Dorio Associates, Marc was managing director of a regional management consulting firm and vice president of organizational development for a start-up software development company. He holds a master's of science degree in Industrial/Organizational Psychology from Stevens Institute of Technology in Hoboken, New Jersey, and dual master's degrees in Human Behavior (M. Div) and Theology (M. Th) from St. Bernard's College in Rochester, New York.

Marc has done graduate study in organizational change at Albert Einstein College of Medicine, Department of Psychiatry. He is the author of two books, the *Personnel Manager's Desk Book* (Prentice-Hall) and *The Staffing Problem Solver* (Wiley), in addition to *The Complete Idiot's Guide to Getting the Job You Want,* as well as many articles on staffing, career development, and training.

Marc is a member of the Society for Industrial/Organizational Psychology, the American Psychological Association, and the New Jersey Psychological Association.

Ten Interview Questions You Should Always Ask

1. **Have you had a chance to review my résumé?** Always open with this one. A staggering number of interviewers do not read your résumé beforehand. A staggering number of interviewers will not admit this fact. While it is unlikely that you will get a simple "no, I haven't" in response to this question, you might hear something like "I haven't had the chance to review it as thoroughly as I'd like to." (Translation: "No, I haven't read a word of it.") You should respond with help, not anger: "Well, then, perhaps you'll find it helpful for me to hit the highlights of my qualifications."

2. **Is there anything else I can tell you about my qualifications?** Should the interviewer answer yes, he or she *has* read your résumé, or after you finish reciting your verbal review of it, invite further questions. The more *time* you can get the target employer to invest in you, the more valuable you will become in the target's eyes.

3. **How would you describe the duties of this job?** You might have memorized the job description in the want ad, but this question specifically asks the *interviewer* to describe the duties, which may be a far cry from what's in the official description. At the very least, the interviewer's response may give you a handle on which job functions really *are* the most important. The answer you get will provide a springboard to launch a description of your particular skills and qualifications. ("Oh, I'm very happy to hear that you consider client contact so major a part of the position. I place a high premium on creating customer satisfaction. It's building a business, each and every day, one client at a time.")

4. **What are the principal problems facing your staff right now?** A dual-purpose question. First, understanding the target employer's problems gives you an opportunity to present yourself as a solution to those problems. Second, the question will help uncover any truly terrible situations that might make you think twice about taking the job. ("The biggest problem is that people just don't seem to be buying buggy whips right now.")

5. **What results would you like to see me produce?** By asking the question, you demonstrate your intention to *do* a job rather than *take* a job. For you, a job means more than earning a living. It means serving the company, creating profit, saving money, solving problems, increasing productivity. Respond point by point to whatever list this question elicits: *This is what* you *want; this is what* I'll *do.*

6. **What do you consider ideal experience for this position?** If the interviewer's response is light-years away from anything you expected, reconsider the job. However, the main purpose of the question is to get the interviewer to describe a profile into which you, verbally, can step. Respond to the *interviewer's* list point by point.

7. **How would you describe the 'weather' in this company? Stormy? Hot? Cool? Breezy? Calm? Brisk? Or what?** A creative question about the work environment. Its primary purpose is to catch the interviewer off-guard and to discover if you are about to walk into a snakepit. The question also gives you a chance to say that you thrive in the target company's environment. "I like intensity, and I'm energized by pressure situations. To me, nothing's more stimulating than stormy weather."

8. **Was the person who held this job before me promoted?** The bad way to put this would be, "What happened to the last marshal of Dodge City?" So don't put it that way. The question aims to find out why the job is vacant. It is also an opportunity to assess the chances for advancement at this particular company and from this particular position.

9. **Might I talk with the person who held this job before me?** What do you do if the answer is no? If the previous incumbent is still with the company, you have to be suspicious of such a response. Ask what the objections are. If the person has moved on, you might ask the interviewer if he or she knows where you might get in touch with the former employee.

10. **Based on what I've told you, don't you think I could give you all that you need in this position?** This invites a positive response and coaxes agreement. At the very least, it prompts the interviewer to tell you more about what he or she wants.

Ten Interview Questions You Should Always Expect

1. **What can you tell me about yourself?**   Don't respond with a full-scale autobiography, but, instead, help the interviewer by focusing the question: "What about me would be most relevant to you and what this company needs?" Then answer this more specific question.

2. **Why do you want to leave your present company?**   If you have a good, *positive* reason for wanting to leave, use it. Avoid negative reasons. Explain why you want to *move to* the target company. For example, instead of answering, "I don't get enough challenges at XYZ Industries," respond: "I am eager to take on more challenges, and I believe I will find them at ABC Industries."

3. **What do you know about us?**   Learn all you can about the target company, using the approaches outlined in **Chapter 18**. If you've done your homework, the question is your chance to shine. If the interview was sprung on you at the last minute, be sure to arrive for the interview early and scan the lobby for information (such as annual reports and brochures). Then sit down and start reading—fast!

4. **How much experience do you have?**   If your pre-interview research has revealed areas in which the company is concentrating its efforts, cite your relevant experience. If your research has failed to reveal any clear-cut areas of concern to the target company, answer the question with a question: "Are you looking for overall experience or experience in some specific area?" The interviewer's response should allow you to frame your answer to directly address the target company's needs.

5. **What do you most like and most dislike about your current job?**   Minimize the negative part of this question by replying, "I like everything about my current position." Then list some vital skills, abilities, and qualifications you've developed or honed in your current position. Conclude with, "I'm ready for new challenges and an opportunity for greater advancement and greater responsibility." Answer the positive part of the question—What do you like?—by citing the opportunity your *present* job has given you to develop assets useful to the *target* employer.

6. **How many hours a week do you need to get your job done?**   If you reply with something like forty hours, you risk labeling yourself as a clock watcher. Instead of pinning yourself down to a specific number, reply "I make an effort to plan my time efficiently. Usually, this works well. However, as you know, this business has crunch periods, and when that happens, I put in as many hours as necessary to get the job done."

7. **How much are you making now and how much do you want?**   You cannot avoid answering the first part of the question, but you can frame the reply effectively: "I'm earning $35,000, but I'm not certain that helps you evaluate my 'worth,' since the two jobs differ significantly in their responsibilities." As to the second part, do not state a specific figure. Instead, itemize the skills, talents, abilities, and responsibilities the target position entails: "If I understand the full scope of the position, my responsibilities would include…." Then: "Given all of this, what figure did you have in mind for someone with my qualifications in a position as important as this?" An alternative is to reply, "I expect a salary appropriate to my qualifications and demonstrated abilities. What figure did you have in mind?" Or: "What salary range has been authorized for this position?"

8. **What's the most difficult situation you ever faced on the job?**   Don't respond by bringing up a situation so difficult that it resulted in personal failure or general disaster. Instead, prepare yourself in advance by thinking of a story with a happy ending—happy for your company. Avoid discussing personal or family difficulties. Avoid discussing problems you've had with supervisors, peers, or subordinates. However, you might discuss a difficult situation with a subordinate, provided that the issues were resolved inventively and to everyone's satisfaction.

9. **What are you looking for in this job?**   You may be looking for money, self-fulfillment, an easy commute… whatever. But don't tell the interviewer any of this. Put words like *contribute*, *enhance*, *improve* in your response. "At ABC Industries, I discovered just how much one person could contribute to a company. As production supervisor, I increased efficiency an average of 14 percent, which meant a quarterly bottom-line increase of $27,000 in net revenue for our department. I'm looking to do even more for XYZ Industries. That's what will give me satisfaction."

10. **Why should I hire you?**   This is really a request for an "executive summary" of what you bring to the company table. Keep the response brief. Recap and repeat, in laundry-list fashion, any job requirements the interviewer may have enumerated earlier in the interview. Point by point, match your skills, abilities, and qualifications to those items.

tear here

alpha
books